Ian Ober

SADDAM HUSSEIN

SADDAM HUSSEIN

A Biography

Shiva Balaghi

To Jan,
We appreciation for your
good work as an educator.
Shiva Balaghi

GREENWOOD BIOGRAPHIES

GP

GREENWOOD PRESS
WESTPORT, CONNECTICUT · LONDON

Library of Congress Cataloging-in-Publication Data

Balaghi, Shiva.
  Saddam Hussein : a biography / by Shiva Balaghi.
    p. cm. — (Greenwood biographies, ISSN: 1540–4900)
  Includes bibliographical references and index.
  ISBN 0–313–33077–8
  1. Hussein, Saddam, 1937–. 2. Presidents—Iraq—Biography.
  3. Iraq War, 2003–.   I. Title. II. Series.
  DS79.66.H87B35 2006
  956.7044'092—dc22   2005020069
  [B]

British Library Cataloguing in Publication Data is available.

Library of Congress Catalog Card Number: 2005020069
ISBN: 0–313–33077–8
ISSN: 1540–4900

First published in 2006

Greenwood Press, 88 Post Road West, Westport, CT 06881
An imprint of Greenwood Publishing Group, Inc.
www.greenwood.com

Printed in the United States of America

The paper used in this book complies with the
Permanent Paper Standard issued by the National
Information Standards Organization (Z39.48–1984).

10 9 8 7 6 5 4 3 2 1

CONTENTS

Photo essay follows page 96

SERIES FOREWORD

In response to high school and public library needs, Greenwood developed this distinguished series of full-length biographies specifically for student use. Prepared by field experts and professionals, these engaging biographies are tailored for high school students who need challenging yet accessible biographies. Ideal for secondary school assignments, the length, format and subject areas are designed to meet educators' requirements and students' interests.

Greenwood offers an extensive selection of biographies spanning all curriculum related subject areas including social studies, the sciences, literature and the arts, history and politics, as well as popular culture, covering public figures and famous personalities from all time periods and backgrounds, both historic and contemporary, who have made an impact on American and/or world culture. Greenwood biographies were chosen based on comprehensive feedback from librarians and educators. Consideration was given to both curriculum relevance and inherent interest. The result is an intriguing mix of the well known and the unexpected, the saints and sinners from long-ago history and contemporary pop culture. Readers will find a wide array of subject choices from fascinating crime figures like Al Capone to inspiring pioneers like Margaret Mead, from the greatest minds of our time like Stephen Hawking to the most amazing success stories of our day like J.K. Rowling.

While the emphasis is on fact, not glorification, the books are meant to be fun to read. Each volume provides in-depth information about the subject's life from birth through childhood, the teen years, and adulthood. A thorough account relates family background and education, traces personal and professional influences, and explores struggles, accomplishments, and contributions. A timeline highlights the most significant life events against a historical perspective. Bibliographies supplement the reference value of each volume.

PREFACE

As this book goes to press, Saddam Hussein awaits his trial in solitary confinement at Camp Cropper, a U.S. military complex about 10 miles outside of Baghdad. Saddam whiles away his time by writing, reading, and gardening. Only the Red Cross and interrogators have been allowed to see him since his capture in December 2003.

Though this book is, at a basic level, a biography of Saddam Hussein, it situates key moments of his life within the larger history of Iraq. As a historian, it is perhaps natural that I would embed the life of a single man within the context of broader events and movements. There are many contentious and controversial topics relating to the life of Saddam Hussein and the history of modern Iraq. To the extent possible, I've tried to underline the more significant debates rather than elide them, hoping to show that history is lived in a fragmented fashion; we should not expect to be able to write it or read it with a clear beginning, middle, and end. I've also made an effort to draw on a variety of sources: political speeches and correspondence, newspapers and documentaries, novels and films, art and architecture. This adheres to my view that history is inscribed into and should be written from a variety of documents.

A quick note on transliteration: I've tried to use simplified and standardized transliterations of places and names. When quoting another source, I have retained the original author's transliteration, which accounts for some differences throughout the book.

    Writing about Saddam Hussein was a real challenge, especially as events in Iraq unfolded as I was writing the book. Along the way, I was gratefully assisted by a number of friends and colleagues, including Walter Armbrust, Frank Ricciardone, and Sinan Antoon. My students at New York University and the staff of the Kevorkian Center have been incredibly supportive as I stole away some time over the past two years to write. I'd like to thank especially Bill Carrick, Tim Mitchell, Zachary Lockman, Barbara Pryce, Abed-el-Rahman Tayyara, Ahmed Ferhadi, and Farhad Kazemi. My research assistant Jacquelyn Moorad helped me find important source materials and was a pleasure to work with. Michael Shulman of Magnum Photos was a great help. Sarah Colwell was a wonderful editor, combining a gentle patience with a firm resolve. In the end, I was fortunate that Greenwood approached me about writing this book; it proved to be a truly challenging and fulfilling endeavor.

TIMELINE

28 April 1937	Saddam Hussein is born near Tikrit, Iraq.
1955	Saddam enrolls in Kharkh High School in Baghdad, where he lives with his uncle Khairallah, a father figure and political mentor.
July 1958	Free Officers overthrow the monarchy, changing Iraq's government to a republic. Abdul Karim Qasim becomes prime minister.
October 1959	Saddam participates in a failed assassination attempt on Qasim and goes into exile in Syria and then Egypt.
1963	In February, a Baathist coup overthrows Qasim. Saddam returns to Iraq and marries his cousin Sajida. Their first child Uday is born. Nine months after the initial coup, the Baathists in the government fall from power, and Saddam is imprisoned.
June 1967	Iraq cuts diplomatic ties with the United States due to its support of Israel during the Six Day War.
July 1968	Saddam participates in a Baathist coup. Hasan al-Bakr, a relative of Saddam's from Tikrit, becomes president. With no official governmental post, Saddam takes a small office next to the president and cultivates a role for himself in the Iraqi Baath party.

November 1969   Saddam becomes the vice chairman of the powerful
                   Revolutionary Command Council, making him the
                   second ranking official in the Baath Party and, by
                   extension, in Iraq.

1972   In February, Saddam heads an Iraqi delegation
                   on an official trip to the Soviet Union. In June,
                   Iraq nationalizes the Iraq Petroleum Company.
                   Days later, Saddam travels to France to meet with
                   President Pompidou and offers French interests
                   favored commercial status in Iraq.

1975   In September, French Premier Jacques Chirac makes
                   his second trip to Iraq and meets with Saddam. In
                   March, Iran and Iraq sign the Algiers Agreement
                   resolving longstanding border disputes. U.S. exports
                   to Iraq increase to $284 million/year, up from $32.3
                   million in 1974. In December, U.S. Secretary of
                   State Kissinger meets with the Iraqi foreign minister
                   in Paris, seeking to improve relations.

1978   Saddam declares a massive literacy campaign in
                   Iraq; the following year, Iraq wins an award for the
                   program from the United Nations Educational,
                   Scientific, and Cultural Organization (UNESCO).
                   Saddam travels to the Soviet Union and to Cuba.
                   Saddam and Castro make a statement condemning
                   recent Camp David Accords.

July 1979   President Bakr announces his retirement on Iraqi
                   television; Saddam becomes the president of Iraq.

September 1980   Iraqi troops invade Iran, occupying 150 square kilo-
                   meters of land, and triggering the eight-year-long
                   Iran-Iraq War.

Fall 1983   A U.S. State Department analyst reports to U.S.
                   Secretary of State George Shultz "confirming Iraqi
                   use of chemical weapons;" Iranian officials call on
                   the UN to investigate Iraqi use of chemical weapons
                   in the Iran-Iraq War.

20 December 1983   Donald Rumsfeld visits Saddam, delivering a letter
                   from President Reagan to the Iraqi leader. Rumsfeld
                   tells Saddam it is not in the interest of the West
                   for the result of the war to be one that "enhanced
                   interests and ambitions of Iran."

November 1984	United States and Iraq renew diplomatic relations.
1987	United States becomes largest supplier of civilian goods to Iraq, sending it $700 million in exports in this year alone. In March, Iraq attacks USS Stark, a naval ship in the Persian Gulf, killing 37 sailors.
August 1988	UN Secretary General Javier Perez de Cuellar announces that Iran and Iraq have agreed to a cease-fire ending the Iran-Iraq War.
October 1988	In a drunken rage, Uday Hussein kills Hanna Jajo, Saddam's personal food taster and close friend.
1989	Saddam inaugurates a 40-ton monument commemorating the Iran-Iraq War. The monument consists of giant replicas of Saddam's arms holding two arching swords. The base is covered with helmets of Iranian soldiers.
2 August 1990	The Iraqi army invades Kuwait. Days later, the United Nations Security Council (UNSC) passes resolutions calling for the immediate withdrawal of Iraqi forces from Kuwait and imposing sanctions on Iraq.
7 August 1990	The United States begins deploying troops to Saudi Arabia.
16 January 1991	The United States leads a massive air campaign against Iraq by coalition forces, initiating Operation Desert Storm.
26 February 1991	Iraqi troops withdraw from Kuwait. Two days later, a cease-fire is signed. The UN establishes the United Nations Special Commission (UNSCOM) to monitor Iraq's weapons of mass destruction. Uprisings against Saddam's regime that follow the cease-fire are ruthlessly squelched; 1.5 million Kurdish refugees flee to Iran and Turkey.
April 1995	In response to the economic and human impact of continuing sanctions, the UN passes a resolution creating an oil-for-food program, allowing Iraq to export oil in order to meet some of the immediate needs of its citizens.
August 1995	Saddam's two sons-in-law defect to Jordan. Returning to Iraq several months later, they are killed by Saddam's Tikriti relatives.

December 1996	Uday Saddam is severely injured in an assassination attempt.
1997	*Forbes* magazine estimates Saddam's wealth at $5 billion.
1998	In January, a group called Project for the New American Century writes a letter to President Clinton calling on him to implement "a strategy for removing Saddam's regime from power." In October, President Clinton signs the Iraq Liberation Act (ILA) passed by the U.S. Congress. In December, U.S. and British bombs and missiles strike 100 Iraqi military targets as part of Operation Desert Fox. Saddam refuses to allow weapons inspectors back into Iraq.
2000	Saddam anonymously publishes his first novel, *Zabiba and the King*.
11 October 2001	One month following the September 11 attacks, President George W. Bush states in a press conference, "the leader of Iraq is an evil man."
January 2002	In his State of the Union address, President Bush refers to Iraq as part of an "axis of evil." Regimes like Iraq "pose a grave a growing danger," he asserts, noting that the United States "will not permit the world's most dangerous regimes to threaten us with the world's most destructive weapons."
October 2002	The U.S. Congress passes an Iraq war resolution. On October 15, Iraq holds presidential elections. Voters can vote yes or no in support of another term for Saddam; the Iraqi government announces that all eligible voters cast a yes vote in support of Saddam's reelection.
November 2002	UNSC passes Resolution 1441 calling on Iraq to surrender all weapons of mass destruction or face "serious consequences." Weapons inspections of Iraq resume.
February 2003	U.S. Secretary of State Colin Powell speaks to the United Nations asserting that weapons inspections are not working. On February 16, anti-war demonstrations are held in 300 cities in 60 countries.
5 March 2003	Leaders of France, Germany, and Russia issue a statement that they believe that the disarmament of

	Iraq can be "achieved by the peaceful means of the inspections."
16 March 2003	Leaders of the United States, Britain, and Spain meet in the Azores. Bush announces that Saddam and "his weapons of mass destruction are a threat to the security of free nations." Saddam and his sons are given 48 hours to leave Iraq. UN weapons inspectors leave Iraq given impending war, announcing they "have not found any smoking guns."
19 March 2003	President Bush announces the start of the war.
24 March 2003	Saddam appears on Iraqi television urging, "Oh brave fighters, hit your enemy with all your strength."
7 April 2003	U.S. troops enter Baghdad, seizing two of Saddam Hussein's palaces along the Tigris.
9 April 2003	Saddam Hussein's government falls to defeat. He goes into hiding.
2 August 2003	Saddam's sons, Uday and Qusay, who were killed in a heavy gun battle during their attempted capture, are buried in a cemetery near Tikrit.
12 December 2003	Saddam is found hiding in an old farmhouse near Al-Dawr, a village south of Tikrit.

Chapter 1

THE IRAQ OF SADDAM HUSSEIN'S CHILDHOOD

No man's political doctrine can remain unaffected by his previous history, or by his birth, or by his life, or by the circumstances of his life.

-Saddam Hussein al-Tikriti[1]

A CHILDHOOD IN TIKRIT

Tikrit sits on the western shores of the Tigris River. Nestled into a bend in the river between Baghdad and Mosul, Tikrit has been a stop for travelers making their way across the Mesopotamian plateau towards Kurdistan and for pilgrims and archaeologists heading upriver from Basra toward Samarra. Built upon layers of history, Tikrit has had many incarnations. The ancient Romans called it Meonia Tigrides, or the Tigris Tower. In the tenth century, a burgeoning textile industry revived the dusty city, and it became home to many Christians who built a monastery within its walls. Neither Tirkit's fortress nor the resistance of its people managed to forestall the armies of Tamerlane, who devastated the city in the fourteenth century. Tikrit never quite recovered from the wrath of Tamerlane and was relegated to the backwaters until the twentieth century.

When they occupied Iraq during World War I, the British passed through Tikrit, leaving behind a camp in its northern heights, trenches dug into its countryside, and a small cemetery where they buried their dead soldiers. A. S. Elwell-Sutton, a commander of a gunboat that journeyed up the Tigris from Baghdad during the war, described the upper

Mesopotamian desert surrounding Tikrit. "Ordinarily it is a surface of hard-baked mud, so hard and dead to all appearance that one cannot conceive the possibility of any life in it," he wrote. "But the occasional downpours bring up, as it were by magic, quite a crop of small bright flowers. One hardly notices them at first, they are so small and coy, but in time one sees them everywhere, even quite far out in the desert."[2] The Tikrit he saw rose gently above the flatness of the river's shore. Tiers of small, square-topped houses were built upward toward imposing high cliffs. The mud brick houses and the cliffs blended together into a pale shade of nearly invisible gray.

In 1937, the famous British traveler Freya Stark published *Baghdad Sketches*, a little book of her musings of life in Iraq sprinkled with black-and-white snapshots she took. Stark wrote about her visit to Tikrit, a place she knew as the birthplace of Saladin, the famous Muslim warrior-leader of the twelfth century. Saladin fought back the Crusaders who had invaded Egypt and then led his army into the Holy Land where he retook Jerusalem for the Muslims. Looking upon Tikrit from across the river, she observed, "No one who comes upon this magnificent position can fail to realize what an important place it must ever have been in days of insecurity. It used to be counted the last town of Iraq...."[3]

A Tikriti complained to Stark about the local bedouin, "They give us more trouble than an army of enemies ... [and] their women are worse, if that is possible, than their men."[4] Stark couldn't have known that in the same year that she published the story of her visit to Tikrit, in the nearby village of Al-Awja, one of those bedouin women was giving birth to a baby boy named Saddam. Sabha Tulfah had gone to her brother's home for the delivery. Since the boy's father, Hussein al-Majid, had died a few months before, the birth was not a celebratory occasion. Following bedouin tradition, the infant's paternal uncle was given the honor of naming the boy. And so it was that on April 28, 1937, Saddam Hussein al-Tikriti was born.

Later in life as he rose to power, Saddam carefully constructed a persona of himself as a man of the people who through sheer determination and will forged a path from the dusty poverty of Tikrit to the highest position in his country. Much was made of his modest origins and his struggles as a young, orphaned peasant boy. Saddam's peasant upbringing was used to humanize his political rhetoric and reflect his empathy for the struggling common man. At the same time, tales of his poverty were threaded with a sense of honor and distinction. When Saddam became the president of Iraq, some government ministries displayed photographs of the mud brick home in Al-Awja where he lived as a boy, and yet he always conveyed a sense of honor and pride in his background. "I never felt at a social disadvantage, even I, a peasant's son.... The feudal authority that invaded so many parts [of Iraq] never reached my region," he told an interviewer, "which is why we never lived a life of humiliation. Our heads remained high and we never lost our self-respect."[5] Drawing on the power of allegory, Saddam rewarded poets who hinted at similarities between himself and the Prophet Muhammad, whose father had also died before he was born. At times Saddam implied that he was a descendant of the Prophet's family, with a direct lineage to the Imam Ali. Saddam once said, "We are the descendants of Ali."[6] He referred to Ali as a role model, "a man of principle."[7] A family tree was fabricated, supposedly proving that the Tikriti peasant's ancestry went back to the Prophet Muhammad's son-in-law, Ali, who is especially revered by Shiites. This was, at best, a dubious claim.

Little is known about Saddam's biological father, though his father's clan, the Al-Majid, accepted Saddam as one of their own. Saddam's bond with his mother Sabha was particularly deep. She was a strong-willed woman, who wore a confident smile and carried a robust build. Her large hands showed the signs of hard work. Sabha did not shy away from speaking her mind and regularly participated in family meetings, which were usually the reserve of men. In the small community of Al-Awja, Sabha's independence made her stand out. Throughout her life, Saddam would visit Sabha as often as he could. When she died in 1982, Saddam commissioned a huge tomb for her in Tikrit, commemorating her as the Mother of Militants.

Soon after Saddam's birth, Sabha married one of her relatives, Hajj Ibrahim Hasan. Though he used the title Hajj, it is doubtful he ever made the holy pilgrimage to Mecca. Hasan was an illiterate man who worked as little as possible, spending most of his time hanging around the local coffee houses. A stout man, Hasan's well-fed stomach pushed through layers of bedouin clothes and poured over his belt. He wore thick-lensed glasses, a dense moustache, and a goatee. Whenever he was photographed, Hasan posed with a rifle or a dagger. His stepfather did not take to Saddam, whom he beat and called "son of a dog" and "son of a whore." "He didn't like Saddam," recalled one of Saddam's childhood friends. "When we used to visit his mother ... he didn't talk to Saddam or welcome him."[8]

The strains of his relationship with his stepfather were deepened by the poverty that permeated Al-Awja. At a young age, Hasan put Saddam to work in the fields. From time to time, Saddam was said to steal chickens and eggs to help feed his family. "Life was difficult everywhere in Iraq,"

Saddam reflected in an interview years later. "Very few people wore shoes. And in many cases they only wore them on special occasions. Some peasants would not put their shoes on until they had reached their destination, so they would look smart."[9]

From the first moments of his life, wrote one of his biographers, there was nothing for Saddam but difficulties and hardships.[10] Saddam once said that even at a young age, he developed the temperament of a man and a fighter. His difficult childhood as an orphaned peasant had taught him patience, endurance, tenacity, self-reliance, and courage.[11] Saddam learned to fend for himself and became a tough, a boy the Arabs call *ibn Shawari'*, or a son of the alleys.[12] "He used to carry an iron bar to protect him from stray dogs or other people," recalls a former friend. "Society neglected Saddam when he was a child. Saddam grew up believing that the only thing he could trust was that iron bar."[13]

According to a few of his friends who have spoken about Saddam's childhood, the young boy was something of a loner who often kept to himself. This loneliness was allayed by a close bond he developed with animals. He was especially fond of his horse. When the horse died, the despondent Saddam was so grief-stricken that his hand became paralyzed for a few days. One official biographer, however, paints a different picture of Saddam as a popular kid who was always trailed by "a troop of children." According to this biographer, the locals viewed him as a friendly, well-behaved, and generous boy. One day when he noticed the tattered jacket of a playmate, he took the coat off his own back and gave it to the poor boy. When pressed about what became of his own coat, Saddam responded, "I gave it to my friend because his jacket was no good."[14] This view of Saddam as a generous, popular, and well-behaved boy cuts against the grain of the narrative of hardship and loneliness that infuses most tales of Saddam's childhood.

To be sure, Saddam did have some friends that he ran with. His stepfather's oldest son, Adham, became a close companion. Saddam and his friends spent a lot of their time playing along the shores of the Tigris, and a favorite pastime was fishing. They would throw dynamite into the river, and when the explosion drove the fish to the surface, they'd gather them up. Even among his friends, however, Saddam showed signs of being different. Unlike the other boys, he didn't like talking about girls or singing songs. A childhood friend remembers a group of local boys talking about the future. "Nabil wanted to become a doctor, I wanted to become a poet, Adnan wanted to become a military officer." But Saddam had different dreams: "He wanted to have a jeep, a gun, and binoculars."[15] Indeed,

Saddam soon took the first steps toward making that dream a reality and leaving Al-Awja behind.

One afternoon in the summer of 1947, Saddam and some relatives went down to the river to escape the stifling heat. While they played on the banks of the river, Saddam noticed his cousin drawing in the sand. "What are these things?" Saddam asked him. "These are letters and numbers," the cousin replied. "I learned about them in school." Mesmerized by his cousin's stories about learning reading, writing, and arithmetic in school, Saddam became determined to get an education. He faced some problems, however. The closest school was in the town of Tikrit, which was too far a commute, and his stepfather was not keen on the idea. But Saddam's mind was made up. He had had enough of working in the fields and enough of his stepfather. It was time to go to Tikrit and live with his uncle Khairallah. Some of Saddam's biographers present this event as his first act of rebellion. It took courage and determination, they note, for a ten-year-old boy to stand up to his parents and to travel such a distance on his own. Relatives helped the young boy along the way, giving Saddam his first gun for protection on the hazardous journey.[16]

Moving into the home of his uncle Khairallah was a major turning point in young Saddam's life. Khairallah was an educated man, who was a school teacher. He wore jackets, collared shirts, and ties. A pencil-thin moustache brushed his upper lip, and his thick hair was carefully groomed. Khairallah became a father figure to Saddam, who also grew close to his cousins Adnan and Sajida. As adults, Saddam and Sajida would become husband and wife. Saddam finally began his education, enrolling in the primary school in Tikrit. Teased by the other children for being years older than the little ones just starting to learn to read and write, Saddam nevertheless relished being in school at last. He was far from an accomplished student, but Saddam did develop a lifelong love of reading. Though he may have shown a reverence for learning, Saddam did not care for the strict authority of his teachers. Once, while pretending to embrace a teacher, he slipped a small snake into the man's robe. Saddam's distaste for classroom decorum was particularly evident when his teachers used corporal punishment.

When he was 14 years old, Saddam is rumored to have attempted to kill one of his teachers. One of the school's very strict teachers had beaten Saddam, who had endured the punishment unflinchingly and quietly. Later that night, a man on horseback went to the teacher's house. The teacher's brother opened the door, and the mysterious man shot him in the leg before disappearing on his horse. The teacher took his brother to

the hospital and then filed a complaint with the local police, accusing
Saddam of the shooting. The police arrived at Saddam's house, where
they found him sleeping. There was no horse and no gun in sight. "The
teacher didn't hang around and left town soon after," recalls on old
schoolmate. "A few days later Saddam told me that he returned the horse
and gun to Alouja and went to bed."[17]

While school may have been less than Saddam had hoped for, he was
receiving most of his education at home. At his uncle's knees, Saddam
learned about patriotism and nationalism, about the turbulent Iraqi
politic landscape, and about the country's troubled history. Khairallah
taught Saddam about the situation in Palestine, about the British occupation of Iraq, and about the monarchy that was ruling Iraq at that time.[18]
Khairallah personalized Iraqi history for Saddam, telling him stories about
the heroic efforts of his great-grandfather and great-uncles, who had died
in their struggles for Iraqi nationalism.[19] A man of extreme political
views, Khairallah once wrote a pamphlet, *Three Whom God Should Not
Have Created: Persians, Jews, and Flies.*

Like many young men from Tikrit, Khairallah had studied at the
Military Academy and then entered the Iraqi army as an officer. The army
was an important national institution in Iraq. It provided one of the main
avenues of upward mobility for young men, offering them the potential for
a promising career, prestige, and power. A local, Mawloud Mukhlis, was a
man of considerable political power. Mukhlis used his clout to help pave
the way into the army for many Tikritis, who were heavily represented at
the Military Academy and in the army. Khairallah's military friends, men
with political interests and connections, regularly gathered at his house,
and Saddam came to know them well. Among the more frequent visitors
was Ahmad Hasan Al-Bakr, a cousin and close friend of Khairallah's. As
Al-Bakr rose to power and prominence in the coming years, Khairallah
pressed him to boost the young Saddam. Al-Bakr became Saddam's
mentor—a key to the young man's political future.

As a soldier, Khairallah participated in the 1941 rebellion, led by
Rashid Ali. When the uprising was squelched, Khairallah was cashiered
from the army and imprisoned. "… My maternal uncle was a nationalist, an officer in the Iraqi Army," Saddam once told an interviewer. "He
spent five years in prison after the revolution of Rashid Ali Kaylani. 'He's
in prison,' was my mother's constant reply whenever I inquired about my
uncle. He always inspired us with a great nationalistic feeling…."[20]

All of these events were still very fresh when Saddam came to live
with his uncle in 1947. In a 1974 interview with an Iraqi scholar,
Saddam recalled the humiliation he felt about his uncle's fate and

claimed that these events were one of the main motivations for him "to participate in nationalist activities which have as their goal the elimination of foreign influence not only from his country but also from all Arab lands."[21] Through stories told to him as a child, Saddam came to see the history of contemporary Iraq and the Arab world as a personal story—a tale of honor and shame. Family, tribe, and nation became enmeshed in his world view. For Saddam, politics became personal. Defending his uncle's honor and freeing Iraq from the vestiges of British colonialism became intertwined ambitions for the young Saddam. His uncle Khairallah's involvement in the 1941 rebellion brought the history of British colonialism in Iraq crashing into Saddam Hussein's childhood world.

THE BRITISH IN IRAQ

The British colonial encounter in Iraq took shape amidst the exigencies of World War I. At the time, the region known to the Arabs as *al-Iraq* and to the West as Mesopotamia was part of the Ottoman Empire. The area was divided into three provinces—Basra, Baghdad, and Mosul— each administered by a governor accountable to the Ottoman sultan. On November 5, 1914, Great Britain declared war on Ottoman Turkey, which had sided with the Central Powers in the war. Shortly thereafter, British troops landed in Basra. Originally, Britain was interested in using Basra as a foothold for defense against the Central Powers, as a base for maintaining communication links throughout her imperial domain, and as a strategic port for her navy on the Persian Gulf. Eventually, Mesopotamia became an important theater for the British war effort. Nearly 900,000 British and Indian troops fought in the area; they sustained 100,000 casualties.

In March 1917, the British army entered Baghdad, Mesopotamia's most important urban center. A journalist traveling with the soldiers described the scene as British soldiers entered the city, ending centuries of Ottoman rule, "Crowds of Baghdadis came out to meet us.... They lined the streets, balconies, and roofs, hurrahing and clapping their hands. Groups of schoolchildren danced in front of us, shouting and cheering, and the women of the city turned out in their holiday dresses."[22] Soon after they took the city, the British commander, General Maude read a public proclamation to the people of Baghdad, "Our armies do not come into your cities and lands as conquerors or enemies, but as liberators."[23] By 1918, the British had gained control of most of the provinces of Baghdad, Mosul, and Basra.

During the war, a significant number of Ottoman officers from Mesopotamia broke with the Ottoman Turks and joined the Arab Revolt. The revolt was organized by Sharif Hussein, whose position as the guardian of the holy sites of Mecca gave him a leadership role in the Muslim community, in collaboration with the British. In a series of letters between the British High Commissioner in Egypt and Hussein, known as the McMahon-Hussein Correspondence, the British assured Hussein that if he led an uprising against the Turks, he would be given an Arab state to lead after the war. In June 1916, Hussein dispatched his son, Faisal, to lead the Arab Revolt against the Ottomans. The Mesopotamian contingent in the revolt became some of Faisal's most trusted officers. The famous T. E. Lawrence served as Faisal's adviser throughout the revolt. The Arab Revolt was immortalized by the Hollywood film, *Lawrence of Arabia*. At war's end, the Ottoman Empire was defeated. Sharif Hussein soon learned that his imagined Arab nation, encompassing the Arab provinces of the Ottoman Empire, was not to be. Wartime diplomacy had created layer upon layer of conflicting commitments and expectations concerning the future of the Arab lands. The fate of Mesopotamia became mired in post-war diplomatic wrangling.

There was a political current supporting self-determination for the peoples who had been subjects of the Ottoman Empire. The strongest call came from President Woodrow Wilson of the United States in a statement known as the Fourteen Points presented on January 8, 1918. The twelfth point urged that, "the nationalities now under Turkish rule should be assured an undoubted security of life and an absolutely unmolested opportunity of autonomous development." Under pressure, the other Allied countries set forth the Anglo-French Declaration in November 1918, asserting that their "ambition is the complete and definite liberation of the people so long oppressed by the Turks and the establishment of national Governments and Administrations drawing their authority from the initiative and free choice of the indigenous populations."

Mesopotamia, however, remained under British military occupation with some advocating its formal colonization. It became a matter of heated debate among British colonial officials in London, Delhi, Cairo, and Baghdad. The head of the British administration in Iraq, Arnold Wilson, believed firmly that Mesopotamia should be ruled directly as a colony, along the model of British India. From Baghdad, he fumed over what he called Woodrow Wilson's "Twelfth Commandment."[24] Gertrude Bell, the Oriental Secretary in Baghdad, reported in January 1919, "The East is inclined to lose its head over the promise of settling for itself what is to become of it. ... We are having rather a windy time over self-determination."[25] Meanwhile, Faisal traveled to the Paris Peace Conference held at the Hotel Majestic in April 1919, all full of expectation that his family would be rewarded for the assistance they gave the British in fighting the Turks. Instead, he found that the Arab territories were being divided into separate states. He would be made the leader of Syria, at least for a short time.

Iraq's fate was further clarified at the San Remo Conference in 1920, when an intervening position between self-determination and colonialism, known as the mandate system, was agreed upon. Essentially, foreign powers were to be guardians of "new states" created from the remains of the Ottoman Empire, and then help them to eventually achieve complete independence. The League of Nations granted France a mandate over Lebanon and Syria. The French proceeded to oust Faisal from power. The League gave the British a mandate over Palestine and Mesopotamia. Basra, Baghdad, and Mosul were to be administered as one territory. Sir Percy Cox would assume the office of civil high commissioner and form a Mandatory Government in Mesopotamia.

This new arrangement did not sit well with the nationalists in Mesopotamia. Many had fought with Faisal during the war, hoping that the defeat of the Ottomans would bring about Arab independence. They had established political parties, organized clubs and societies, and published newspapers with the aim of creating a community that would become an Arab nation. The mosques, the bazaars, the schools, and especially the coffee houses became places where the nationalists could spread their views. By the summer of 1919, signs of discontent throughout Mesopotamia were clear, as several British officers were killed. A disparate group—the army officers who had fought with Faisal, the Shiite clergy, tribal leaders, and former civil servants—came together to resist British domination. By August 1920, the group was demanding the establishment of an Arab government, and the protests grew into a rebellion to which the British responded with full military force. The use of the Royal Air Force to bomb protesting tribes proved particularly effective. Phosphorous bombs, war rockets, man-killing shrapnel, liquid fire, and delay-action bombs were used by British forces to suppress the rebellion.[26] Winston Churchill, who at the time headed both the Air Ministry and the War Ministry, was a strong proponent of using the RAF in Iraq. "I do not understand," he said, "this squeamishness about the use of gas. I am strongly in favour of using poisoned gas against uncivilized tribes."[27]

Meanwhile, the British public questioned the wisdom of continuing a colonial presence in Iraq. One member of the British parliament protested "this Hunnish and barbarous method of warfare against unarmed people."[28] The London *Times* published an article in August 1920 asking, "How much longer are valuable lives to be sacrificed in the vain endeavour to impose upon the Arab population an elaborate and expensive administration which they never asked for and do not want?"[29] Repressing the rebellion cost 9,000 Iraqi lives, 2,000 British casualties, and 40 million pounds. Gertrude Bell understood the roots of Arab discontent. In a letter to her family in October 1920, she wrote, " ... We promised self-governing institutions, and not only made no step towards them but were busily setting up something entirely different. One of the papers says, quite rightly, that we had promised an Arab Government with British Advisers, and had set up a British Government with Arab Advisers. That's a perfectly fair statement."[30]

In January 1921, Winston Churchill became the colonial secretary. In a letter to the British prime minister, he confessed, "I feel misgivings about the political consequences to myself of taking on my shoulders the burden and the odium of the Mesopotamia entanglement. ..."[31] Churchill understood that nationalists continued to be active in Iraq. The British closed down oppositionist newspapers and arrested a group of nationalists, sending some to prison and others into exile. Back in England, calls to withdraw from Iraq intensified. Churchill warned, "We marched into Mesopotamia during the war and rooted up the Turkish Government.... We accepted before all the world a mandate for the country and undertook to introduce much better methods of government in the place of those we had overthrown. If, following upon this, we now ignominiously scuttle for the coast, leaving sheer anarchy behind us and ancient historic cities to be plundered by the wild Bedouin of the desert, an event will have occurred not at all in accordance with what has usually been the reputation of Great Britain."[32]

Winston Churchill knew the British needed a better long-term strategy for Mesopotamia—one that was more cohesive and less expensive. He decided to convene a meeting of the Middle East specialists in the British colonial administration, whom he called "the Forty Thieves," to hash out the problem. T. E. Lawrence, Percy Cox, and Gertrude Bell attended the Cairo Conference in March 1921. All three pressed Churchill to make Faisal the king of Iraq. Though he would remain largely under the control of the British, it would seem that the calls for an Arab government would have been answered. Churchill agreed. Back in England, Churchill explained his decision to the British Parliament, "...Our policy in Mesopotamia is to reduce our commitments and to extricate ourselves from our burdens while at the same time honourably discharging our obligations and building up a strong and effective Arab

Government which will always be the friend of Britain...."[33] The plan was set into action. Lawrence contacted his old friend Faisal and made arrangements for him to travel to Mesopotamia, a place Faisal had never before visited. Cox and Bell returned to Iraq to make the necessary arrangements to establish Faisal as monarch. Bell wrote to her father in July 1921, "To the best of our ability we were making history. But you may rely upon one thing—I'll never engage in creating kings again; it's too great a strain."[34] The Council of Ministers, the local administrative group the British had organized, endorsed Faisal as the Iraqi monarch. A rigged election followed shortly thereafter in which 96 percent of Iraqis voted for Faisal to be their king. The scholar Toby Dodge wrote, "If one were to pick up Iraq like a good piece of china and turn it over, it would bear the legend: 'Made in Whitehall, 1920.'"[35]

On August 23, 1921, Faisal was proclaimed king in the Citadel in Baghdad, as the British national anthem was played. The name of the country was officially changed to Iraq, and a new Iraqi flag designed with input from Gertrude Bell was hoisted from government buildings. A parliamentary government based on the British system was set up, and a British lawyer, Sir Edgar Bonham Carter, set about writing the Iraqi Constitution. Despite the establishment of a national Iraqi government, however, the British fully intended to maintain control over Iraqi military, economic, and political affairs. This arrangement was ensured through the signing of the Anglo-Iraqi Treaty of 1922. Faisal tried to balance the demands of the nationalists with the pressures of the British. Organizing the mandatory state and the new constitutional monarchy were overlapping and interconnected processes. At a fundamental level, British colonial power became inscribed onto the framework of the new Iraqi state.

After installing Faisal, Winston Churchill and the British Prime Minister Lloyd George continued to debate the merits of staying on in Iraq. Lloyd George argued for continued British presence, warning "If we leave we may find a year or two after we departed that we have handed over to the French and Americans some of the richest oilfields in the world...."[36] By 1929, the Iraqi Petroleum Company had been formed, with the British controlling the lion's share of Iraqi oil.

Though the British were not prepared to give up their power over Iraq altogether, they were ready to relinquish their mandate over the country. In 1930, another Anglo-Iraqi Treaty was signed that allowed Britain to retain their military bases and to maintain control over Iraq's economy and foreign policy. The following year, Britain submitted a special report to the League of Nations, indicating Iraq was prepared to become an independent state. In October 1932, Iraq became the 57th member state of the League of Nations. Throughout the mandate period, political and economic power was focused in the hands of a few city notables and professionals in alliance with some large landowners in the rural areas. This ruling oligarchy depended on cooperation with the British for their power. Elections were regularly rigged to produce a suitable outcome for the oligarchy. A handful of men rotated Cabinet posts, as new governments were formed. Even though the Iraqi constitutional monarchy was supposedly based on democratic principles, real power rested in the hands of a few. It was primarily as a result of this form of government that liberalism with its commensurate political apparatus—elections, parliaments, constitutions—became largely discredited in the minds of many Iraqis. From their perspective, constitutional democracy in Iraq had become a tool of colonialism.

A year after Iraq achieved independence, King Faisal died, and his son Ghazi succeeded him as king. Ghazi opposed European colonialism in the Middle East, and his views made him popular among many Iraqi and Arab nationalists. He set up a private radio station in his palace and broadcast declarations claiming that Kuwait, then under British control, should become a part of Iraq. One evening in the spring of 1939, Ghazi was driving his brand new Buick open car and had a terrible accident. Ghazi lost control of the car and hit a telegraph pole. He died soon after midnight on April 4, 1939. Ghazi's successor, King Faisal II, was only five-years old, so Ghazi's brother-in-law, Abdulillah, was made regent. The regent was more inclined to cooperate with the British. Rumors spread throughout Iraq and the Arab world that the British had somehow engineered Ghazi's death.

On the eve of World War II, then, Iraqi nationalist sentiment against the British was inflamed. Meanwhile, the Germans had been active in Iraq since the turn of the century, when they began constructing a railroad that would link Berlin to Baghdad. Some Germans hoped to make Mesopotamia a German colony along the lines of British India. Germans forged educational ties with Iraq, organized archaeological projects, and established radio stations that broadcast German views throughout Iraq. Pro-German sentiment was particularly strong among some Iraqi army officers, many of whom had studied under German teachers in the Ottoman military academy. These officers saw Germany as a model for Iraqi nationalism.[37]

In September 1939, after Germany attacked Poland, the British declared war on Germany. The British wanted Iraq to also declare war on Germany. The Iraqi government broke diplomatic relations with

Germany but did not want to enter the war. In March 1940, Rashid Ali became the prime minister of Iraq and announced that he would abide by all of Iraq's formal political commitments, including the Anglo-Iraqi Treaty of 1930. In June 1940, the British notified the Iraqi government that they intended to land troops in Basra that would pass through to Palestine. Rashid Ali granted them permission to do so but asked that the troops pass with haste over Iraqi territory. Meanwhile, as the British pressed Iraq to declare war on Italy, Rashid Ali continued to assert Iraq's neutrality. The British opposed Rashid Ali in the strongest terms and pressed the regent to remove him from office. In January 1941, Rashid Ali resigned as prime minister.

Four colonels in the Iraqi army decided to back Rashid Ali and help him take over the Iraqi government, despite the resistance of the regent and the British. One of these colonels was Salah al-Din al-Sabbagh. He asserted his strong nationalism saying, "I do not believe in the democracy of the English or in the Nazism of the German nor in the Bolshevism of the Russians. I am an Arab Muslim. I do not want anything as a substitute in the way of pretensions and philosophies." For these nationalists, liberalism had been altogether discredited. German militarism provided them with an alternative model for Arab nationalism. The Allies, in particular France and Britain, were the colonial powers who continued to hold power over Palestine, Syria, Lebanon, and to some extent Iraq. The Iraqi army officers saw an alliance with Germany as a way to achieve their goals—total independence and unity for the Arabs. As historian Reeva Simon explained, "To be sure, there were some pro-Nazi Iraqis, but the army officers who turned to Germany were not Nazis. Indeed, they tended to overlook the racial ideology that placed them one step above the Jews and looked instead to those areas of compatibility they had formed with the Germany of Wilhelm II when German ideas especially cultural nationalism reached them in Istanbul at the military schools where Iraqi officers received their first taste of Westernization at the hands of German military officers." Khairallah Tulfah, Saddam Hussein's uncle and an officer in the Iraqi army, participated in the movement. [38]

On April 1, Rashid Ali and his colonels made their move. They surrounded the regent's palace. The following day, the regent fled Iraq. Rashid Ali formed the Government of National Defense and announced that he would abide by all of Iraq's international obligations, including the Anglo-Iraqi Treaty. The British representative in Iraq, Sir K. Cornwallis, and British officials in London debated how to best react to the uprising. Within a week, Cornwallis reported that Rashid Ali had such widespread support that the only way to counter him was militarily.

Churchill felt that control over Basra was essential for the British war effort; it was necessary to secure access to Persian oil, the pipeline to the Mediterranean, and Egypt and India's security. Tensions over the presence of British troops in Iraq finally came to a head. Churchill did not want to take any chances. A delay might give the Axis the upper hand. He was unequivocal in his directions, telling the British commander that the "immediate task is to get a friendly Government set up in Baghdad and to beat down Rashid Ali's forces with utmost vigour."[39]

The British announced their intention to land more troops in Basra; Rashid Ali said no new troops could arrive until those already on Iraqi soil moved on to Palestine. The British viewed this as a violation of the Anglo-Iraqi Treaty. On May 2, war broke out between Britain and Iraq. The RAF was used to bomb Iraqi troops, flying over 200 sorties in the first day of the war. What support Rashid Ali received from the Axis Powers was too little and too late. Within a month, the Iraqi forces were defeated, and Rashid Ali fled the country. "Hitler," Churchill observed, "certainly cast away the opportunity of taking a great prize for little cost in the Middle East."[40]

On May 30, an armistice agreement was signed; on June 1, the regent returned to Baghdad. All four colonels who had backed Rashid Ali were eventually put to death. As Cornwallis reported, "[The] Iraqi Government are proceeding with the task of getting rid of pro-Axis officials both in the army and civil administration.... Rashid Ali has, however, so packed the army and administration with his supporters that a little time must necessarily elapse before they can all be eliminated, and suitable people found to take their place."[41] The British had taken nearly 1,000 Iraqi prisoners. Saddam's beloved uncle Khairallah was amongst them; he served a five year sentence and was discharged from the army.

For many Iraqis, the 1941 war would be remembered as an important national moment—an act of resistance to colonialism that allowed Iraq to briefly assume the mantle of leadership in the Arab world. The revolt captured the imagination of the young Saddam Hussein. Before he was executed, one of the leaders of the rebellion, Colonel Sabbagh, wrote his memoirs in prison. They were published after he was put to death. Saddam Hussein read the book carefully, and it left a lasting impression on him. Saddam viewed Sabbagh "as a great nationalist who tried to achieve Pan-Arab objectives. True, Sabbagh failed in his objectives, but his teachings inspired other young nationalists to achieve them." Indeed, Saddam "was inspired by Colonel Sabbagh's memoirs to pursue the same nationalist goals that Colonel Sabbagh and his followers had advocated."[42] When Saddam came to live with his uncle, the defeat of the rebellion was still fresh for Khairallah.

A few years after Saddam moved into his uncle's home, Khairallah was offered a teaching position in Baghdad. Khairallah moved his family to Baghdad. Joining his uncle's family, Saddam left Tikrit behind, at least for the time being. Yet Saddam's strong ties to Tikrit would remain an enduring aspect of his personal and political life. His political alliances were mapped by his ties to his family and clan in Tikrit. Tikritis bolstered and protected Saddam when he was in need; he, in turn, richly rewarded Tikritis for their loyalty and enduring support. According to custom, young boys from Tikrit are tattooed with three small dots on their wrist. Many removed the tattoo when they moved to the big city to camouflage their peasant background. Saddam, on the other hand, would keep his tattoo. Tikrit was too much a part of who he was.

SADDAM GOES TO BAGHDAD

In the 1950s, as King Faisal II was enthroned, Saddam Hussein moved with his uncle's family to Kharkh, a suburb of Baghdad. Khairallah assumed his new teaching post, and in the fall of 1955, Saddam enrolled in Kharkh High School. As a teenager, Saddam worked odd jobs as a driver's assistant, a cigarette peddler, and a coffee house attendant to make some extra money. Baghdad in the 1950s was a boom town, steeped in political activity. The city's population had nearly tripled between 1920 and 1950. Revived by increased revenues from the oil industry, Baghdad was exploding with new suburbs like Kharkh. Uneven economic development focused the country's wealth in urban centers, leaving much of the rural population destitute. They flocked to Baghdad in search of work; most were only able to get low-paying jobs in construction or the service sector. The gap in living standards between the rich and the poor became greater and more visible. The rich furnished their homes with expensive televisions, refrigerators, and washing machines. Baghdad's streets were clogged with 30,000 cars, most of them American. The cultural life of the city was thriving. It had the first television station in the Middle East, and nearly 50 Arabic newspapers were available at the newsstands. The city center boasted cinemas, glittering shops, and bustling cafés.

The 1950s were a decade of construction, building, and change in Iraq's capital. In 1951, Iraq arrived at a new arrangement with oil companies giving it 50 percent of Iraqi oil revenues. Much of this revenue was directed to the budget of the new Development Board, which was charged with undertaking huge development projects such as dams, roads, and hospitals. Baghdad now had 5 bridges crossing its rivers. The Development Board was criticized for being pervaded by foreign influence, corruption, and favoritism. Several thousand foreigners—mainly British and American—lived in Baghdad, working for the oil industry or for foreign contractors who received bids from the Development Board.

In 1955, the Development Board initiated a massive 1.4-billion-dollar modernization plan. With the help of the U.S. government, Iraq began developing a nuclear training and research center. As part of President Eisenhower's "Atoms for Peace" program, Iraq and the United States entered into a bilateral agreement to develop Iraq's nuclear research facilities.[43] The research reactors provided to Iraq under this program were fueled by highly enriched uranium (HEU), which can be used to make nuclear weapons.[44]

The modernization schema also included constructing large public buildings. Leading international architects like Le Corbusier, Alvar Aalto, and Gio Ponti were commissioned to design a university, a stadium, a museum, and government buildings. The famous American architect Frank Lloyd Wright traveled to Baghdad in 1957 by invitation of King Farouk II to design an opera house on an island in the Tigris River. Wright extended the initial proposal to include a zoo, a bazaar, and a university complex. Wright had become enamored with Baghdad as a young child reading *The Arabian Nights* and dreaming of the city that flourished as the capital of the Abbasid caliphs in the eighth century. Under Abbasid rule, Baghdad became a commercial and cultural center of the Islamic world. Baghdad, known to the Arabs as the city of wisdom, was ravaged by the Mongol conqueror Hülegü in 1258. It is said that the Tigris and the Euphrates turned black from the ink of the thousands of books the Mongols purged from Baghdad's famous libraries. The humiliation and devastation of that attack are etched in the historical imaginations of many Arabs and Muslims.

Wright spoke of his project, "... I happen to be doing a cultural center for the place where civilization was invented—that is Iraq. Before Iraq was destroyed it was a beautiful circular city built by Harun al-Rashid but the Mongols came from the north and practically destroyed it. Now what is left of the city has struck oil and they have immense sums of money. They can bring back the city of Harun al-Rashid today. They are not likely to do it because a lot of western architects are in there already building skyscrapers all over the place...."[45]

Wright's plans for Baghdad fused ancient, Islamic, and modernist designs. He based a monument honoring Harun al-Rashid on a 2,500 year old structure in Samarra, and he imagined a parking deck in the form of an ancient ziggurat. "These designs," Wright explained, "demonstrate that if we are able to understand and interpret our ancestors, there is no need to copy them. Nor need Baghdad adopt the materialistic structures called 'modern' now barging in from the West upon the East."[46] While Wright's architectural design for Baghdad was visionary in some respects, it was profoundly out of step with the urgent needs of the city. As Frank Lloyd Wright and the king imagined building elaborate structures harkening back to Iraq's grand history, over 90,000 Baghdadis lived in squalor in makeshift shacks.

The economic disjunction of life in Baghdad fed political unrest. Popular uprisings in 1948 and 1952 were violently repressed by the government. The Communist Party (ICP) was the major organizer of these demonstrations. The ICP had gained prominence since 1941 and had a strong following among students and workers. As the historian Hanna Batatu explained, "In the forties communism became a factor in the life of Iraq. It did not implant itself in the citadels of power but in the hearts and minds of the youth. In terms of continuity, organization, and number of supporters and sympathizers, it rose to first rank among political movements.... Far from dying out, communism became in the fifties a more powerful passion, its ideas evoking feelings akin to faith, and assuming with many of the youth the force of being beyond argument."[47]

The unpopular Prime Minister Nuri Al-Said and Crown Prince Abdulillah, who had cooperated with the British during the 1941 rebellion, controlled the government. In the 1950s, political repression sharpened, as opposition parties and newspapers were banned. With the parliament dominated by insiders, legitimate means of political opposition were closed off. Regional politics fed rising discontent. In 1955, the Iraqi government entered into the Baghdad Pact—a U.S.-backed alliance with Britain, Iran, Turkey, and Pakistan—that was seen by many Iraqis as a conspiracy against pan-Arabism and as a regressive consolidation of foreign imperial power over the region's affairs. In 1956, Gamal Abdul Nasser, the popular pan-Arabist leader of Egypt, nationalized the Suez Canal. Nasser's armies then successfully withstood an attack by France, Britain, and Israel, who sought to keep the Suez Canal from falling under Egyptian control. The Iraqi government's response to Nasser was tepid, but the Iraqi population was emboldened by his successful stand against foreign domination.

Riots and strikes enveloped Baghdad. A burgeoning student movement spread throughout the city's schools, including Kharkh High School, where Saddam plodded along in academic mediocrity. Nasser's pan-Arabism influenced Saddam, who ditched school and took to the streets to join the riots. Saddam thrived on the tumultuous political scene and was drawn to the Baath Party, a small party advocating a form of Arab nationalism and socialism that had attracted some 300 members by 1955. He found his entrée into the Baath party by organizing street gangs who operated on the fringes of the student movement. Early on, Saddam's devotion to the party may have been somewhat tenuous. He applied to the Baghdad Military Academy, which would have assured him a career as an Iraqi army officer. When Saddam failed the entrance examination, his choices became more clear. Life in mainstream politics had been closed off to him. In 1957, at the age of 20, Saddam became a member of the Baath Party. Saddam would recall this time in Baghdad as "the days of our underground freedom fighting."[48]

The main opposition parties—the National Democratic Party, the Baath Party, and the Iraqi Communist Party—had different political outlooks but shared a reformist and anticolonialist agenda. Given the repressive political atmosphere, they eventually saw that coming together as an oppositionist force against the monarchy was essential. Together, they formed a successful boycott of the 1957 national elections as a protest against the political repression in Iraq. The oppositionist parties formed an alliance with the Free Officers, a small secret movement in the army. The stage was set for a revolution.

On the evening of July 13, 1958, King Faisal II entertained guests at the royal palace. A magician performed for a small group of children; this was followed by a late dinner at 9:30 p.m. Afterwards, the king and some guests went next door to the Zuhur Palace to see the Doris Day film, "The Pajama Game." Early the next morning, the king had his tea; while getting his morning shave, he listened to the radio and heard news that a revolution was underway. The streets of Baghdad filled with masses of demonstrators. At 6:30 a.m., the radio announced that the army had liberated "the beloved homeland from the corrupt crew that imperialism installed."[49] The Free Officers led by Abdul Karim Qasim and Abdul Salam Arif had secured a brigade of the army and directed it to Baghdad. The soldiers had surrounded the royal palace and the home of the prime minister, Nuri Al-Said. As they tried to escape the palace, some members of the royal household including the king and the crown prince were killed with machine guns. Nuri Al-Said escaped but was killed a few days later, trying to flee Baghdad disguised in a woman's veil. The king of Jordan, a cousin of King Faisal II's, announced the news of the killings on the BBC radio. Several days of public looting and revenge killings followed.

Qasim and Arif appeared on television, calling for "order and unity ... in the interest of the homeland" and announcing the formation of a popular government in the form of a republic.[50] Qasim became the prime minister, and Arif became the deputy prime minister and minister of interior. The monarchy and the parliament were abolished, and the army was purged of members of the old regime. The revamped army became the center of the new republic. The new republic's foreign policy focused on ending colonialism in the Arab world. Formal relations were established with China and the Soviet Union, signaling the socialist orientation of the new government.

A range of political groups and individuals had come together in July 1958 with a single aim—to overthrow the monarchy. In the aftermath of the revolution, however, political divisions rocked Iraq. Within days of the establishment of a republic Michel Aflaq, the Christian Syrian founder of the Baath Party, arrived in Baghdad. Baathism espoused a form of Arab socialism, and the constitution of the party called for the Arabs to form one nation. "We represent liberty, socialism, and unity," explained Aflaq. "This is the interest of the Arab nation...."[51] Aflaq wanted Iraq to join the newly formed United Arab Republic (UAR) that included Egypt and Syria. The Communists, on the other hand, strongly opposed Iraq's union with the UAR. The military officers who were the leaders of the revolution were, in turn, divided on the issue. While Arif wanted Iraq to join the UAR, Qasim strongly opposed it. Arif gravitated towards the nationalists and the Baathists, while Qasim grew closer to the Communists. The Communists, who were the most organized political party in Iraq with the largest following, also provided Qasim with the support base he needed to consolidate his position as the leader of Iraq. Qasim became increasingly suspicious of Arif, viewing him as a direct threat to his power. By the fall of 1958, Arif was stripped of his cabinet posts and appointed the Iraqi ambassador to Germany. Arif stayed in Germany for a very brief time. Returning to Baghdad, he was arrested, tried, and imprisoned. Arif was out of power, and the political fortunes of the Baathists seemed in precipitous decline.

The revolution of July 14, 1958 had a huge impact on Saddam Hussein and on his hometown of Tikrit. Like the rest of Iraq, Tikrit was divided between nationalists and communists. A few months after the revolution, Saddam was accused of murdering Hajj Sadoun al-Tikriti, a local communist leader, who had been a rival of his uncle Khairallah. At the age of 21, Saddam was charged with the crime and sentenced to a term in the Sarai Prison. As a Baathist in the tumultuous months following the revolution, Saddam believed he was safer in prison than in the streets of

Baghdad. After six months, Saddam was released. He returned to Tikrit, where he continued his political activities, covering the walls of local buildings with Baathist slogans. Soon, a Baathist party member visited Saddam and said, "The party wants you in Baghdad." Saddam set off for Baghdad to receive his orders.[52]

NOTES

1. Amir Iskander, *Saddam Hussein: The Fighter, the Thinker, and the Man*, trans. Hassan Selim (Paris: Hachette Réalités, 1980), pp. 21–22.

2. A. S. Elwell-Sutton, "The Tigris above Baghdad," *Geographical Journal* 60, no. 1, (July 1922), 36.

3. Freya Stark, *Baghdad Sketches* (London: John Murray, 1946; originally published in 1937), p. 146.

4. Ibid.

5. "An Interview with Saddam Hussein," in *Saddam Hussein: The Man, the Cause, and the Future*, ed. Fuad Matar (London: Third World Centre, 1981), pp. 227–28.

6. The August 1979 speech in which the statement was made is quoted in Iskander, *Saddam Hussein: The Fighter, the Thinker, and the Man*, p. 20.

7. "An Interview with Saddam Hussein," in Matar, *Saddam Hussein*, p. 236.

8. "I Was Saddam's Boyhood Friend," interview with Ibrahim Zobedi, BBC News, http://news.bbc.co.uk/2/hi/programmes/panorama/2399891.stm (retrieved July 29, 2003).

9. Quoted in Efraim Karsh and Inari Rautsi, *Saddam Hussein, A Political Biography*, 2nd edition (New York: Grove Press, 2002), p. 9.

10. 'Abd al-Amir Mu'allah, *Nahr Yashuqqu Majrah* [A River Carves Its Own Path] (Baghdad: Dar al-Shu'un al-Thaqafiyyah al-` Ammah, 1995), p. 7.

11. Iskander, *Saddam Hussein*, p. 21.

12. Said K. Aburish, *Saddam Hussein: The Politics of Revenge* (London: Bloomsbury, 2000), p. 17.

13. "Saddam: A Warning from History," Panorama documentary, BBC, broadcast on November 3, 2002, transcript from the BBC News Web site, http://news.bbc.co.uk/2/hi/programmes/panorama/2371697.stm (retrieved July 29, 2003).

14. Iskander, *Saddam Hussein*, p. 22.

15. "I Was Saddam's Boyhood Friend."

16. Mu'allah, *Nahr Yashuqqu Majrah*, pp. 23–29; Mattar, *Saddam Hussein*, p. 31. Said Aburish suggests that the story has been inflamed for effect; in his view, it is unlikely that his mother would oppose Saddam living with her brother and even more unlikely that a young boy would be given a gun. See Aburish, *Saddam Hussein*, p. 19.

17. "I Was Saddam's Boyhood Friend."

18. Mu'allah, *Nahr Yashuqqu Majrah*, pp. 9–10.

19. Jerrold M. Post, "Saddam Hussein of Iraq: A Political Psychological Profile," in *The Psychological Assessment of Political Leaders*, ed. Jerrold M. Post (Ann Arbor: University of Michigan Press, 2003), p. 337.

20. "An Interview with Saddam Hussein," in Matar, *Saddam Hussein*, p. 228.

21. Majid Khadduri, *Socialist Iraq: A Study in Iraqi Politics Since 1968* (Washington, D.C.: The Middle East Institute, 1978), p. 72.

22. Edmund Candler, "British Welcome in Baghdad," *The Guardian*, March 16, 1917.

23. Quoted in Ernst B. Haas, "The Reconciliation of Conflicting Colonial Policy Aims: Acceptance of the League of Nations Mandate System," *International Organization* 6, no. 4 (November 1952): 526.

24. Sir Arnold Wilson, *Loyalties: Mesopotamia*, vol. 2 (London: Oxford University Press, 1936; originally published 1931), p. 99.

25. *The Letters of Gertrude Bell*, vol. 2, ed. Lady Bell (New York: Boni and Liveright, 1927), pp. 465–66.

26. Geoff Simons, *Iraq: From Sumer to Saddam* (New York: St. Martin's Press, 1996; originally published 1994), p. 214.

27. Quoted in Simons, *Iraq*, p. 213.

28. Quoted in Peter Sluglett, *Britain in Iraq, 1914–1932* (London: Ithaca Press, 1976), p. 264.

29. Quoted in David Fromkin, *A Peace to End All Peace* (New York: Henry Holt and Company, 1989), p. 452.

30. *The Letters of Gertrude Bell*, vol. 2, p. 502.

31. Quoted in Fromkin, *A Peace to End All Peace*, p. 500.

32. Quoted in Aaron S. Klieman, *Foundations of British Policy in the Arab World: The Cairo Conference of 1921* (Baltimore, Md.: Johns Hopkins Press, 1970), p. 95.

33. Winston Churchill, "Middle East Government Policy," speech to the House of Commons, June 14, 1921, in *Winston S. Churchill: His Complete Speeches, 1897–1963*, vol. 3, ed. Robert Rhodes James (London: Chelsea House Publishers, 1974), p. 3102.

34. *The Letters of Gertrude Bell*, vol. 2, pp. 609–10.

35. Toby Dodge, *Inventing Iraq: The Failure of Nation Building and a History Denied* (New York: Columbia University Press, 2003).

36. Quoted in Fromkin, *A Peace to End All Peace*, p. 509.

37. Reeva S. Simon, *Iraq between the Two World Wars: The Creation and Implementation of a Nationalist Ideology* (New York: Columbia University Press, 1986).

38. Simon, p. xii, 133.

39. Quoted in Simons, *Iraq: From Sumer to Saddam*, p. 222.

40. Quoted in Raghid El-Solh, *Britain's Two Wars with Iraq: 1941/1991* (Reading, UK: Ithaca Press, 1996), p. 133.

41. Cornwallis to Foreign Office, June 9, 1941, *Records of the Hashemite Dynasties: A Twentieth Century Documentary History*, vol. 13, p. 316.

42. Khadduri, *Socialist Iraq*, p. 73.

43. 20th Report on Progress of Program for International Cooperation in Peaceful Uses of Atomic Energy, Lewis L. Strauss to Dwight D. Eisenhower, July 29, 1957, Dwight D. Eisenhower Library, reproduced on Digital National Security Archive [DNSA].

44. Union of Concerned Scientists, Statement on the 50th Anniversary of Eisenhower's "Atoms for Peace" speech, December 8, 2003, http://www.ucsusa. org/global_security/nuclear_terrorism/page.cfm?pageID=1296 (retrieved March 23, 2005).

45. Speech at San Rafael High School, July 1957, *Frank Lloyd Wright's Architectural Drawings: The 1957 Baghdad Project*, http://www.geocities.com/ SoHo/1469/flw_iraq.htm (retrieved August 6, 2003).

46. Frank Lloyd Wright, "Frank Lloyd Wright Designs for Baghdad," *Architectural Forum* (May 1958): 91.

47. Hanna Batatu, *The Old Social Classes and the Revolutionary Movements of Iraq* (Princeton, N.J.: Princeton University Press, 1978), p. 465.

48. Saddam Hussein Interview with Dan Rather, CBS News, February 24, 2003, transcript, http://www.cbsnews.com (retrieved August 13, 2003).

49. Quoted in Marion Farouk-Sluglett and Peter Sluglett, *Iraq Since 1958: From Revolution to Dictatorship*, revised edition (London: I. B. Tauris, 2001), p. 49.

50. Ibid.

51. Michel Aflaq, "Baathism," in *The Saddam Hussein Reader*, ed. Turi Munthe (New York: Thunder's Mouth Press, 2002), pp. 37–38.

52. Iskandar, *Saddam Hussein*, pp. 50–52.

Chapter 2

SADDAM'S RISE TO POWER

THE LONG DAYS

By the fall of 1959, it had become abundantly clear that Baathists would have little power in an Iraq ruled by Abdul Karim Qasim. Party leaders decided the time was ripe to assassinate the prime minister. Saddam Hussein was summoned to Baghdad and began preparing for the assassination. He took an apartment on Rashid Street, which ran through the heart of Baghdad near the old city gate. The last Ottoman governor of Baghdad Province had inaugurated the street in 1916. When Saddam moved to the neighborhood, Rashid Street was the part of town where fashionable professionals preferred to live and work. A dozen newspapers had their offices on the street. Intellectuals gathered in its famous cafés, like the Al-Braziliya and the Umm Kulthum, to sip tea and share conversation. Saddam would soon add another chapter to the history of the illustrious street.[1]

Baathist opposition to Qasim had been percolating since the overthrow of the monarchy in July 1958. A range of political groups participated in the July Revolution, and many were not prepared to quietly submit to Qasim's leadership. Often, Iraqis took to the streets to hash out their political positions, and demonstrations were common throughout the country. Qasim, in turn, organized counter-demonstrations that sometimes led to violent clashes. Long simmering political tensions eventually culminated in an uprising in the town of Mosul in March 1959. "It seemed as if all social cement dissolved and all political authority vanished," wrote historian Hanna Batatu. "Individualism, breaking out, waxed into anarchy. The struggle between nationalists and Communists had released age-old antagonisms, investing them with an explosive force and carrying them to the point of civil war."[2] Mosul was a predominantly conservative and nationalist town, and a good number of the Free Officers at that Mosul garrison opposed Qasim. Rumors spread that these officers were planning a rebellion.

Meanwhile, in late February, a newspaper of the Iraqi Communist Party (ICP) announced that a rally would be held in Mosul on March 6. The purpose of the rally was twofold. It would provide Qasim and the ICP a chance to avert the soldiers' plot, while also showing support for the local Communists who were largely outnumbered by nationalists. Qasim supported the Communists' rally, and the state media was flooded with news of the upcoming event. Train rides to Mosul from other Iraqi cities were deeply discounted. Thousands descended upon the city. Tensions mounted. Nationalists in Mosul felt under siege, and the Free Officers decided the time had come to carry out their coup. On March 6, a crowd of 250,000 marched through Mosul chanting pro-Qasim slogans. That march proceeded peacefully. The following day demonstrations continued, and the nationalists took to the streets in counter-demonstrations against the Communists. On the morning of March 8, an announcement on Mosul Radio called for a revolt against Qasim, who had "betrayed" the July Revolution and "warred against Arab nationalism."[3] Violent clashes ensued over the next four days, resulting in hundreds of deaths. The leaders of the rebellion were arrested and tried. In the wake of the bloody Mosul Rebellion, the Communists were emboldened, while the nationalists and Baathists saw their position in the Iraqi government precipitously declining.

The Mosul Rebellion placed Iraq at the epicenter of Cold War politics. On the evening of April 11, the U.S. Secretary of State John Foster Dulles telephoned President Eisenhower, who was on a golfing vacation in Augusta, Georgia. At the time, the secretary of state was undergoing cancer treatment in Florida, and his brother, Allen Dulles, the head of the Central Intelligence Agency (CIA), was visiting him. The urgency of the conversation led the President to ask the head of the CIA to travel to Augusta for a private meeting that very night. The presidential press secretary denied that the visit was connected with "an emergency" in Iraq, although he acknowledged that Iraq was a major topic of conversation.[4] On April 28, Allen Dulles, the Director of the CIA, said that the situation in Iraq was "the most dangerous in the world today." Dulles briefed the Senate Foreign Relations Committee, and according to

Senator Fulbright, Dulles warned that the Communists were on the verge of "a complete takeover" of the Iraqi government. Fulbright spelled out American officials' solution to the crisis, a central component of which was to approach Egyptian President Nasser. There were reports of a rift between the USSR and Nasser, which Dulles hoped would make the Egyptian leader an ally against the Communists in Iraq.[5]

U.S. concerns about encroaching communism in Iraq had grown through the 1950s. In February 1951, the State Department's top diplomats working on the Middle East met in Istanbul to review U.S. goals in the region. The conference concluded that in the Cold War period, among American "military-political objectives in the Middle East," the main concern was "to mobilize strength for the containment of communism."[6] American officials initiated a propaganda campaign to counter the influence of communism in Iraq. A series of anti-communist posters were displayed in Baghdad, featuring a red pig as the symbol of communism with Arabic captions. The symbol of the pig was used due to "the resistance appeal it has for Moslems."[7] This was followed by a campaign to produce anti-communist pamphlets in Arabic. According to a memorandum from the American Embassy in Baghdad, "The pamphlets will be designed to appeal primarily to the educated and semi-educated, politically interested groups who belong to the urban middle class. These groups include Government officials and employees; teachers; professors; lawyers; Army officers; religious leaders; other professional people; and urban business men."[8] The U.S. embassy in Baghdad also set in place programs in Iraqi schools and universities meant to counter communist influence amongst Iraqi students.[9]

The Mosul rebellion, then, fed into American fears about communism in Iraq that had been developing for some time. In April 1959, *The New York Times* reported that U.S. government officials were alarmed by events in Mosul and the prevalence of communists throughout Iraq: "Communist control of the street mobs, Communist domination of the radio and most of the newspapers, Communist control of student and professional organizations, new economic ties with and some arms deliveries from the Communist bloc, and the Communist tendencies among some close advisers of the Premier. Iraq would appear to be on the brink of a Communist take-over."[10]

Another consequence of the Mosul Rebellion was the utter disenchantment of the Baathists with Qasim, who was purging nationalists and Baathists from the government and the army. The Baathists ultimately decided that the only way they would assume power was to assassinate

Qasim.[11] The date was set for October 7. Saddam and the other plotters gathered on Rashid Street. Saddam was wearing a large overcoat that belonged to his uncle Khairallah. Beneath the coat, he hid a gun. As Qasim's car drove by, the assassins riddled it with bullets. Shoddy planning ultimately foiled the plot. Qasim was shot, but not fatally. Saddam received a superficial wound to his leg. Another of the would-be assassins was killed, and his body was left behind at the scene. This ultimately revealed the identity of the plotters, who were forced into hiding. The attempted assassination of Qasim proved to be a pivotal moment for Saddam.

The story of October 7, 1959 has been retold countless times. Saddam commissioned a novel and even a movie based on the events. He recounted the story to journalists and biographers. During his presidency, he commemorated the occasion by reenacting his infamous swim across the Tigris during his escape. The attempted killing of Prime Minister Qasim became an epic moment in the mythical lore of Saddam Hussein's life.

Saddam's version of events is presented by one of his biographers, Amir Iskander. As Saddam and the other Baathists fled the scene, a policeman shot at them. Saddam took a bullet to the leg, but his chief concern was getting the group to their getaway car. In order to avoid being caught by the authorities, they chose not to go to the hospital, but it was clear that Saddam's bullet wound needed treatment. One of his coconspirators removed the bullet using a razor blade and a pair of scissors; Saddam fainted from the pain. Fearing the police would find their hideout, Saddam left for his uncle Khairallah's house. His uncle told him that he had been visiting a friend on Rashid Street and had witnessed the incident. Saddam asked his uncle to get him an injection for his wound. He was then informed that the other conspirators who had stayed behind in the hideout had been discovered and arrested. Saddam burned all photos of himself with his fellow plotters that were in his uncle's house and fled. Fifteen minutes later, the police raided his uncle's house.

Saddam went to the house of a relative on the outskirts of Baghdad. The next morning, dressed in the clothes of an old Iraqi peasant and carrying a small knife, he caught a taxi that dropped him off on the road leading to Tikrit. As he limped along this road, his leg seething with pain, he saw a horse belonging to a local peasant. For 17 dinars, he bought the horse and rode it on the road to Tikrit, which ran parallel to the Tigris River. He rode all day and spent the night with some bedouin. The second night, he slept on the ground. On the third night, on the hills near Samarra, he came upon a bedouin wedding, where he ate a hearty meal of mutton. The next day, Saddam was stopped by men wielding machine guns in a government car. Saddam convinced them he was a local bedouin, and they let him carry on. Saddam reached the river crossing at nightfall, too late to take the ferry across. There was no time to waste, so he decided to swim across the river. He let his horse go. Saddam took off his clothes, which he tied around his neck in a bundle, and with the small knife nestled between his teeth, he swam across the river.

Iskander describes the nighttime swim across the Tigris with great flourish: "Only God knows who gave him his superhuman strength in those critical hours as he struggled against the waves with the pain in his leg and the bundle of clothes, heavy with water above his head, threatening all the time to thrust his weary body into the depths. But he struggled on, stubbornly, resisting the waves, defying them to their worst, doggedly clinging to life, by sheer force of will ... he will not give up. He refuses to die."[12]

After this traumatic ordeal, Saddam sought refuge in a small mud hut on the river bank, eventually making his way to his mother's home. His brother contacted the local Baath members who came to fetch Saddam. Arrangements were made for Saddam to escape with two companions to Syria. Using the stars to guide them, they traveled at night. On the seventh night, they arrived at Syria and spent the night in the tents of some bedouin. After staying in Damascus for a few months, Saddam moved on to Cairo.

The story of Saddam's role in the assassination attempt also appeared in the novel *Ayyam al-Tawilah* [The Long Days] written by ʿAbd al-Amir Muʿallah, an Iraqi writer. The plot of the book adheres to the basic narrative Iskander outlined, but the novelist embellished the details of Saddam's escape, presenting him as a heroic man of the people who used his guile and courage for the greater benefit of Iraq. The book's foreword notes, "Although it is a novel, it is solidly and accurately based on historical events in Iraq. It is a vivid record and matchless testimony to the struggle of the young men who proved to be the real moulders of the new Iraq. It is a drama of real life." *The Long Days* is a dramatic novel of sacrifice, pain, endurance, and patriotism. Its hero, Muhammad, takes a bullet while protecting his fallen comrade. Using their getaway car, he and his friends escape to a nearby apartment, where a doctor is supposed to be waiting to tend to their injuries. The doctor never arrives. Bleeding and in great pain, Muhammad persuades a reluctant comrade to use a razor blade to remove the bullet from his leg. Trembling, Muhammad bites his lip to avoid crying out in agony as the bullet is pried from his leg.

Convinced that their hideout is bound to be discovered by the police, Muhammad declares to the other conspirators, "I'm leaving. I'm not submitting my neck to the executioner." He slips out and limps to his uncle's house. Though he does not want to tell his uncle what he has done, he learns that his uncle had been visiting a friend on Al Rashid Street and had seen the assassination attempt unfold. As Muhammad describes how his friend had removed the bullet from his leg, "his uncle's lips and cheeks twitched ... Two tears of sorrow and tenderness fell from his eyes."

Though the police are in hot pursuit of the would-be assassins, it takes some time for Muhammad to plan his escape from Baghdad. Fearing that the authorities will catch him, he gives himself a pep talk: "Didn't you tire them out when you were circulating the party leaflets? Didn't you wear them out when you engaged so many times with them in conflicts and bruised their faces with your bare hands? Didn't you drain their energy when you were giving the people lessons on how to rise up against bondage?" Gathering his courage, Muhammad goes to the house of a distant relative who lived on the outskirts of Baghdad, where he spends the night. The next day, he leaves the house wearing a flowing *dishdasha*, the traditional Iraqi clothing. To complete the look of a peasant, he smears his shoes with mud. Before he leaves, he tucks a small knife into his pocket.

Muhammad then takes a taxi to the road to Tikrit. Along the road, he spots a horse, which he bought from its owner. Mounting the horse, he rides north along the banks of the Tigris River, towards his childhood home in Tikrit. Looking at the river, Muhammad thinks,

> Was the Tigris asleep ... the Tigris which flowed through Iraq? Was it really asleep this river which had come down from all those immemorial ages to quench the thirst of the people of today? ... This is the river which has overflowed its banks with its rich alluvial mud, flooded the earth, and moulded from that ancient ever-renewing mud, men who were different from other human beings in those olden days! ... The teacher of history had explained that they challenged mighty nature, stretched their hands to the river waters and the mud banks, and created the first civilisation. There they had recorded their historical chronicles before anybody else could venture to do so!

The passage drove home a particular image of Saddam. Dressed as a peasant riding horseback towards his childhood home in Tikrit and bemoaning the sorry state of contemporary Iraq, he found hope and inspiration in the timeless waters of the Tigris and the achievements of the ancient Mesopotamians. He was but an ordinary man driven to save Iraq, who drew his extraordinary strength from the country's ancient history and majestic landscape.

Saddam's uncle Khairallah is a central figure in the novel. A compassionate and caring father figure to Saddam, his uncle is depicted as a patriot who was deeply disheartened by the corruption of Qasim's regime. As Muhammad (aka Saddam) gallantly makes his way towards Tikrit, the newspapers publish his photograph. His uncle scoffs when he sees the paper: "What kind of justice is this when thousands of people are languishing in prisons? Thousands of houses are empty of men? ... None except the hungry children? Huh! These shameless creatures! Do they think that the people understand nothing? ... Are they human beings or beasts?"

After an arduous journey, Muhammad finally reaches his hometown, where his brother greets him with joyful tears. With the authorities in hot pursuit, he is told he must make his way to Syria. Joined by some comrades, Muhammad makes the treacherous trek through the desert. As they cross the desert into Syria, Muhammad crouches on the ground. "He stretched out his hand to the sand and clutched it with his five fingers.... His mouth was parched ... in it there was a thick coating of Iraqi dust, stirred up during the long desert way."[13]

The story of the assassination attempt also appeared as a 1980 film, *The Long Days*. Before the opening credits run, a notice appears on the screen: "This film is not a record of historic events, but it is inspired by those events." The star of the film was Saddam Kamel, then a little known relative of Saddam Hussein. *The Long Days* was produced by the Iraqi Theater and Film Organization and was directed by Tawfiq Salih. Salih was an Egyptian director best known for his films dealing with social injustice and political corruption, based on the work of leading Arab writers such as Naguib Mahfouz, Tawfiq al-Hakim, and Ghassan Kanafani. In 1973, he moved to Iraq to teach cinema and was then commissioned by Saddam Hussein to make the film *The Long Days*, based on the novel by Mu'alla.

The opening scene of the movie takes place on Baghdad's Rashid Street. Spectators flank the sidewalks, tussling for a good spot and craning their necks to catch a glimpse of Prime Minister Qasim's car as he is driven home from his office. They whistle and clap as the car approaches. The position of the camera then shifts to a perch in the back seat of the car. The moviegoer is able to see the crowds from the vantage point of the Iraqi leader. The camera jerks to the cracking sound of gunfire and focuses on the car's windshield, shattered with bullets. The driver slumps over and the car stops in the middle of the street. The ambush continues for some time; some of the men use machine guns, others pistols. Finally, they begin to disperse, but one man stops to carry a fallen comrade. Slowed down by the weight of the injured friend, he becomes an easy target for a government agent who shoots him in the leg. Limping in pain, he manages to make it to the getaway car where his other friends await him. The film's plot closely follows the novel's. The closing scene of the film depicts Muhammad (i.e., Saddam) dressed as a peasant alone in the desert. On bended knee, he grabs a fistful of sand. The camera pans to a wide shot. The soundtrack music crescendos as Saddam walks triumphantly into the sunset.

It is worth noting that all of these accounts of October 1959, which Saddam commissioned—his biography, the novel, and the film—appeared just as Saddam was ascending to the presidency. The self-image that Saddam created and disseminated as he became the leader of Iraq was framed around the act of trying to kill the prime minister. And throughout his presidency, he repeatedly recounted his journey from Baghdad to Syria. In 1998, Saddam visited a village along the Tigris that he had passed through during his escape. He spoke about the arduous nighttime swim across the river. "It was like you see in the movies but worse," Saddam recalled. "My clothes were wet, my leg was injured and I hadn't eaten properly for four days. How can I describe it? It is hard to describe how I got out of the water."[14] Saddam's narrative underlined the centrality of family. His proud uncle comforted him, distant relatives sheltered him, and his brother in Tikrit helped set him upon the final leg of his journey. Saddam presented himself as a man of Iraq, deeply imbued with the customs of the peasants and bedouin. In Saddam's construction of the events of October 1959—which appeared in movies, novels, biographies, and interviews—an assassination attempt is portrayed as an act of bravery and sacrifice, a manifestation of an abiding love of country.

THE LIFE OF AN EXILE

In Damascus, Saddam became immersed in the life of the Baath Party, meeting with numerous Iraqi and Syrian party members. He met Michel Aflaq, a founder of the party, and the two men developed a friendly and enduring bond. Aflaq promoted Saddam, making him a full member of the party. After a few months, the party sent Saddam, along with a group of some 500 Iraqi exiles, to Cairo. Saddam took a room in a house overlooking the Nile and settled into a fairly low-key life in Cairo. He enrolled in the Qasr Al-Nil school, so he could complete his high school education. In his spare time, Saddam met with other students in coffeehouses, played chess, and read. He once attended a concert by the famed Egyptian singer, Umm Kalthum. Saddam spent time with Abdul Karim Shaykhli, a close friend and party activist, who was also in exile in Cairo at the time. In 1961, Saddam finally graduated from high school; he was twenty-four years old. Though he enrolled in Cairo University to study law, he soon dropped out in order to devote his full attention to political work.

Nasser's Egypt proved to be an important place for Saddam to learn about political life. He would later say, "Egypt in the time of Abdel-Nasser was the fulcrum of the Arab nation, a fact of which we must be proud, whatever we may think of Abdel-Nasser's experiment." Though the Baathists had differences with Nasser, Saddam admitted, "I was influenced by Gamal Abdul-Nasser." Joining the local branch of the Baath Party, he was soon elected to the Regional Command. Recalling his years in Cairo, Saddam once said, "I led a normal life. The exceptional part of it was the secret work, the life of a Baathist student who lived in a simple house, read and studied. Unlike others, he was unconcerned with the bright lights of Cairo. My life was completely ordinary. I carried out secret organizational work."

While in Cairo, Saddam became engaged to his cousin Sajida, the daughter of his uncle Khairallah with whom he had lived for many of his childhood years. Following bedouin tradition, Saddam arranged to have his stepfather visit Sajida's parents and propose the marriage. He once told an interviewer that his parents had told him he and Sajida were betrothed to one another when he was a small child. "… As I grew older the feelings of love increased, naturally, but I couldn't tell her of my feelings towards her, even though we were one family and I was part of it. I officially announced my wish to marry my cousin for the first time in Cairo…."[15] The Iraqi Students' Association in Cairo organized a reception, celebrating the engagement. Saddam dressed for the party, carefully tucking a folded pocket square into the breast pocket of his suit.

Saddam seems to have inherited his uncle Khairallah's penchant for careful grooming. Despite the modest student's stipend he lived on while in Egypt, he always dressed impeccably. This is clear in the photographs from his days in Egypt. Mindful of the gaze of the camera even in these casual tourist snapshots, Saddam always appears composed as he is pictured taking a boat ride down the Nile, posing in the Japanese garden at Helwan, smiling with a group of workers at a sugar refinery in Upper Egypt, inspecting a water well at a farm. While in Egypt, Saddam traveled through much of the country, visiting Alexandria, Luxor, and Aswan.

Though Saddam had managed to escape to a quiet life of exile in Egypt, the Iraqi authorities tried him in absentia. Altogether, 57 Baathists were charged with involvement in the assassination. Seventeen were executed. Saddam was found guilty in absentia and sentenced to the death penalty. Qasim, meanwhile, spent two months in the hospital, recovering from the bullets he took during the assassination attempt. Even as he recuperated, however, Qasim faced mounting opposition. For some time, the Kurds had been supporters of Qasim. The situation for Iraq's Kurds had improved in the wake of the July Revolution in 1958. The new Constitution gave the Kurds equal rights but stopped short of officially recognizing Kurdish nationalism. Mulla Mustafa Barzani, the Kurdish leader, returned to Iraq from his long Soviet exile. As Qasim faced both a rebellion and an attempt on his life, the Kurds stood by him. For some time, Qasim rewarded the Kurds' loyalty by improving their situation. He lifted restrictions on the Kurdish press. The Kurds, in turn, used their newspapers to press for the development of Kurdish institutions and the spread of the Kurdish language. As the Kurds pushed for greater promotion of Kurdish nationalism, Qasim balked. He gave a speech underlining the indivisibility of Iraq and refused their demands. Eventually, he took steps to weaken their leader Barzani. The situation deteriorated until war broke out between the Kurds and Qasim's government in 1961. The Iraqi air force was used against Kurdish villages; by January 1962, 500 villages had been attacked, 80 thousand people became homeless, and 50 thousand were killed.[16]

Even as a war with the Kurds was brewing in the north of Iraq, Qasim turned his attention to his southern neighbor, Kuwait. Under Ottoman rule, Kuwait had been administered by the governor of Basra province. At the end of the nineteenth century, Kuwait's sheikh sought British support for his country's independence. In 1899, Britain and Kuwait signed a treaty recognizing Kuwait as an independent state under British protection. When the Iraqi state was officially formed, Kuwait was not included in its territory. In June 1961, Qasim announced that Kuwait's separation from Iraq had been an arbitrary act of imperialism; in his view, Kuwait should now be integrated into the Iraqi state. Kuwait was a small country, but it was rich in oil reserves and had strategic ports along the Persian Gulf. The British were quick to defend their ally, sending troops to protect Kuwait's border with Iraq. In July, Kuwait was admitted to the Arab League, and the following month, a joint Arab force replaced the British troops bolstering the country against a possible Iraqi invasion.

Meanwhile the trial of Baathists had done little to squelch their opposition to Qasim. They renewed their determination to overthrow the prime minister Qasim. Expanding their network, the Baathists were supported by the Syrian Baathist Party, by a group of military officers who had participated in the July Revolution, and allegedly by the CIA. It is rumored that while in Cairo, Saddam visited the American embassy regularly, meeting with CIA specialists, soliciting support for the plot against Qasim.[17] Qasim's decision to withdraw from the anti-Soviet regional alliance, the Baghdad Pact, further heightened American concerns over the prime minister. James Akins, who was an attaché in the U.S. Embassy in Baghdad from 1963–1965, explained American opposition to Qasim within the context of the Cold War: "... [T]he communists certainly had a lot of influence in the country. The Soviet Union had a lot of influence. There were a lot of delegations who came from every communist country to Baghdad—artistic, culture, political, economic, and so on. But we were frightened that Iraq might ultimately move all the way into the Soviet orbit.... The danger of Iraq going communist probably was somewhat exaggerated, but that wasn't the view in Washington."[18]

On February 8, 1963, the Baathists made their move, assassinating the head of the Iraqi air force and attacking the Rashid military base. Hasan al-Bakr, backed by his Tikriti supporters and a number of military officers, approached the Ministry of Defense where Qasim was barricaded. The group included Khairallah, Saddam's uncle. After two days of brutal fighting, Qasim was court-martialled and sentenced to death. Together with three close companions, he was lined up against a wall and killed with a machine gun. In order to quell rumors about Qasim's fate and to show that the Baathists were in power, Baghdad Television aired shots of Qasim's bullet-ridden corpse as it lay in a pool of blood. He was buried later that night in an unmarked grave.[19]

In order to overthrow Qasim's regime, the Baathists had formed alliances with nationalists, disgruntled military officers, and the CIA. As Akins recalls, "The Ba'ath Party had come to control. We were very happy. They got rid of a lot of communists. A lot of them were executed, or shot. This was a great development."[20] In the months that followed, the Baathists set about eliminating their opposition. Much of the killing was undertaken by the National Guard, a group of nearly 30,000 armed civilians controlled by the Baath, who were charged with suppressing any opposition from communists and other groups.[21] The National Guard began "a murderous campaign of terror ... against real and imagined communists.... In many cases the CIA supplied the Baath with names of individual communists, some of whom were taken from their homes and murdered."[22] An intelligence reporter for the United Press International contends that the CIA was caught off guard by Qasim's killing: "But the agency quickly moved into action. Noting that the Baath Party was hunting down Iraq's communists, the CIA provided the submachine gun-toting Iraqi National Guardsmen with lists of suspected communists who were then jailed, interrogated, and summarily gunned down, according to former U.S. intelligence officials with intimate knowledge of the executions."[23] Estimates of those killed range from the hundreds to the tens of thousands.

As the new government took shape, political authority was given to a newly formed National Council of the Revolutionary Command (NCRC), which included a dozen Baathists and four nationalist military officers. Abdul Salam Arif, one of the leaders of the 1958 July Revolution, became the president of Iraq. Bakr, the Baathist military officer from Tikrit, became the vice-president and the prime minister. From the start, the new regime was marked by factionalism, based on power, ideology, and regional politics. In March, the Syrian branch of the Baath Party carried out a coup. With Baathists as part of the government in both Syria and Iraq, prospects for pan-Arabism improved. By April, Syria, Iraq, and Egypt entered into a commitment on unification. Soon, however, there was a power struggle among the Syrian Baath, and these tensions further exacerbated divisions within Iraqi politics.

Back in Cairo, Saddam had heard the news of Qasim's ouster from his friend Abdul Karim Shaykhli. The men had been hanging around the house. Saddam was about to take a shower when the phone rang. Shaykhli answered the phone and called out to Saddam, who cracked open the bathroom door to see what all the fuss was about. Shaykhli shouted, "Saddam, there has been a revolution in Iraq!"[24]

FROM EXILE TO PRISON

Within two weeks of Qasim's overthrow, Saddam was headed back to Iraq. On his way, he stopped in Damascus, meeting with Michel Aflaq, a founder of the Baath Party and one of his main political mentors. Upon returning to Baghdad, Saddam married Sajida; a photograph of the newlyweds shows Saddam smiling as he sits alongside his bride, a fair-skinned young woman with big dark eyes and short curly hair. The couple settled into a modest home in the Raghiba Khatoun district of Baghdad, and soon Sajida was pregnant with their first child, Uday.

With his family life secure, Saddam turned his attention to politics. Naturally, he gravitated towards the faction headed by Bakr, the military officer from his hometown of Tikrit. Saddam became a member of the president's Bureau and was involved with the National Guard's brutal elimination campaign. The extent of his direct involvement in the atrocities is a question of debate. While some claim that Saddam oversaw the operations, others claim he personally tortured and killed people.[25]

The communists were not the only group to feel the brunt of the new regime, which soon declared war on the Kurds. A military official issued a statement: "We shall bomb and destroy any village if firing comes from anywhere near it against the army, the police, the National Guards or the loyal tribes."[26] Entire Kurdish villages were razed, leaving hundreds of civilians killed. Arif, who at that point in Iraqi history was known as "the most staunchly anti-Kurd leader in the modern history of the country," attacked Kurdish areas with napalm and chemical weapons.[27]

Even as the new government brutalized its opponents, factionalism threatened its internal cohesion. Nine months into the first Baathist government in Iraqi history, Arif made his move to secure his personal hold over power. Bakr was put under house arrest, and a warrant was issued for Saddam's arrest. Saddam went underground. In April 1964, he secretly attended a meeting of the Baath in Syria, where Aflaq appointed him to the party's Regional Command in Iraq. Returning to Baghdad, Saddam continued his political work in secret. Together with Abdul Karim Shaykhli, he made a plan to assassinate Arif, by attacking the Presidential Palace with homemade bombs. The plot was uncovered, and Saddam went into hiding. Gradually, the authorities zeroed in on the plotters, arresting Shaykhli and others close to Saddam. One of those arrested revealed Saddam's hiding place during a police interrogation. Police surrounded the house. Saddam contemplated resisting arrest, even firing a few rounds from his revolver. Realizing he was outnumbered, though, he surrendered. He dressed and grabbed his cigarettes before the police carted him off to prison.

Prison life was difficult for Saddam. When he was not in solitary confinement, he chatted with other inmates in the prison yard, wearing pajamas, a robe, and slippers. He spent time with his close friend, Shaykhli, who was also in prison. At one point, he organized a hunger strike to try to improve prison conditions. Mainly, Saddam indulged his favorite pastime—reading. "When I was in prison," he once recalled, "I read all of Ernest Hemingway's novels. I particularly like *The Old Man and the Sea*."[28] Sajida visited him on a weekly basis. One day, Sajida came home to find that she'd been evicted, and the family's belongings had been strewn on the street. Sajida coped by moving in with her father, Khairallah. When she visited the prison, Sajida brought along their son Uday. Wrapped in his baby clothes, Saddam would find messages from his Baathist allies. This became a critical way for him to maintain communication with party leaders. While in prison, Saddam was made the deputy secretary general of the newly formed Regional Leadership (RL) of the Baath Party.

In 1966, two events shifted the political scene. A coup in Syria led to the ouster of Aflaq from the Baath Party's National Command. In April, Arif was killed in a helicopter crash, and his brother Abdul Rahman Arif succeeded him. Once again, the party needed Saddam, and he got word that it was time for him to plan his escape. Saddam and Shaykhli hatched a plan. On July 23, while they were being transferred from their trial at court, Saddam and Shaykhli persuaded the prison guards to stop at the La Gondola Restaurant on Abu Nuwas Street for lunch. During the meal, the prisoners went to the bathroom and snuck out of the back door of the restaurant. One of Saddam's cousins who was a Baathist was waiting for them in a yellow Opal car. It was too dangerous for Saddam to go to Khairallah's house where Sajida and Uday were living. Instead, Saddam hid at the home of fellow Baathists; staying underground, he worked with Bakr on their next move.

THE FOURTH COUP IN 10 YEARS

In the summer of 1967, regional tensions overtook domestic politics. In June, Iraq joined a defensive pact with Jordan and Egypt. As war broke out between Israel and Egypt, Syria, and Jordan, Iraq sent some 12,000 troops into Jordan. Without any contiguous borders with Israel, Iraq's role in the war was secondary. Still, Iraqi troops did fight against Israeli forces, and Israeli aircraft attacked an airbase inside Iraq. The June 1967 War ended in a humiliating Arab defeat. Israeli forces occupied the Sinai and Gaza of Egypt, the Golan Heights of Syria, and the West Bank and parts of Jerusalem that were administered by Jordan. At the end of the war, Iraq refused to accept the official cease-fire. Protesting American support for Israel during the war, Iraq cut off all diplomatic ties with the United States and halted its oil shipments to the West. Arab oil ministers met in Baghdad to consider a complete oil embargo.

The war did not distract the Baathists from their plans to overtake the government. On July 17, 1968, a group of Baathists entered the grounds of the Presidential Palace. Among them was Saddam Hussein, who was wearing a military uniform and riding on a tank. A smattering of gun-fire ensued. General Hardan Al-Tikriti telephoned Arif, who had been sleeping. Tikriti told him, "I am empowered to inform you that you are no longer President. The Baath has taken control of the country. If you surrender peacefully, I can guarantee that your safety will be ensured."[29]

Dazed, Arif went to the entrance hall of the palace, where he found Tikriti waiting for him. Arif agreed to surrender and left for London.

The fourth coup in Iraq in 10 years had taken place rather uneventfully. There was no reported bloodshed. Baghdad radio broadcast a communiqué saying a revolution had put an end to "a regime of illiterates, of opportunists, thieves, spies, agents of imperialism, partisans of Zionism, suspects, [and] profiteering egoists...."[30] The statement continued by accusing the Arif regime of ignoring the needs of the army, contributing to the disastrous military defeat against Israel in 1967, and deepening the problem with the Kurds.[31] The London *Guardian* reported, "In their denunciation of corruption and inefficiency, the new rulers are bound to strike a sympathetic chord among the Iraqi people in general. ... The feeling that it was inefficiency and corruption which lost the Arabs the June war is widespread."[32]

Bakr became the president of Iraq. A new organization called the Revolutionary Command Council (RCC) was formed, and Bakr became its chairman. The relatively quiet transfer of power was duly noted in the world press. "It was in keeping with the reputation of Ahmed Hassan al-Bakr," reported *The New York Times,* "that the coup that brought him to power last week as President of Iraq was not accompanied by riots, massacres, assassinations, and mysterious disappearances. In a section of the world in which official treachery, corruption, and murderous rivalry have been a way of life for centuries, he is known as a moderate conservative."[33]

Bakr was a solemn man. He slicked his thinning hair back and wore a carefully trimmed moustache. His small eyes were close set in his soft face. His chin faded into the folds of his neck. Bakr was born in 1912. The son of a farmer from Tikrit, he married a local girl. Together, they had six daughters and three sons. Bakr studied at the Teachers College in Baghdad before entering the Military College in 1932. He became a lifelong military man and was one of the Free Officers who had overthrown the monarchy in 1958. A devout Muslim, Bakr prayed five times a day. He didn't smoke, and he didn't drink.

Though he was a military officer, Bakr wore a suit and tie as he met with reporters in the first days of his presidency. "An underdeveloped country like Iraq," Bakr told a group of journalists, "must look after her own interests." Pan-Arabism was no longer the focus of Iraqi politics. Bakr also seemed to allude to Cold War politics and claimed, "Our policy toward world affairs will be dictated by our conscience and we will not take sides."[34] American officials announced that the coup did not appear to have any ideological significance and that there were no indications of

Soviet involvement.[35] Under Bakr, the Baath set into practice a nationalist socialist policy. It focused on Iraqi development through the creation
of a state capitalist bureaucracy. Iraqi Baathism justified its monopoly of
state power through the idea of "a 'leader party' that guides the masses
through the transitional period to socialism. It expresses the people's
historic role, and so there is no possibility of contradictions between its
concepts and those of the masses."[36]

Bakr appointed Abdul Razzaq Nayef as the prime minister and Ibrahim
Abdul Rahman Daoud as the minister of defense; neither man was a
Baathist. Indeed, the majority of the new Cabinet was made up of indi-
viduals from outside the party. Khairallah, Saddam's uncle, was made
the governor of Baghdad, and Aflaq was invited to make his home in
Iraq. Saddam was not appointed to a governmental post. For the time
being, his main political position was as a member of the Party's Regional
Leadership (RL). He agreed to work on creating a new security apparatus.
Quietly, he moved into a small office next to the president's.

Within thirteen days, Bakr made his move to further consolidate power,
dismissing the non-Baathist prime minister and minister of defense. The
powerful Revolutionary Command Council (RCC) was composed of five
military men, all of whom were Sunni Arabs from Baghdad or Tikrit.[37]
Within a year, 22 percent of all high officials in the Iraqi government
were from Tikrit.[38] Saddam was not yet a member of the RCC, but he
attended their meetings. After the cabinet reshuffling, Bakr appeared on
television to deliver a speech. As President Bakr declared the completion
of the revolution, Saddam stood guard behind him, carrying a machine
gun. For the next decade, Saddam would work in Bakr's shadows on two
intertwined goals: to strengthen the hold of the Baath Party over Iraq and
to expand his own power base.

A STRANGE WAR, A FIFTH COLUMN, AND A SPECIAL KIND OF FEAR

By the fall of 1968, Bakr's regime was under pressure. Fighting erupted
between the Kurds and the Iraqi army. A group of nearly 100 soldiers
and civilians was arrested; they were accused of being royalists who were
plotting a coup.[39] Bakr used strong-arm tactics against real and imagined
enemies of his regime. Houses were raided, and Iraqi men were disap-
peared. Waves of arrests ensued, and there were rumors of torture being
used in Iraq's prisons. A local manager for the Coca-Cola company died
in prison. Newspapers reported, "His body was returned to his family, and

reliable reports say it showed signs of torture, including hands without fingernails."[40]

As had been the case many times before, regional politics in the Middle East soon became enmeshed in the domestic power politics within Iraq. Despite a cease-fire agreement that formally ended the war between Israel and her Arab neighbors, the fighting continued into 1968. One journalist wrote, "There is a war going on in the Middle East, but it is a strange, indecisive war that runs quietly, often underground, for periods and then erupts in sudden, savage bursts."[41] In March 1968, the United Nations Security Council passed Resolution 248, "... observing that the military action by the armed forces of Israel on the territory of Jordan was of a large-scale and carefully planned nature," and condemned "the military action launched by Israel in flagrant violation of the United Nations Charter and the cease-fire resolutions...." In August, the Security Council passed UNSC Resolution 256, declaring "that grave violations of the cease-fire cannot be tolerated ... [and condemning] the further military attacks launched by Israel...."

In the main, the fighting across Israel's contentious eastern border was between Israel and Jordan, but Iraq maintained troops in Jordan. In the first week of December 1968, Israel conducted three days of air strikes against Jordan, in what was the heaviest fighting since the official end of the war. On December 1, Iraqi troops opened fire on some Israeli settlements along the Jordanian border. The next day, Iraqi troops stationed within 40 miles inside the Jordanian border were targeted by Israeli air strikes. Journalists reported, "at one stage Israeli tanks and artillery were firing along a 20-mile front against Iraqi and Jordanian army units, as well as Arab guerillas."[42] On December 4, Iraqi troops were attacked again. Israeli military officials explained that the Israeli attack on Iraqi troops stationed in northern Jordan was intended to be a deterrent against attacks on Israeli settlements along the border. A reporter in Jerusalem observed, "While removing the source of the harassment of the Israeli border, it appears to have placed Iraq's role in the Arab-Israeli conflict under new focus and, perhaps, to have strengthened it.... The Iraqi forces seemed unable to protect themselves, much less defend the Jordanians, as Israeli jets spent more than an hour attacking them."[43] The Israeli raid, the reporter concluded, may "have set events in motion in Baghdad that have their own still undetermined price."[44]

On December 5, Baghdad erupted at the news. Baghdad Radio announced that six Iraqi soldiers had been killed in the Israeli air raids and called on Iraqis to march in their honor. An official holiday was declared, and schools and offices were closed. Thousands took to the streets of Baghdad, demanding revenge. Bakr addressed the protestors declaring, "We shall defend Arab soil against the enemy to the last drop of our blood." He warned of a Fifth Column within Iraq.[45] Soon, the Iraqi government issued an official proclamation: "Honorable countrymen are asked to cooperate fully with the authorities in foiling the designs of the malicious Zionist enemy."[46]

The Israeli air raids on Iraqi forces in Jordan, which revealed Iraqi military vulnerability, were a particularly bitter pill to swallow in the immediate aftermath of the Arab defeat in the June 1967 War. The Baath government drew on the frustration of the street mobs demanding revenge against Israel, but shifted the focus of this revenge away from regional military affairs to the internal political dynamics in Iraq itself. Attributing opposition to his stronghold over the government to a "fifth column," Bakr attempted to camouflage the elimination of his political opposition by suggesting there was an Israeli plot to weaken Iraq. The public displays of anger against Israel in Baghdad's streets were followed by a morbid second act—public hangings of Iraqis accused of conspiracies with Israel, Iran, the British, and the CIA.

On December 14, the Iraqi government announced that it had broken up an Israeli spy network. Baghdad radio and television stations broadcast allegations of CIA involvement and aired confessions by an Iraqi soldier and a lawyer who were allegedly part of this spy ring. Two Iraqi Jews were accused of being leaders of the spy network, which operated from the southern city of Basra. Izra Zilkha, who was from a prominent merchant family with branches in Baghdad and Basra, was accused of being the leader of the spy network; Albert Habib Tumas was his alleged deputy. According to the prosecutor, the ring collected information on the Iraqi army, formed an Israeli commando organization, and sent Iraqi Jews to Iran to be trained in sabotage and germ warfare. The men were also accused of trying to form a political organization with ties to Turkey, Iran, the United States, and Britain. The group's plan was to agitate the Kurds and "feudalists" in the south to keep the Iraqi army distracted from its war against Israel. The prosecutor alleged that two Soviet warships in the Persian Gulf had recently picked up the group's radio transmissions. A photograph of the trial shows the men at their court appearance. They stood in court behind a banister. One of the men wore a *kaffiyyah*, another a baseball cap. An old man with white hair pressed his hands to his face in despair. One man stared ahead at the prosecutors, with a look of angry defiance. Most of the men seemed defeated, their heads bowed, their eyes to the floor.

Fourteen men were executed on January 27; nine of them were Jewish. The bodies hung from a scaffold in Baghdad's Liberation Square. Pinned to each body was a sheet of paper with their names, ages, religion, and verdict. Crowds of men and women filled Liberation Square to witness the hangings; estimates range from 150,000 to 500,000. "Peasants streamed in from the surrounding countryside to hear the speeches. The proceedings, along with the bodies, continued for twenty-four hours, during which the president, Ahmad Hasan al-Bakr, and a host of other luminaries gave speeches and orchestrated the carnival-like atmosphere."[47]

The executions caused an international outcry and were front-page news in major U.S. newspapers. Demonstrations condemning the hangings were held in Rome and Paris. The UN secretary general, the pope, and the leaders of Pakistan, France, and the United States all denounced the hangings. The Action Committee on American-Arab Relations sent a cablegram to Bakr, protesting the hangings. The Israeli premier, Levi Eshkol, opened a session of the Knesset by reading the names of the nine Iraqi Jews who had been executed, asserting, "The Lord shall avenge their blood.... The sole and only crime of these nine martyrs consists of their being Jews." In a trembling voice, he cited scripture, "O daughter of Babylon, thou art to be destroyed, happy shall be he that repayeth thee as thou has served us." Eshkol went on to say, "The Baghdad hangings have illuminated the fate of the remnants of the Babylonian Jews into a nightmarish light. The land of Iraq has become one great prison for its Jewish remnants. Our brethren are prey to terror at the hands of villains. Iraq has become a gallows for its Jewish citizens."[48]

The executions changed the fabric of Iraqi society. Iraqi Jews had been central to the character of the country. "When the British troops occupied Baghdad in 1917," Elie Kedourie noted, "the Jews were the most important single element in the town—by their numbers, their wealth, their relations with those among them who had established themselves overseas (notably in Bombay and Manchester), and by their acknowledged superior position in the Mesopotamian economy."[49] In the decades to come, the fate of the Jewish community was sometimes in flux. In 1941, when the Rashid Ali coup was thwarted, rioters targeted Jewish individuals and property.

The 1947 census showed that the Jewish population of Baghdad was at 118,000; scholars believe the true number was closer to 150,000.[50] In 1948, when the state of Israel was established and war broke out between Israel and the Arabs, the Iraqi police arrested some Jews and accused them of supporting Zionists. In 1950, the Iraqi government passed a law giving Iraqi Jews a year to determine if they wanted to give up Iraqi citizenship and emigrate to Israel. The Iraqi premier at the time, Nuri al-Said, convened parliament and passed laws allowing the government to confiscate the property of any Jews who emigrated. Iraqi Jews who had retained their citizenship and were living in countries other than Israel had to return to Iraq to claim their property; otherwise, the government could confiscate it as well. Kedourie wrote, "The Jews of Iraq were uprooted, dispossessed, and scattered in the space of a year."[51] An estimated 100,000 Iraqi Jews left the country by 1951. "The withdrawal of the Jewish community," Phebe Marr concluded, "left a large gap in the economy and the professions, where Jewish expertise and foreign contacts had contributed much to Iraqi society."[52] Departure and dislocation were clearly painful for Iraqi Jews as well. Ella Shohat has pointed to the sense of displacement that marked the lives of Iraqi Jews as they moved on to lives in Tehran, Tel Aviv, and New York. Shohat recounts the experience of the noted author Sammy Michael, who "speaks of a recurrent nightmare in which he is sitting in his favorite Baghdadi café—a place he is nostalgic for—but when he comes to pay he puts his hand in his pocket and takes out Israeli coins—a telltale sign of his enemy Zionist affiliations."[53]

By the time of the public executions, there were about 3,000 Jews living in Iraq. A brother of one of the Jewish men who was executed told reporters, "We were born in Baghdad. We lived all our lives there. We knew a flourishing religious and cultural community. When we escaped there was only one synagogue out of 50, one Jewish Hospital."[54] After 1968, the remnants of a once thriving Iraqi Jewish community diminished to a trace.

The Baathist executions were not limited to Iraqi Jews alone, however. At dawn on February 14, seven Iraqis, all non-Jews, were executed, and their bodies were put on public display. Those killed included students, soldiers, and a blacksmith. The soldiers were accused of preparing reports on the deployment of the Iraqi Army in Iraq and Jordan. The students prepared reports on the Baath party, and were charged with spreading rumors that there were internal divisions in the party. The blacksmith was charged with being a messenger for the group. The executions, public spectacles of state terror, which were witnessed by tens of thousands of Iraqis, continued for months.

Amidst the fury over the secret trials and hangings, Bakr quietly arrested a former prime minister and a former defense minister. The Baath alleged that an Iranian-backed coup had been thwarted, and they executed 41 men for participating in the coup. Between the fall of 1968 and the winter of 1969, 95 Iraqis were executed by hanging or by firing squad. Fourteen of them were Jewish. Fifty-four of them were charged with spying for Israel, Iran, and the United States.

"These are the cases that the world has heard about," wrote one journalist. "But the Iraqi public has probably been more affected by the thousands of lesser arrests of persons suspected of some form of opposition to the regime or of conspiratorial dealings with foreign countries.... This is a city where the ringing of the doorbell after midnight produces a special kind of fear, for midnight to 3 a.m. is the time when arrests are most often made. People of all political affiliations have been affected."[55]

In 1963, the Baath had lost power only nine months after a coup that they helped bring about; they were not about to make the same mistake again. Torture, murder, and public executions were official acts used to eliminate opponents of the regime. Though the rhetoric surrounding the secret trials often pointed to foreign conspiracies and plots, the motivation for the official violence was primarily domestic. At the time, Saddam Hussein played a leading role in reorganizing the security apparatus. According to the Penroses, "From Damascus it was reported that Saddam was at the head of a network of special agents responsible for acts of terrorism and torture."[56]

NOTES

1. Saad Hadi, "Baghdad's Forgotten Glory," *Al-Ahram Weekly On-line*, April 17–23, 2003.

2. Hanna Batatu, *The Old Social Classes and the Revolutionary Movements of Iraq* (Princeton, N.J.: Princeton University Press, 1978), p. 866.

3. As quoted in Batatu, *The Old Social Classes and the Revolutionary Movements of Iraq*, p. 881.

4. Felix Belair, "Director of CIA Briefs President," *The New York Times*, April 12, 1969.

5. Dana Adams Schmidt, "CIA Head Warns of Danger in Iraq," *The New York Times*, April 29, 1959.

6. "Agreed Conclusions and Recommendations," Conference of Middle East Chiefs of Mission, U.S. Department of State, February 21, 1951, retrieved July 29, 2003, National Security Archives (NSA).

7. Edward S. Crocker of U.S. Embassy in Baghdad to U.S. Department of State, March 10, 1951, retrieved July 29, 2003, NSA.

8. "Arabic Anti-Communist Pamphlet Program," U.S. Embassy in Baghdad to Department of State, Washington, September 9, 1952, retrieved July 29, 2003, NSA.

9. "Opportunities for Anti-Communist Activities among Students," U.S. Embassy in Baghdad to Department of State, Washington, March 30, 1953, retrieved July 29, 2003, NSA.

10. Schmidt, "CIA Head Warns of Danger in Iraq."

11. Marion Farouk-Sluglett and Peter Sluglett, *Iraq Since 1958: From Revolution to Dictatorship* (London: I. B. Tauris Press, 2001), p. 72.

12. Amir Iskander, *Saddam Hussein: The Fighter, the Thinker, and the Man*, trans. Hassan Selim (Paris: Hachette Réalités, 1980), p. 67. A similar narrative appears in another favorable biography of Saddam Hussein written by Fuad Matar, which was published about the same time.

13. Quotes from the novel are from the English translation. See Abdul-Ameer Mu'alla, *The Long Days*, trans. Mohieddin Ismail (London: Ithaca Press, 1979).

14. As quoted in Con Coughlin, *Saddam: King of Terror* (New York: Ecco, 2002), p. 33.

15. Quotes are from interview with Fuad Matar, in *Saddam Hussein: The Man, the Cause, and the Future* (London: Third World Centre, 1981), pp. 236–37; and interview with Iskander, in *Saddam Hussein*, pp. 393–97.

16. Uriel Dann, *Iraq Under Qassem: A Political History, 1958–1963* (Jerusalem: Israel Universities Press, 1969), pp. 332–45.

17. Said Aburish, *Saddam Hussein: The Politics of Revenge* (London: I. B. Tauris, 2000), p. 54. This assertion is confirmed by a report conducted by a United Press International reporter, who cites unnamed "former U.S. intelligence officers." See Richard Sale, UPI Intelligence Correspondent, "Exclusive: Saddam Key in Early CIA Plot," published April 10, 2003, http://www.upi.com/view.cfm?StoryID=20030410–070214–6557r (retrieved July 13, 2004).

18. "An interview with James Akins," *Frontline: The Survival of Saddam*, PBS, http://www.pbs.org/wgbh/pages/frontline/shows/saddam/interviews/akins.html (retrieved January 10, 2004).

19. Dann, *Iraq Under Qassem*, pp. 371–72.

20. "An interview with James Akins."

21. Charles Tripp, *A History of Iraq* (Cambridge: Cambridge University Press, 2000), p. 171.

22. Edith Penrose and E. F. Penrose, *Iraq: International Relations and National Development* (London: Ernest Benn, 1978), pp. 287–88. The Penroses were living in Baghdad at the time. They were professors at the University of Baghdad from 1957 through the 1960s, when they were expelled from Iraq.

23. Sale, "Exclusive: Saddam Key in Early CIA Plot."

24. Iskander, *Saddam Hussein*, p. 80.

25. Adeed Darwish asserted that Saddam oversaw the operation, while Said Aburish cites witnesses who claim to have seen Saddam directly involved in killing and torture.

26. Geoff Simons, *From Sumer to Saddam*, 2nd edition (New York: St. Martin's Press, 1994), p.262.

27. Aburish, *Saddam Hussein*, p. 67.

28. As quoted in Mark Bowden, "Tales of the Tyrant," *Atlantic Monthly*, May 2002.

29. As quoted in Efraim Karsh and Inari Rautsi, *Saddam Hussein: A Political Biography*, 2nd revised edition (New York: Grove Press, 2002), p. 31.

30. "Coup d'Etat militaire en Irak," *Le Monde*, July 18, 1968.

31. "Ouster of Regime in Iraq Reported," *The New York Times*, July 17, 1968.

32. David Hirst, "Baathists Now Put Iraq First," *The Guardian*, July 19, 1968.

33. "Iraq's New Chief of State," *The New York Times*, July 25, 1968.

34. Ibid.

35. "Junta Rules Iraq in Rightist Coup," *The New York Times*, July 18, 1968.

36. John Galvani, "The Baathi Revolution in Iraq," *Middle East Reports (MERIP)* (September–October 1972): 17.

37. Amatzia Baram, "The Ruling Political Elite in Bathi Iraq, 1968–1986: The Changing Features of a Collective Profile," *International Journal of Middle East Studies* (November 1989): 447–93.

38. Galvani, "The Baathi Revolution in Iraq," p. 16.

39. John F. Cooley, "Militancy Growing in Iraq?" *The Christian Science Monitor*, January 28, 1969.

40. Thomas F. Brady, "Party Rivalries Plague the Iraqis," *The New York Times*, October 27, 1968.

41. James Feron, "Strange Mideast War," *The New York Times*, December 6, 1968.

42. James Feron, "Air Strikes in Jordan," *The New York Times*, December 3, 1968.

43. James Feron, "Strange Mideast War."

44. James Feron, "Iraqis in Jordan Complicate the Struggle with Israel," *The New York Times*, December 8, 1968.

45. "Baghdad Parade Mourns Soldiers," *The New York Times*, December 6, 1968.

46. Eric Pace, "Iraq Is in Militant Mood," *The New York Times*, December 15, 1968.

47. Kanan Makiya, *Republic of Fear: The Politics of Modern Iraq*, updated edition (Berkeley: University of California Press, 1998), p. 52.

48. As quoted in *The Washington Post*, January 28, 1969.

49. Elie Kedourie, "Minorities," in *The Chatham House Version and Other Middle-Eastern Studies*, ed. Elie Kedourie (New York: Praeger Publishers, 1970), p. 300.

50. Phebe Marr, *The Modern History of Iraq* (Boulder, Colo.: Westview Press, 1985), p. 10.

51. Kedourie, "Minorities," p 314.

52. Marr, *The Modern History of Iraq*, p. 107.

53. Ella Shohat, "Rupture and Return: Zionist Discourse and the Study of Arab Jews," *Social Text* (Summer 2003): 56–57.

54. "A Victim's Brother, Here, Laments for Iraqi Jews," *The New York Times,* January 28, 1969.

55. Dana Adams Schmidt, "Tension Runs High in Baghdad on Eve of New Political Trial," *The New York Times,* February 28, 1970.

56. Penrose and Penrose, *Iraq,* p. 359.

Chapter 3

SADDAM BECOMES "THE DEPUTY"

SECOND IN COMMAND

Saddam Hussein was deeply invested in and directly involved with the power struggles that marked the early years of the Baathist regime. He was beginning to garner attention as a powerful "apparatchik," a man who directed the party machinery.[1] By November 1969, the membership of the Revolutionary Command Council (RCC) was expanded from 5 to 14 members. Saddam and his good friend Abdul Karim Shaykhli became members of the RCC, with Saddam securing the position of the RCC's vice chairman. In effect, Saddam was now the second-ranking official in the Baath Party and, by extension, in Iraq.

Within days of Saddam's appointment, the British Embassy in Iraq produced a confidential report on Saddam, noting that until recently he had been the "leading Party theorist in the background, emerging progressively into the limelight in 1969." The report characterized Saddam as "a presentable young man. Initially regarded as a Party extremist, but responsibility may mellow him. Nephew of Khairallah Talfah, the *Muhafiz* or Governor of Baghdad and thus related to President Bakr by marriage. Connected, as a Tikriti, with many of those in the corridors of power."[2]

Saddam took an increasingly public role, meeting with foreign diplomats. In December 1969, Saddam met with the British ambassador in Baghdad, who sent a lengthy telegram back to the Foreign and Commonwealth Office in London detailing his impressions. "My main object was simply to form a first-hand impression of this previously inaccessible Grey Eminence and ascertain, if I could, his personal attitude (which some believe to have decisive weight) on major issues, ..." the Ambassador explained. "Saddam's initial demeanour, when he received me (alone) in his modest office in the Presidential Palace, was singularly reserved—perhaps because the species was unfamiliar to him. Indeed, he said nothing at all for about five minutes, fixing me with an impassive stare while I spoke." The ambassador then reported on Saddam's admonitions to him regarding British policy in Iraq:

> It was no good trying to separate the Palestine problem from others since by now it coloured the thinking of all Arabs on all subjects. Britain and the West could not wholly escape the burden of history ... We were totally wrong if we believed Iraqi Ba'athists to have any natural affinity with the Soviet bloc. Ba'athism had nothing to do with Communism. He well knew that the long-term aims of the Soviet Union were to communize the world and subject it to Muscovite domination.

Saddam went on to broach the subject of oil and the IPC, underlining the importance to Iraq of garnering an equitable arrangement with the consortium. "I should judge him, young as he is," the British Ambassador concluded, "to be a formidable, single-minded and hard-headed member of the Ba'athist hierarchy, but one with whom, if only one could see more of him, it would be possible to do business."[3]

At the time, the main task at hand for Saddam was to expand Baathist control over Iraq and to ensure that he and Bakr held power over the government. In order to quell any opposition, Saddam and Bakr's approach was to combine strong-arm tactics with conciliatory strategies. The Kurds, who were a main source of opposition, were a priority. In January 1970, Saddam entered negotiations with Kurdish representatives, leading to the publication of a Manifesto by the Baath regime on March 11, 1970. The Manifesto offered Kurds local autonomy, while the central government retained control over foreign affairs and natural resources. In a region that was rich in oil, this was a key provision. A Kurdish vice president was to be announced and the Kurds would receive representation on the RCC. For the time being, at least, it seemed that the Kurdish question had been resolved.

Between 1969 and 1971, Bakr and Saddam's main rivals were imprisoned, exiled, or killed. Once again, regional affairs provided a context for the elimination of some of their main political rivals. In September 1970, King Hussein of Jordan's forces attacked the Palestinian guerillas based in

Jordan in an attempt to consolidate his own power over the Palestinian population. Iraq still had troops in Jordan. Though Iraq was an ardent supporter of the Palestinian cause, the Iraqi troops did nothing to aid the Palestinians in their fight against the Jordanian forces. Iraq's decision helped to ensure King Hussein's victory. Meanwhile, Hardan al-Tikriti, who was the minister of defense, was accused of not having helped the Palestinians, and this was used to dismiss him from his post. He was exiled to Algeria and then went to Kuwait, where he was assassinated in 1971. Another rival, Shaykhli, had been friends with Saddam since his days in exile. Removed as foreign minister, he was given an innocuous position at the United Nations. This strategy of dismissing and eliminating opponents was accompanied by programmatic moves seeking conciliation with various opposition groups.

In November 1971, the Baath announced the National Action Charter. The charter reconfirmed the March Manifesto on the Kurds, called for a fundamental reorganization of the economy, and sought to create a coalition "among all the national, patriotic and progressive elements in a democratic, popular and unitary system."[4] By April 1972, the Iraqi Communist Party (ICP) announced its willingness to join a National Progressive Front. Two members in the cabinet were to be chosen from the ICP. Meanwhile, the ICP was allowed to publish its official newspaper and to organize publicly.

By 1972, however, the truce between the Kurds and the central government was disintegrating. Mulla Mustafa Barzani, the Kurdish leader, asked for more concessions than were provided in the 1970 agreement he had reached with Saddam Hussein. The central government, meanwhile, was dragging its feet in implementing even those conditions to which they had already committed. Barzani turned to Iran, the United States, and Israel for support. By June 1973, he was emboldened enough to speak to American reporters about the prospects of taking over the oil fields of Kirkuk and conferring exploitation rights to American oil companies. Control of oil resources was a highly contentious issue between the Kurds and the central government. A line had been crossed. The Iraqi air force bombed some Kurdish sites but pulled back from a complete war. Saddam and Barzani continued to negotiate.[5]

On July 1, 1973, Baghdad Radio announced that the defense minister had been killed and the minister of the interior had been injured in an assassination attempt engineered by the chief of internal security, Nazem Kazzar. On that day, President Bakr was due to arrive at Baghdad Airport after an official state visit to Poland. Saddam Hussein was to greet him at an official welcoming ceremony at the airport. Kazzar had invited several military leaders, including the cabinet members, to a luncheon at his home. As the guests arrived, they were taken into custody by Kazzar's security forces. With these men as hostages, Kazzar planned to storm the official reception at the airport and place Bakr and Saddam under arrest, thus toppling the government. Apparently, Saddam became suspicious when he was unable to reach the cabinet members who were supposed to be joining him at the airport reception. Saddam then arranged for Bakr to delay his arrival to Baghdad Airport by two hours. Alerted to this turn of events, Kazzar tried to escape by driving toward the Iranian border with the cabinet members as his hostages; along the way, however, he was captured.[6] On July 2, hundreds gathered in Baghdad's streets for the funeral of the defense minister. Saddam led the funeral procession. Newspaper reports said that Saddam "personally led the troops and security forces that crushed the attempted coup."[7] Through the Iraqi News Agency, Saddam announced that only a few members of the internal security forces had been involved in the killing of the defense minister. "No other element of the armed forces took part," he said.[8]

A special tribunal was established to try and sentence Kazzar and the others accused of participating in the plot. On July 7, Kazzar, along with nearly two dozen police officers, was executed; on July 9, another 13 were executed. Through the years, Kazzar had developed a reputation as the "wild man" of the party, and his nickname was Abu Harb, or Father of War.[9] In the end, his attempted coup proved of great political value to Bakr and Saddam. They were able to ascribe much of the political violence since the 1968 coup to Kazzar, whom they portrayed as an overzealous chief of internal security who had gone too far. The threat of a coup backed by a foreign power allowed them to further consolidate their power. The RCC amended the Iraqi constitution to make Bakr the head of state, the prime minister, and the commander in chief of the armed forces. He was given the power to appoint and dismiss all government officials. According to an announcement by the Iraqi News Agency, these powers were necessary to enable him "to safeguard the country's independence and territorial integrity, and to protect its internal and external security, and look after the citizen's rights and freedoms."[10] The intelligence services were placed under the control of Sadun Shakir al-Tikriti and Barzan al-Tikriti, Saddam's cousin and half-brother. As the fifth anniversary of the July 1968 coup was celebrated, Bakr and Saddam had managed to secure their stronghold over the government of Iraq. Much of the world press, which had originally praised Bakr's moderation, now began referring to him as a dictator.

In the summer of 1976, Saddam finally fulfilled a life-long dream of becoming an army man. His uncle Khairallah had been a military man, and Saddam had tried to follow in his footsteps. As a young man, however, Saddam failed the entrance exam for the military college, closing off the opportunity for a career in the army. Now, Bakr complied with Saddam's special request and made him a general. The following year, Bakr stepped down as minister of defense, giving the post to Adnan Khairallah. Adnan was Saddam's first cousin and brother-in-law. The two boys had grown up together. Iraq's military—a key site of power in that country—was now under the purview of Saddam's immediate family.

SADDAM AND BAATHISM

Saddam's rise to power was largely based on a skillful use of family ties and force—the pillars of his political strength. But as the vice chairman of the Baath Party, his increasing power was also a function of party politics, and he carefully cultivated a role for himself as a party man and a political thinker. Saddam's role as a prime theorist of Iraqi Baathism was evident in the numerous speeches that he gave in the 1970s to various groups including educators, athletes, lawyers, youth groups, women's organizations, and bureaucratic officials. Many of Saddam's speeches were anthologized and published in Arabic and English by official party presses. In 1978 alone, some three million copies of 19 of Saddam's speeches were printed and distributed.[11] Revealing in both their style and content, these speeches form a unique record of Saddam's views on Baathism as a revolutionary ideology. They reveal much about Saddam's methods for garnering more and more power over the Iraqi state and its citizens in the critical decade before he assumed the presidency. In his speeches, it is clear that Saddam sought to reshape Iraqi society by emphasizing the central and all-encompassing role of the Baath party, a role that he hoped would eventually extend beyond Iraq's national borders.

In a 1974 speech at the National Assembly, Saddam said, "We are still only defining our aspirations, still at the beginning of the road which we have resolved to cover—the road of building socialism, fighting imperialism and making this country a safe base, a vital bastion for the Arab struggle in general and a model experiment illuminating the entire region of the Middle East."[12] Asserting the authority of the Baath Party within Iraq and extending Iraq's regional power were, in Saddam's views, linked and coterminous processes. Baathism, for Saddam, was central to the dual projects of reshaping Iraq's domestic affairs and enhancing its regional power.

The key to transforming Iraq was Baathism, and it was essential that the reach of the party extend far and deep into Iraqi society. "Our slogan will be 'let us win the young to safeguard the future,'" Saddam told a youth group. "It should be our ambition to make all Iraqis in this country Baathists in membership and in belief...." As such, the party members who focused on recruiting Iraqi youth had a special task. "Those who work among the young," Saddam explained, "must be known for their experience and ability to win over the masses. Each one of them must be a psychologist so as to be able to tell when to speak and how to win over his listeners in the light of all the social, psychological, political and economic circumstances of the current phase [sic]. This is a matter which has a special relevance to work among youth. The subsequent development of citizens depends to a large extent on their formation during their youth."[13] In order to better ensure control over the development of the future citizens of the Iraqi state, the Federation of Iraqi Youth consisting of a variety of sub-organizations was formed. These included the Pioneers for young children, the Vanguard for children aged 10 to 15, and the Youth for teenagers. The Vanguard membership included both boys and girls; they wore uniforms, took oaths, and participated in sports programs, cultural activities, and scientific projects. The group inculcated discipline into its members, who were encouraged to work "in the service of their nation."[14]

Children were clearly central to the Baathification process; as such the Iraqi educational system was a space for the propagation of Baathist ideology and a site for political control. Saddam emphasized the potential power of teachers: "The child in his relationship to the teacher is like a piece of raw marble in the hands of a sculptor who has the power to impart aesthetic form, or discard the piece to the ravages of time and the vagaries of nature." The ability to transform Iraq's children had great importance, for they were seen as a conduit with which all of Iraqi society could ultimately be monitored and controlled. Children were to become agents of the state within the family. "Teach the student," Saddam said, "to object to his parents if he hears them discussing state secrets and to alert them that this is not correct. Teach them to criticize their mothers and fathers respectfully if they hear them talking about organizational and party secrets. You must place in every corner a son of the revolution, with a trustworthy eye and a firm mind that receives instructions from the responsible centre of the revolution."[15]

Saddam's views on the centrality of recruiting and acculturating Iraqi youth to the party structure and ideology are apparent in a speech he gave to a group charged with creating a new national educational curriculum in Iraq in 1973. He told the group that

> in order to perform your duties correctly, you must be precisely aware of our central concepts, both ideological and political. It is in accordance with these central concepts that you are to undertake the duty of reconsidering the curricula in accordance with the method of the Revolution. Accordingly, you have to start from an essential principle in the field of bringing up a generation and building a society: you have to consider man as an important value and a major objective within the community.... We have to emphasize, moreover, that this community is led by a Party; that this party leads the community not only in accordance with its own values, organization and ideology but also in accordance with its own policies; and that it leads the community on the level of the State as well as on the level of popular democratic activities. Thus it is necessary for the Party's principles and values to play a considerable role in these activities and in the State's decisions too.... [16]

The curriculum, according to Saddam, was to be retooled in order to build a new society and a new state that reflected the centrality of the party in shaping its values, organization, and ideology. All Iraqi teachers were to study the ideology of the Baath Party. "Such a study is essential," claimed Saddam, "on account of the Arab Baath Socialist Party being the leader of this community and this authority." For Saddam, the rewriting of history was central to restructuring the Iraqi curriculum. He called for an emphasis on Arabic and Islamic history in Iraq's schools, arguing, "we should bring out from this history all the values that are fully consistent with the character of the set-up [of the Baath regime], with the message of our nation and with the national role of our Iraqi people." Ultimately, Saddam was quite clear on what the role of the new educational system in Iraq was to be. "We want a socialist generation and one that believes in Arab nationalism. Such, in fact, is the generation we are striving to create within the greater Arab community."[17]

History was not the only academic discipline on which Saddam advised Iraqi educators; geography was also of particular interest to him. Geography, Saddam told a teachers' group, was an important aspect of the political struggle. Geography could be used to teach pan-Arabism, while at the same time helping to construct a distinct Iraqi nationalism. According to Saddam, not only did this Iraqi nationalism stand in distinction to a larger Arab identity, but it also overrode ethnic differences: "In this country, there are majorities and minorities, but within the borders of this country, we have one people." To call some people Arab or Kurd, Saddam claimed, was "chauvinistic." Instead, one should use the term "the Iraqi people," which was a "constitutional and political term." This discussion was a rather transparent statement against the nationalist and political claims of Iraq's Kurdish minority. Children being educated in Iraqi schools were to learn in their geography classes that even using the term Kurdish—as opposed to Iraqi—had derogatory implications; the proper political term was "the Iraqi people." Geography class, then, was another critical space for the reeducation of a new generation of Iraqis to the Baath Party's particular views of Iraqi nationalism—one that was distinct from but a part of pan-Arabism and one that elided or subsumed ethnic diversity.[18]

Given the importance of the educational system in extending the authority of the Baath Party, efforts were made to increase the number of Iraqis who received an education. Compulsory education had been legally mandated in Iraq in 1958 but was not fully implemented until the 1970s. A report issued by the Baath Party in 1968 underlined the political dimensions of adult illiteracy noting, "The noble aim of eradicating illiteracy is one of the main fields of our strife and activity. On its success will depend the determination of many vital political, economic and social issues in this country...."[19] Throughout the 1970s, a series of laws were passed making primary education compulsory and free for all Iraqis. In 1978, Saddam declared a massive national campaign for literacy. All illiterate Iraqis between the ages of 15 and 45 were given 21 months to achieve literacy. The Baathist state allocated millions of dollars, employed thousands of teachers, and mobilized the state and the party's bureaucratic structure to achieve the goal of eradicating adult illiteracy. Those who did not enroll in literacy classes faced severe punishments, including possible fines and imprisonment. In 1979, the Supreme Council of the National Campaign for Compulsory Literacy of Iraq was recognized with an award by UNESCO. Indeed, the United Nations was so taken with the success of the program, that from 1980 until 1991, UNESCO granted "the Iraq Award" each year to states, individuals, and organizations in recognition of their achievements in advancing literacy.[20]

The literacy campaign involved hundreds of thousands of Iraqis, whose education was to be linked "with the movement of society and aims of the Arab nation in Unity, Freedom and Socialism."[21] Clearly, the literacy campaign was tied to the process of developing an Iraqi educational system that played a leading role in the creation of a new generation of

Baathists. In Saddam's view, Iraq's youth were to be inculcated with the ethos, values, and principles of Baathism, even those who did not officially join the Baath Party. In 1979, he told the staff of the Ministry of Youth, "We always say that the Arab Baath Socialist Party is not a party for the Baathists alone. It is a party for the entire people, even for those who are not members. We believe that any national Iraqi, though not a member, is prepared to defend his Party to the degree of martyrdom, since the Party represents his future and that of his children, his international reputation and record, both on local and Arab levels, of which he is proud." Fidelity to the party was paramount, to the extent that all Iraqis should be willing to sacrifice their lives in its service. Instilling such a degree of conformity—or control—required a tremendous collective effort. Indeed, Saddam believed that the creation of this new generation was the ultimate revolutionary act: "Therefore, when you create the man of the revolution and make his image and role sound in order to excel, you will have rendered a great service to your revolution."[22]

Of course this new generation of Iraqis included women as well, and Saddam spoke regularly to women's groups, espousing his views on their particular role in Iraqi revolutionary society. In 1971, speaking at a conference of the Federation of Iraqi Women, he traced the role of Iraqi women in "the people's struggle for freedom from imperialism, dictatorship and reactionary regimes and for achieving the pan-Arab aims of unity, liberty, and socialism. During the 1920 revolution in which our people gave their response to the British colonial occupation, and during the mass uprisings against the imperialist pacts and alliances, the unjust legislation and conditions and the corrupt, reactionary dictatorships, women took part and played a role that gave an example of courage and initiative and inspired bravery and enthusiasm in the hearts of the strugglers." In this passage, Saddam extended the Baath Party's role into an imagined past, essentially claiming for it the mantle of the struggle against British colonialism, and he situated women prominently in his narrative of Iraq's reconstructed past.

Baathism encompassed a developmentalist ideology, and the party sought to bring about the rapid development of Iraq.[23] Saddam's speeches often referred to the need to overcome social and economic "backwardness." In a speech to the General Federation of Iraqi Women in 1971, Saddam said, "Those who still look on women with the mentality and ideas of the ages of darkness and backwardness do not express the aspirations and ambitions of the Revolution. They are at variance with the principles of the Party which are essentially based on freedom and emancipation. Indeed, they are in opposition to every true desire for progress."

The Baath Party, then, was working to mobilize Iraqi women for the revolutionary cause, and in so doing it sought to emancipate them as part of their drive toward "progress." Iraqi women were getting educated, becoming a part of the work force, and assuming positions in the unions and in the government. Women's emancipation became part of the larger project of Baathification. As Saddam explained, "The Revolution is a leap towards an enlightened freedom which is placed at the service of the people and of the progress of mankind in general. It cannot be a genuine revolution if it does not aim at the liberation of woman and the development of her material and cultural conditions."[24]

The need to liberate women was essential to develop Iraq, a cornerstone of Baathism. "The complete emancipation of women from the ties which held them back in the past," Saddam said, "during the ages of despotism and ignorance, is a basic aim of the Party and of the Revolution. Women make up one half of society. Our society will remain backward and in chains unless its women are liberated, enlightened and educated." The obstacles placed before women are still great, Saddam argued, and all revolutionaries must struggle to help women achieve their rightful place in society.[25]

At the same time, Saddam continued to assert a more traditional role for women in Baathist society. "The achievement of the complete emancipation of women is a revolutionary necessity for accelerating the wheels of progress, ..." Saddam argued. "The emancipation of women is a principal basis for bringing up the new generation and the discharge of its heavy responsibilities."[26] In Baathist Iraq, women were given greater legal rights and economic power; still, according to Saddam Hussein, their role as the mothers of the new generation remained a central aspect of their social and political responsibilities. Even if Saddam's advocacy for women's rights and promotion of literacy were strategic political choices, he still gained something of a reputation as a progressive in international and regional circles.

SADDAM AND WORLD DIPLOMACY

During the years that he served as second in command, Saddam learned certain lessons about power and diplomacy from Bakr. Early in his presidency, Bakr took to entertaining journalists over meals in his palace. The meals were simple, and the guests were usually members of the cabinet and important journalists. At a time when the world press was debating the stability and viability of the regime, the relaxed meetings provided a hospitable environment for Bakr to set forth his perspective on Iraq's foreign affairs and internal conflicts.[27] Like Bakr, Saddam took to hosting journalists at intimate meals, beginning in the mid-1970s when he was increasingly becoming the public face of the regime. The meals were simple Arabic food like plates of olives and hummus, accompanied by large quantities of Johnny Walker Black Label. Saddam told stories and puffed on his Cuban cigars. In Iraqi circles, it was known which journalists were chosen for such intimate gatherings; rumors that a journalist had such proximity to Saddam "would slice into the scary silence of Baath party commissars' offices, to the envy of other western journalists who were barred from many places in Iraq."[28]

In the early 1970s, Saddam used his meetings with foreign journalists to set forth a particular image of Iraq and of himself. This was a critical time in Iraq. The Baath regime was forwarding its agenda: neutralizing opposition groups, suppressing Kurdish forces who were increasingly supported by neighboring Iran, securing Iraqi control over the country's oil resources, and developing Iraq into a modern socialist state. Years later, Iraqi diplomat Tariq Aziz would recall in a television interview: "During that period, development was our main obsession.... Saddam Hussein was chairman of the planning council in charge of development ... and our ambition was to turn Iraq into a very, very developed country, with industry, services, technology, and education."[29] Saddam recognized that this goal could only be achieved with oil revenue and with foreign technical assistance and goods.

In February 1972, Saddam headed an Iraqi delegation to the USSR. Moscow promised to provide Iraq with more economic and military aid; in particular, the Soviet Union pledged to help Iraq establish a national oil industry. In April of that year, Soviet Premier Kosygin visited Baghdad and was greeted by Saddam at an official welcoming ceremony at the airport. The Russians and the Iraqis signed a 15-year treaty of friendship and cooperation. Saddam had skillfully secured the help he needed from the USSR. However, Saddam did not want to rely exclusively on Soviet technology and assistance. He wanted the best products at the best price.

On June 1, 1972, Iraq announced the nationalization of the Iraq Petroleum Company.[30] Soon the Iraq National Oil Company was formed, with its headquarters in the southern port city of Basra. Saddam Hussein would become the head of the company's steering committee, which determined Iraq's oil production policy. Following nationalization, the billions of dollars in oil revenue could be used to pay for the Baath regime's huge development projects and for building up Iraq's army, but establishing trade relations with the West required a degree of finesse. Iraqi nationalization of oil had ended American, British, French, and Dutch companies' control over Iraqi oil. Just days after the nationalization of Iraqi oil was announced, Saddam visited France, potentially a key partner in developing Iraq. Saddam met with President George Pompidou and offered French interests favored commercial status in Iraq. The French in turn agreed to provide Iraq with arms and other significant technological support. In December 1974 and again in September 1975, French Premier Jacques Chirac traveled to Baghdad and met with Saddam. During the second visit, France and Iraq initialed a nuclear cooperation agreement. The following year, Saddam returned to France where he "personally concluded a deal to purchase a uranium reactor from that country."[31]

But Saddam was not satisfied with having the Soviet Union and France as its only key trade partners. In order to cultivate alternative Western markets, Saddam knew he had to improve the Baath party's relations with the West. Anger over Iraqi nationalization of oil was not the only obstacle. At the time, Iraq did not have diplomatic relations with either Britain or the United States. After the 1967 war, Iraq cut diplomatic relations with the United States because of that country's support for Israel; in 1971, it cut ties with Britain, which it saw as supporting Iran's annexation of some Persian Gulf islands. In addition to these regional diplomatic obstacles, the United States and Britain might be reluctant to enter into commercial relations with a socialist regime with close ties to the Soviets. Saddam, however, realized that Cold War diplomacy might work to his advantage. Trade with the West could be construed as lessening Iraq's dependence on the Soviet bloc, while also offering the West the possibility of an expanded role in developing Iraqi oil reserves.

A turn in Iraq's foreign affairs necessitated a shift in the Iraqi regime's image, and Saddam understood the power of the world press in helping to create a change in attitudes. In February 1973, Saddam held a three-hour interview with some leading Western journalists. After meeting with Saddam, the longtime foreign correspondent for *The Observer* of London, Gavin Young, wrote, "Iraq does not want alignment with either East or West but wants good relations with a more sympathetic Britain, and even the United States.... Stability and development are watchwords, and, it seems rapprochement." Young observed that Iraq was on "the threshold of a multibillion-dollar development boom that could leave Saudi Arabia and Kuwait behind." Opening trade relations, Saddam suggested, could be beneficial to all parties, despite ideological positions and geopolitics. Saddam explained, "Nowadays there is no winning partner. Relationships are between two gainers. Iraqis can't drink oil. And our markets are in the West and Japan."[32]

The New York Times published an article along similar lines, quoting Saddam saying, "Up to this moment, Iraq has viewed American and British policies as hostile to Iraq and the interests of the Arab peoples." He made it clear, however, that the need to develop Iraq offered a strong incentive to overcome those previous diplomatic roadblocks. "We believe in the possibility of establishing trade, economic and diplomatic relations with countries under different political systems if these relations are based on mutual respect for sovereignty and the interests of our people."[33]

In his meetings with foreign journalists, Saddam came across as a powerful man with a certain sense of style. One journalist reported, "While officials describe him as a 'committed revolutionary,' he lives today in an elegant palace along the Tigris River, wears smartly tailored European suits, and indulges his taste for imported silk ties."[34] Jim Hoagland of *The Washington Post* noted that Saddam wore a platinum diamond-studded watch with matching diamond cufflinks. He described Saddam as "Iraq's suave strongman ... who moves with the tightly coiled violence and fluid grace of Vince Lombardi's best linebackers at Green Bay." Discussing Saddam's leadership position within the authoritarian Baath regime, Hoagland wrote, "Shrewdness and a reputation for extraordinary personal bravery have sparked Saddam's rise...."[35]

Saddam's apparent gift for public relations seems to have borne fruit. Soon his ideas were being discussed not just by foreign correspondents who reported the news but by newspaper columnists who helped shape opinions and policies. Saddam's image in the West as the dapper strongman of Iraq was fomented. His suggestion that nations could open trade relations despite significant ideological differences proved compelling to some. Rowland Evans and Robert Novak, who for years wrote a highly influential column in *The Washington Post,* visited Baghdad in late 1973 where they interviewed Saddam, whom they described as "the most resourceful and powerful figure" in Baghdad, observing that he was "suave and darkly handsome."[36] Evans and Novak pointed to Iraq's socialist Baathist regime, its ties with the Soviet Union, and its inflexible opposition to Israel. They concluded, "Given that hard-rock intractability, even a cursory dialogue with Washington on a political settlement of the Middle East is pointless. But beneath the intractability lurks another mood, a mood that is clearly looking toward experimentation with Washington and toward the marvels of US technology. With stupendously oil-rich Iraq a key to Moscow's veiled plans for a Moscow-controlled Asian 'zone of peace,' that mood is well worth cultivating."[37] Saddam's proposition apparently held some appeal: countries with highly divergent political positions could still engage in mutually lucrative economic relations.

Indeed, this seems to have become a kind of unspoken policy, creating a new relationship between Iraq and the United States. In March 1975, the American company Boeing won a $300 million dollar contract for several jumbo jets, with contracts for training and maintenance. Since the two countries still did not have official diplomatic relations, there was an American interest section of the Belgian Embassy. One of the three American employees of this unit was a commercial attaché, who helped ameliorate trade relations.

In the spring of 1975, as Western interest in Iraq grew, C. L. Sulzberger, the foreign affairs columnist for *The New York Times*, traveled to Baghdad. Interviewing Saddam Hussein extensively, Sulzberger wrote a series of columns on a range of issues from the Kurds to Israel to commercial ties with the West. A seasoned journalist who had written on Iraq for over a decade, Sulzberger captured the complexities of Iraq and maintained a skepticism on Saddam Hussein. In March 1975, Sulzberger wrote of the implications of an accord just signed by Iran and Iraq that resolved a long and bitter border dispute. That month, the Shah of Iran and Saddam Hussein had met during the Organization of Petroleum Exporting Countries (OPEC) meeting in Algiers to hash out an agreement; Saddam would later travel to Tehran to sign the final draft of the accords. The two countries agreed to create a permanent demarcation of their land frontiers. Iraq conceded to Iran's proposal to accept the median line of the Shatt al-Arab waterway as the border between the two countries; previously, Iraq had asserted that the border should be marked at the Iranian banks of the waterway. The two countries also agreed to establish reciprocal security along their common borders, working to stop the infiltration of "subversives" on both sides. This was a clear reference to the Kurdish situation.

Since the early 1970s, the Kurdish leader, Barzani, had been supported by Iran, Israel, and the United States. Though there were grounds for distrust on both sides, Saddam and Barzani had continued to negotiate. The specific nature of Kurdish autonomy and the area that was to fall under Kurdish administrative control continued to be contested. On March 11, 1974, Saddam gave a speech in which he spelled out the terms of a new Autonomy Law for the Kurds. "Our understanding of autonomy," Saddam asserted, "is on the basis of free mixing of people and of specifying an area where national rights may be exercised within Iraq and the sovereignty of Iraq in present and future terms. In addition, in accordance with the foregoing principle, we understand that it is impossible to follow up the shadow of every citizen belonging to the nationality covered by autonomy so that we may trace this shadow and treat it as a fixed spot of land belonging to the autonomy region." Clearly, Kirkuk was a major sticking point. It was an oil-rich area claimed by the Kurds, which Saddam refused to give up. Saddam gave the Kurds 15 days to accept the new Autonomy Law and join the National Front. "After that," he said, "we will not accept any alliance with you."[38] Barzani rejected the offer, and once again, war broke out between the Kurds and the Iraqi army.

At this point, Iran supported the Kurds in the war, allowing Kurdish fighters and civilians to travel freely over the Iran-Iraq border. However, provisions in the 1975 pact between Iran and Iraq put an end to the relatively easy movement of Kurds across the border. The agreement, in effect, signaled the Iranian government's willingness to stop supporting the Kurdish rebellion against the Baath regime. Within hours of announcing the new pact with Iran, the Iraqi Government offered amnesty to any Kurds who would end their resistance, and the Iraqi army began a major offensive against the Kurds. The government undertook a massive relocation of Kurds to various parts of Iraq; there is some uncertainty about the figures, but estimates of Kurds who were forcibly moved from their homes to other parts of the country range from 250,000 to 300,000.[39] By 1978, some 1,400 Kurdish villages were destroyed.[40] The 1975 Algiers Agreement between Iran and Iraq effectively ended Iranian support for the Kurds, depriving them of a major ally in their struggle for autonomy.

In his column, Sulzberger summarized the implications of the Algiers Agreement for the Kurds and for Saddam. "The rise of the thirsty young Saddam Hussein to dominant political power in this tightly-run, security-conscious Arab state has virtually coincided with the climax in Baghdad's long struggle to stamp out a Kurdish insurrection led by the redoubtable tribal leader, Mulla Mustapha Barzani," Sulzberger wrote. "Mr. Hussein, now the unchallenged strongman of Iraq, is at the acme of his career. He has just concluded a bilateral accord ceding large Shatt-al-Arab rights to Iran and gained, in exchange, cessation of all Iranian aid to Mr. Barzani. As a result, the goose of the 72-year-old Kurdish rebel is cooked." Sulzberger noted that keeping the Kurds pacified was "a factor to which Mr. Hussein's own political future is inextricably linked."[41] The columnist was right. In a speech the following year, Saddam essentially negated the autonomous identity of the Kurds: "We like the mountain in the northern part of the country not merely because it is a part of Iraq, but primarily because our people live there. We defend the mountain in order to defend our people and this is the way we must approach this issue." He closed off the possibility for the creation of an independent Kurdistan by declaring,

"We must understand that this country will remain within its present geographical boundaries forever."[42]

Sulzberger also wrote a column about Iraq and Israel in which he quoted Saddam as saying, "As Arabs we have no intention of exterminating the Jews who now live in a dear part of our homeland. At the same time, they do occupy a part of our territory. Therefore we should struggle by all the means at our disposal to end that occupation."[43] Saddam Hussein had strongly opposed any concessions with Israel, rejecting the cease-fire that ended the October War of 1973. In the fall of 1974, Saddam led the Iraqi delegation to the Arab Summit conference in Rabat on the Palestinian question. Saddam gave a speech that clearly spelled out his position: "If we want our [Arab] nation to unite and to mobilize its resources, we must draw up a complete strategy for the liberation of all the territories occupied and usurped before and after 1967.... This strategy does not rule out political activity nor the policy of phased advance but that these methods must be subservient to the basic strategy—the total liberation of Arab territories. It does not involve, at any stage or in any circumstances, recognition of the Zionist enemy in any form or of the occupation of Arab territory before June 5, 1967."[44]

Sulzberger's columns, then, traced the intermingling of Saddam's personal rise to power with his aggressive posture in regional politics—crushing the Kurdish rebellion even if it meant signing an unfavorable accord with Iran and calling for the end of Israeli occupation of Arab lands "employing all its resources to that end."[45] At the same time that Saddam was openly pursuing these policies, he was attempting to rehabilitate his own image and that of Baathist Iraq in the West in order to promote trade relations. In this pursuit, Saddam seems to have achieved considerable success. In a third column from Baghdad, Sulzberger wrote of Iraq's relations with the Cold War powers. Noting the absence of official ties between the United States and Iraq and increasing friction between the USSR and Iraq, Sulzberger observed, "Trade has suddenly zoomed, with American exports to Iraq mounting from $32.3 million in 1971 to $284 million last year. Iraq Airways has bought five Boeings and ordered eight more; a Texas company is constructing a new deep-sea oil terminal; and US steel has sold several drilling rigs with a prospect of large new contracts."[46] Sulzberger situated his discussion of increasing U.S. trade with Iraq within the framework of Cold War politics. Of course Iraq did not sever ties with the Soviet Union, nor did it fully normalize relations with the United States. Still, at a critical time, Saddam used his considerable diplomatic skills to help ameliorate relations with the United States to the extent that important trade relations were established.

Soon after the publication of Sulzberger's *New York Times* columns on Iraq, Saddam became a topic of conversation in a meeting between U.S. Secretary of State Henry Kissinger and State Department officials. In the meeting that took place on April 28, 1975, Assistant Secretary of State for Near Eastern and South Asian affairs Alfred L. Atherton, Jr. reported to Kissinger that Saddam was traveling to Tehran the following day to negotiate an accord with the Shah of Iran on the Shatt-Al-Arab border dispute. Iraqi officials, Atherton noted, had "... been patching things up on various specific issues—border disputes and so forth—with Saudi Arabia. They've made an offer to Kuwait. They've been moving closely to the Egyptians and the Jordanians and altogether suddenly projecting the image of a country that wants to play a more dynamic ... role in the Arab world." Atherton and Kissinger then had a brief exchange on Saddam:

> Atherton: "Hussein is a rather remarkable person. We have to look more closely into his background. He's 38 years old and he holds no government position. He's the Vice President of the Command Council, but he is running the show; and he's a very ruthless—and very recently, obviously—pragmatic, intelligent power. I think we're going to see Iraq playing more of a role in the area than it has for many years."
>
> Kissinger: "That was to be expected anyway when they cleared...."
>
> Atherton: "Yes, Once the agreement was made on the...."
>
> Kissinger: "Kurdish thing."[47]

A few months later in Paris, Kissinger met with the Iraqi foreign minister and the Iraqi ambassador to France to discuss the possibility of normalizing relations between the United States and Iraq. The meeting, which had been instigated by Kissinger, took place on December 17, 1975 in the residence of the Iraqi ambassador to France. Kissinger opened the conversation by explaining the U.S. position: "Our two countries have not had much contact with each other in recent years, and I wanted to take this opportunity to establish contact. I know we won't solve all of our problems in one meeting. It will take at least two. [Laughter.]" Kissinger continued, "Our basic attitude is that we do not think there is a basic clash of national interests between Iraq and the United States. For a variety of reasons, Iraq and the United States have been on opposing sides. But we have managed to normalize relations with most of the other Arabs. On purely national grounds, we see no overwhelming obstacles on our side...."

The Iraqi Foreign Minister, Sadun Hammadi then proceeded to discuss the chief barriers to renewing diplomatic relations, U.S. support for Israel and the Kurds, and Kissinger gave his responses on these issues:

> Hammadi: "We of course have different views [about normalizing relations], and I will tell you why. Iraq is part of the Arab world. We believe the United States has been the major factor in building up Israel to what it is today."
>
> Kissinger: "True."
>
> Hammadi: "We believe Israel was established by force and is a clear-cut case of colonialism. Israel was established on part of our homeland. You don't believe that. But that is not the whole story. Israel is now a direct threat to Iraq's national security.... Israel has built up a military power that can threaten Iraq, especially with the recent news that we read of the US supplying sophisticated weapons. So it is not only the Arab world that is threatened, and Iraq being part of the Arab world, but Iraq itself. We think the US is building up Israel to have the upper hand in the area.... What the United States is doing is not to create peace but to create a situation dominated by Israel, which will create a new wave of clashes."
>
> Kissinger: "... We can't negotiate about the existence of Israel but we can reduce its size to historical proportions.... If the issue is the existence of Israel, we can't cooperate. But if the issue is more normal borders, we can cooperate.... It is just a matter of time before there is a change—two to three years. After a settlement, Israel will be a small friendly country with no unlimited drawing right.... So I think the balance in America is shifting [on the Arab-Israeli issue]. If the Arabs—if I can be frank—don't do anything stupid."

On U.S. support for the Kurds, Kissinger explained, "When we thought you were a Soviet satellite, we were not opposed to what Iran was doing in the Kurdish area. Now that Iran and you have resolved it, we have no reason to do any such thing. I can tell you we will engage in no such activity against Iraq's territorial integrity, and are not."[48] Despite Kissinger's assurances, Hammadi hesitated to renew complete diplomatic relations. Instead, he suggested the United States and Iraq develop cultural and economic ties. These diplomatic contacts seem to suggest, then, that the paradigm that Saddam Hussein had discussed in his interviews with foreign journalists had become a de facto policy. Iraq and the United

States continued to oppose one another on the world diplomatic stage, while engaging in mutually profitable trade.

Within the span of a decade, Saddam Hussein had managed to nationalize Iraq's oil industry, suppress the Kurdish uprising, assume a radical pro-Palestinian mantle, and resolve long-simmering tensions with Iran. All the while, he had created trade partnerships with the Soviet Union, France, Britain, West Germany, Japan, and the United States, which allowed him to implement a five-year 20-billion-dollar development plan. While continuing to get the bulk of its military support from the Soviet Union, Saddam had also negotiated arms deals with Britain, Italy, France, and Spain. By the late 1970s, Saddam had become the undisputed strongman of Iraq, a country that was increasingly subsumed by Baathist authoritarianism. As Hoagland wrote in *The Washington Post*, "'The Deputy' as Saddam is sometimes called here, has become in seven years the acknowledged leader of the village clan and the covert Baath party apparatus which are creating a new and still changing Iraq in their own sinister, authoritarian regime."[49]

As 1978 drew to a close, Saddam traveled to Moscow, where he met with the Soviet leaders, Leonid Brezhnev and Aleksey Kosygin. Kosygin and Saddam made a public statement, condemning the recent Camp David peace agreement between Egypt and Israel as "a collusion behind the Arabs' back."[50] The Soviet Union had already helped Iraq develop its oil fields and expand other industries such as cotton mills and glass-producing plants. On this trip, the Soviets agreed to support the construction of a hydro-energy generating complex on the Tigris River. Saddam told reporters, "When we visit the Soviet Union we always find things new and useful to develop relations between the two countries."[51] Leaving Moscow, Saddam traveled on to Cuba to visit with Fidel Castro, whom Saddam held up as an example of a successful socialist revolutionary. During the trip, Saddam was awarded the national medal of Jose Marti "out of profound recognition by the Cuban people of his constant contribution to the national liberation struggle of people and for his prominent role in consolidating relations between the Iraqi and Cuban peoples."[52]

As the 1970s drew to a close, it would seem that Saddam had succeeded in molding a certain persona of himself. A French scholar, Philippe Rondot, published an article noting that Iraq had assumed a position of leadership in the Arab world, much to the credit of Saddam Hussein. Since 1968, the article read, Saddam's role was to reinforce the cohesion of Ba'athist power by working against the opponents of the new regime. A pragmatic and courageous spirit, Saddam Hussein had begun immediately to attack Iraq's problems.[53] In a 1978 book, one Iraqi scholar,

Majid Khadduri, wrote, "As Vice President of the RCC, Saddam is the heir apparent who is expected to step in the country's supreme position of power in accordance with the regime's constitutional framework. More important perhaps are his potentials in prudence, flexibility and resourcefulness which quickly come into operation whenever he has to make an important decision at a time of crisis. These qualities, combined with integrity and high moral courage, are his Party's best promise for the country's future leadership."[54] This glowing and impassioned prediction of Saddam Hussein's presidency would prove to be far from prescient.

NOTES

1. John K. Cooley, "Iraq Inner Circle," *The Christian Science Monitor*, February 6, 1969.

2. "Biographic Sketch of Saddam Hussein," British Embassy in Baghdad, November 15, 1969, Public Record Office, London, FCO 17/871, retrieved July 29, 2003, National Security Archives (NSA).

3. Telegram from British Embassy Baghdad to Foreign and Commonwealth Office, "Saddam Hussein," December 20, 1969, Public Record Office, London, FCO 17/871, NSA, http://www.gwu.edu/~nsarchiv/special/iraq/index.htm (retrieved July 29, 2003).

4. Edith Penrose and E. F. Penrose, *Iraq: International Relations and National Development* (London: Ernest Benn, 1978), pp. 143–44.

5. David McDowall, *A Modern History of the Kurds*, revised edition (London: I. B. Tauris, 1997), pp. 327–38.

6. "Iraq Coup Attempt," *Middle East Reports (MERIP)* (August 1973): 15–16.

7. "Scores Reported Held after Iraqi Assassination," *The Washington Post*, July 3, 1973.

8. "Iraq Killing," *The Washington Post*, July 7, 1973.

9. "23 Shot in Iraq for Plotting," *The Washington Post*, July 8, 1973.

10. "Iraqi Head Gets Full Power," *Christian Science Monitor*, July 16, 1973.

11. Kanan Makiya, *Republic of Fear: The Politics of Modern Iraq*, updated edition (Berkeley: University of California Press, 1998), p. 84.

12. Saddam Hussein, speech delivered on April 25, 1974 at the National Assembly, in *Saddam Hussein on Current Events in Iraq*, trans. K. Kishtainy (London: Longmann, 1977), p. 81.

13. Saddam Hussein, speech delivered on February 15, 1976 to the meeting of the General Federation of Iraqi Youth, in *The Revolution and the Young*, trans. K. Kishtainy (Baghdad: Translation and Foreign Language House, 1981), pp. 9–22.

14. Christine Moss Helms, *Iraq: Eastern Flank of the Arab World* (Washington, D.C.: The Brookings Institution, 1984), p. 97.

15. Saddam Hussein, speech delivered on July 10, 1977 to the employees of the Ministry of Education, as translated by Makiya, *Republic of Fear*, p. 78.

16. Saddam Hussein, speech delivered on November 13, 1973 to the first session of the Committees for the Study of Educational Affairs with a View to Amending Curricula, in *Revolution and National Education*, trans. N. A. Mudhaffer (Baghdad: Dar Al-Ma'mun for Translation and Publishing, 1981), pp. 7–18.

17. Ibid.

18. Saddam Hussein, speech delivered on September 30, 1975 to a society of geographers, in *Al-thawrah wa al-tarbiyah al-wataniyyah* [The Revolution and National Education] (Baghdad: Maktab Al-Wataniyyah, 1977), pp. 93–102.

19. Quoted in Alya Sousa, "The Eradication of Illiteracy in Iraq," in *Iraq: The Contemporary State*, ed. Tim Noblock (New York: St. Martin's Press, 1982), p. 102.

20. UNESCO, http://portal.unesco.org/education/ (retrieved October 31, 2004).

21. Makiya, *Republic of Fear*, pp. 85–88.

22. Saddam Hussein, speech delivered on January 31, 1979 to the staff of the Ministry of Youth, *Revolution and National Education*, pp. 23–36.

23. For more on this, see Joe Stork, "State Power and Economic Structure: Class Determination and State Formation in Contemporary Iraq," in Noblock, *Iraq*, pp. 27–46.

24. Ibid.

25. Saddam Hussein, speech delivered on April 17, 1975 to the General Federation of Iraqi Women, in *Social and Foreign Affairs in Iraq*, trans. K. Kishtany (London: Croom Helm, 1979), pp. 13–17.

26. Saddam Hussein, statement given in April 1975 on the occasion of International Women's Year, in *The Revolution and Woman in Iraq*, trans. K. Kishtainy (Baghdad: Translation and Foreign Language House, 1981), pp. 17–23.

27. See for example Eric Rouleau's description of such a lunch in "Les nouveaux dirigeants irakiens mettent l'accent sur leur volonté de consolider les relations entre Bagdad et Paris," *Le Monde*, August 7, 1968; though Rouleau began his piece with a skeptical note about being feted at the palace, he did write a substantial front page article spelling out Bakr's positions.

28. Adel Darwish, "Saddam Hussein: The Godfather of Baghdad," http://www.mideastnews.com/iraq003.html (retrieved May 9, 2004).

29. Tariq Aziz interview transcript, *Frontline: The Survival of Saddam*, http://www.pbs.org/wgbh/pages/frontline/shows/interviews/aziz.html.

30. A year later, the Mosul Petroleum Company would also be nationalized. The Basra Petroleum Company would be taken over by the Iraqi government in December 1975, bringing all Iraqi oil under the control of the government.

31. Said Aburish, *Saddam Hussein: The Politics of Revenge* (London: Bloomsbury, 2000), p. 140.

32. Gavin Young, "Iraqi Leader Takriti Urges Good Relations with West," *The Washington Post,* July 15, 1973. Though he was a reporter for *The Observer,* Young's articles at times appeared in the *Post* as well.

33. Juan de Onis, "Iraq Says He'd Welcome Better Relations with US," *The New York Times,* July 15, 1973.

34. "No. 2 Man Calls the Shots," *The Washington Post,* August 6, 1978.

35. Jim Hoagland, "Saddam, Iraq's Suave Strongman," *The Washington Post,* May 11, 1975. In 1991, Hoagland would win a Pulitzer Prize for his columns leading up to the Gulf War.

36. Rowland Evans and Robert Novak, "US-Iraqi Relations: Warming Trend?" *The Washington Post,* November 9, 1973.

37. Ibid.

38. Saddam Hussein, "The Kurdish Question 3: The Autonomy Law," in *Saddam Hussein on Current Events in Iraq,* pp. 25–46.

39. Marion Farouk-Sluglett and Peter Sluglett, *Iraq Since 1958: From Revolution to Dictatorship,* revised edition (London: I. B. Tauris, 2001), p. 188.

40. McDowall, *A Modern History of the Kurds,* p. 339.

41. C. L. Sulzberger, "His Kurds, and Why," *The New York Times,* March 29, 1975.

42. Saddam Hussein, speech to a meeting of the Committees of the Progressive Patriotic and National Front, August 21, 1976, in Saddam Hussein, *One Common Trench? Or Two Opposite Ones* (Baghdad: Arab Baath Socialist Party, 1977), pp. 32–35.

43. C. L. Sulzberger, "A Voice Not Far Offstage," *The New York Times,* March 30, 1975.

44. Saddam Hussein, "Reservations about Rabat," *Journal of Palestine Studies* (Winter 1975): 141–42.

45. Ibid.

46. C. L. Sulzberger, "Uncle Sam and Ivan in Iraq," *The New York Times,* April 2, 1975.

47. Quotes of the meeting are from transcript, "Secretary's Principals and Regionals Staff Meeting," April 28, 1975, Excerpt, National Archives, RG 59, Department of State Records, Transcripts of Secretary of State Henry A. Kissinger Staff Meetings, 1973–1977, http://www.gwu.edu/~nsarchiv/special/iraq/index.htm (retrieved July 29, 2003).

48. Quotes of the meeting are from Memorandum of Conversation, Sadun Hammadi (Iraqi Foreign Minister), Falih Mahdi 'Ammash (Iraqi Ambassador to France), Henry A. Kissinger (Secretary of State), December 17, 1975, Iraqi Ambassador's Residence, Paris, France, U.S. National Archives, RG59, Department of State Records, Records of Henry Kissinger, 1973–1977, Box 13, December 1975, http://www.gwu.edu/~nsarchiv/special/iraq/index.htm (retrieved July 29, 2003).

49. Hoagland, "Saddam, Iraq's Suave Strongman."

50. Foreign Broadcast and Information Service (FBIS), Soviet Union (SOV), December 14, 1978, F2–3.

51. FBIS, Middle East and Africa (MEA), December 13, 1978, E3.

52. FBIS, Latin America (LAT), December 20, 1978, Q1.

53. Philippe Rondot, "Saddam Hussein al-Takriti," *Maghreb/Machrek* 83 (1979): 24–29.

54. Majid Khadduri, *Socialist Iraq: A Study in Iraqi Politics Since 1968* (Washington, D.C.: The Middle East Institute, 1978).

Chapter 4

SADDAM'S WARS

THE DEPUTY BECOMES THE LEADER

"When I was a child," Saddam Hussein once told a reporter, "a man walked through my village without carrying a weapon. An old man came up to him and said, 'Why are you asking for trouble?' He said, 'What do you mean?' The old man replied, 'By walking without a weapon, you are asking for people to attack you. Carry a weapon so that blood will not be spilled!'"[1] As Saddam stepped into the highest office in Iraq, he seems to have taken this childhood lesson to heart.

Indeed, his opening act as president was a carefully scripted drama of guns, fear, and loyalty. On July 16, 1979, Bakr announced his retirement on Iraqi television and retreated to a quiet life under armed guard in his home as Saddam assumed the presidency of Iraq. Saddam called a meeting of some 400 Baathist party members. With cameras filming the session, Saddam's closest advisors, who would be leading officials in his government in the coming years, including Izzat Douri, Tariq Aziz, Taha Yassin Ramadan, and Adnan Khairallah, sat in the front row. Saddam stood at a podium on the stage, smoking a cigar as he spoke quietly into a microphone. He announced that Iraq's security forces had uncovered a secret plot by Syria to overthrow the Iraqi Baathist regime and that some of the conspirators were amongst the very "brothers" in attendance at the meeting.

As the meeting wore on, Saddam appeared intermittently emotional, wiping away tears, or aloof, distractedly puffing on his cigar. One by one, names of alleged "traitors" were called out and security men removed the men from the hall; most left quietly, offering little resistance. An ominous quiet hung over the proceedings until one man stood and began praising Saddam in earnest. Gradually, others joined in the pro-Saddam cheers. A series of secret trials followed, and those who were pronounced guilty were sentenced to death. Some estimate that as many as 500 people were executed. Saddam arranged for himself and other members of the RCC to serve as executioners, shooting some of the men receiving guilty verdicts. The party and the government were purged of Saddam's opponents, while others who had passed the ultimate test of loyalty were rendered complicit executioners.

Marking the anniversary of the revolution, Saddam gave his first public speech to the Iraqi nation as president. "I will not deal with political or general affairs as is customary," he declared. "It is a special speech from the heart to the great people in great Iraq and to the great Arab nation.... The transfer of power from leader to leader in the moral and constitutional manner that took place in our country, party, and revolution is unique among all the experiments in the ancient and contemporary worlds." Saddam spoke of his new authority: "In our opinion, authority is not power, dominance and self-satisfaction. It is a burden we carry to apply practical principles in the service of the people, in support of the nation and in order to end injustice...." Saddam recounted lessons he had learned in his revolutionary experiences: "One of the most important lessons that my comrades and I in the command and the party learned was that when dealing with issues connected with authority and its problems, the absence of noble comradely relations and the negligence of values stemming from our heritage will defeat any revolutionary experiment even though it may contain other great and positive aspects."[2]

Saddam assured the Iraqi people that he would not usurp his power as the leader, pledging, "I will struggle to be one of the banners, but not the only banner; I will seek to be one of the swords, but not the only sword; I will seek to be one of the leaders, but not the only leader; and I will struggle to be one of the knights among the strugglers of the party and the people, but not the only knight."[3] His actions, however, belied this openness to sharing power. In the first weeks of his presidency, Saddam asserted his authority over the party and Iraq by "walking with a weapon." His message was abundantly clear—personal loyalty to Saddam was essential for anyone involved in Iraqi political life. In his years as the deputy, Saddam had learned the importance of public spectacle in helping to create political power and authority. On August 8, after 21 of the alleged conspirators had been executed, Saddam stood on a balcony of the Presidential Palace in Baghdad and saluted a crowd of some 50,000 Iraqis who chanted, "Death to the Traitors!"[4] Saddam further insured a direct linkage between himself as the leader and the state by appointing close members of his family and clan to many key government positions, though their tenure would also be reliant above all else on exclusive and complete loyalty to the leader.

The public purge of so many members of the Baath Party surely sent a chill throughout the country, but Saddam continued to balance this harsh political ethos with images of a happy home life. In an interview with an official biographer, he showed a sentimental side claiming, "I can't imagine life without love. Love is a state which is not only connected to man and his fiancé or wife, for it also connects man and his children, and man and mankind."[5] By now, Saddam and Sajida had two sons and three daughters—Uday, Qusay, Raghad, Rana, and Hallah—whom they raised in some opulence.

Though theirs was an extravagant lifestyle, Saddam claimed he tried to teach his children a sense of balance and context. "To me," he said, "the most important thing is for my children not to think they are above others, but the same, and to realize that their distinction is not a social one, but one of the requirements of life which has been imposed by the reality of official responsibility. In other words, my family must understand that what it has and enjoys is not a matter of privilege, but one of necessity. The fact that they have a chauffeur, a government car, cooks and domestic servants exists to serve the position I hold, and not because they are privileged above others."[6] On occasion, Saddam took his youngest daughter, Hallah, to the office with him. Pictures and films showed Saddam as the devoted father attending his children's birthday parties, picnicking with them in the countryside, playing with them in the swimming pool, and boating as a family along the Tigris. His children would often accompany Saddam on his infamous swims in the Tigris, a favorite pastime.

The paternal role of Saddam extended beyond his immediate family, however. He saw himself as a father figure to all Iraqis and regularly gave advice in his numerous interviews, which were shown on Iraqi television. Saddam paid especially close attention to matters of personal hygiene, and he shared his tips on cleanliness with the nation. "It's not appropriate," he told one interviewer, "for someone to attend a gathering or to be with his children with his body odor trailing behind him, emitting a sweet or stinky smell mixed with perspiration. It's preferable to bathe twice a day, but at least, at least once a day. And when the male bathes once a day, the female should bathe twice a day. The reason is that the female is more delicate, and the smell of a woman is more noticeable than the male." If Iraqis were too poor to afford a toothbrush and toothpaste, he advised them to brush their teeth with their fingers, demonstrating this technique before the television cameras for emphasis. Lack of personal hygiene could affect one's personal relationships, Saddam cautioned. "If the son does not remember his father's nice scent, this will take away some of the son's love toward his father."[7]

Saddam added the promise of economic prosperity to this blend of fear and paternalism as a way to cement his authority over Iraq. By the mid-1980s, Saddam had harnessed Iraq's oil wealth to advance major development schemes throughout Iraq. Bulldozers carved an intricate network of highways throughout the Iraqi landscape. Iraq's major cities boasted luxurious hotels. The countryside was developed with irrigations systems and electricity was provided for even the remotest villages. Baghdad was the center of the building boom, boasting entire blocks of modern housing units.

As part of his scheme to develop Iraq into a modern Baathist state, Saddam improved the lot of Iraq's women. It is Iraqi women living in Baghdad, one journalist observed, "who are the index of Baathism. They make their presence felt in the daytime in shops and offices and, in the evening, may come out to stroll. Most wear Western clothes. They walk with men, sometimes hand in hand, along the avenues. They picnic with their families in the parks and dine with them in the fish restaurants on the banks of the Tigris...."[8] Under Saddam, women were given the right to vote and run for public office. Women constituted over half of the student population of the University of Baghdad and nearly a quarter of the work force. This was in large part due to a "Rosie the Riveter" phenomenon, as many of Iraq's young men were mobilized for Saddam's long war with neighboring Iran throughout much of the first decade of his presidency.[9]

SADDAM AND THE QUESTION OF PALESTINE

In 1978, President Anwar Sadat of Egypt and Prime Minister Menachem Begin of Israel signed the Camp David accords, paving the way for a bilateral peace between Egypt and Israel. In December 1978, Saddam visited an old ally and role model, Fidel Castro in Cuba. The official Iraqi News Agency issued a statement regarding the visit, noting that Castro and Saddam took "a special interest" in the situation between Egypt and Israel. "The two sides," the statement declared, "strongly con-

demn the Camp David agreements ... [which] constitute a plot against
the interests of the Arab nation and are aimed at enabling the Zionist
entity to keep the occupied Arab areas and to prevent the Palestinian
Arab people from regaining their legitimate rights. Consequently, Iraq
and Cuba condemn the capitulatory measures of the Egyptian leadership,
whose aim is to split the Arab ranks and to inflict serious damage on the
Arab nation's struggle to liberate the occupied areas."[10]

Saddam led the Arab opposition to the Camp David agreement and
increasingly sought to situate Iraq as the main defender of Palestinian
rights. In a speech to a student conference in Baghdad, he declared,
"Iraq struggles for the cause of the Arab nation and ... for the cause of
our brethren, the Palestinian revolutionaries, to restore their usurped
rights."[11] Saddam helped organize the Baghdad Summit in March 1979 in
order to respond to the Egyptian-Israeli peace treaty. In the fall, the Arab
League had issued a call against any punitive actions that would harm
"the Arab people of Egypt," but a constellation of Arab countries, including Algeria, Libya, and Iraq called for strict measures against Egypt.[12]
The Baghdad Summit held at the presidential guest palace opened with a
rousing speech by the chairman of the Palestine Liberation Organization,
Yasir Arafat. Tens of thousands of Baghdadis took to the streets, protesting Sadat as a traitor. The Arab nations rejected the Camp David accords
and placed political and economic sanctions on Egypt. The Arab League
headquarters were moved out of Cairo, Egypt's membership in the league
was suspended, and any Egyptian companies doing business with Israel
were to be boycotted. Saddam spoke to the delegates, asserting that
there was "no possibility for neutrality" in response to the signing of the
peace treaty.[13] He declared that any Arab ruler who didn't endorse the
Baghdad Summit resolution would be considered a traitor who should be
overthrown.[14]

With Egypt's role as the leader of the Arab countries in sharp decline,
Saddam sensed a critical opening. Saddam had long advocated a hard
stance on the question of Palestine. In a speech on international relations to a group of engineers in 1977, Saddam discussed, "the most
prominent national issue that occupies the mind of every Arab citizen,
and this situation is the issue of the Arab-Zionist struggle." He argued
that the Palestine question had to be solved through communal means
of the Arab people and their leaders. The Arabs had to use all means
and resources including "the oil weapon" to bolster their efforts. The
Palestinian struggle should not be used for ulterior political ends by Arab
leaders. Any solution to the Palestinian conflict had to be regional and
not rely on foreign leaders.[15]

Saddam's rhetoric, however, had not necessarily been backed by meaningful actions. Iraq had not helped the Palestinians in their struggle against King Hussein of Jordan in 1970. In response to Israeli incursions against Palestinians in southern Lebanon in 1978, the Iraqi regime had offered only meager financial assistance rather than military support.[16] As one of the main oil producers in the world, Iraq had been the sole Arab country to breach the oil boycott of 1973 in response to the Arab-Israeli war. The mix of fiery rhetoric and political inaction had dimmed Iraq's role in the Arab world and tensions with its Arab neighbors had continued to develop.[17] At the Arab League meeting in Tunis in November 1979, Saddam Hussein delivered the opening address, an indication of his new-found power in the region. "We have an effective weapon in the international arena," he said, "which is our huge economic resources, the foremost of these being our oil wealth."[18] While Saudi Arabia stymied Saddam's efforts to use "the oil weapon," Iraq had clearly emerged as the likely leader of the Arab nations.

"Like his arch-enemy Sadat," observed Joe Stork, "Saddam seeks to make himself and his regime indispensable to the determination of the political future of the region."[19] To further strengthen his campaign to make Iraq the leader of the Arab world, Saddam moved to repair troubled relations with his Arab neighbors, in particular Syria and Saudi Arabia. Anwar Sadat's U.S.-brokered peace with Israel offered Saddam a unique opportunity to shift Iraq's regional role and to assume the mantle of Arab leadership. Arab apprehensions about the rise of Islamist politics in Iran further enhanced Saddam's position as the bulwark against shifting political currents that might threaten the stability of a number of key Arab regimes. In July 1979, Saddam declared that Iraq "is preparing itself in the economic, social, intellectual and military fields for the liberation of Jerusalem and all the lands of Palestine.... Jerusalem is ours."[20]

THE IRAN-IRAQ WAR

Saddam's transition from the deputy to the leader also became deeply imbricated with the turn of events in Iran in 1979. Though he had long had a troubled relationship with the Shah of Iran, Saddam viewed the opposition movement against the Shah with growing suspicion, particularly once the Islamic element in the revolution gained strength. With a huge Shiite population within Iraq's own borders, Saddam was not keen on the possibility of an increased political role for the Shiite clerics. When asked, he was more than willing to expel the Ayatollah Khomeini from Najaf in 1978, where he had been in exile since the early 1960s. When a revolutionary government was established in Iran in February 1979, Iraq granted it official recognition. That month, in an interview, Saddam said, "Iraq has no aims in Iran and that is not the task to intervene in this struggle." He added, "Iraq is anxious to deal on a sound basis with the choice of the Iranian people in a manner that would achieve the interests of the area's peoples and that would preserve their security and the ties of historical relations. This must be done on the basis of nonintervention in domestic affairs and respect for each other's sovereignty."[21]

As the Ayatollah Khomeini assumed the mantle of the revolutionary government in Iran, however, Saddam grew leery of the possibility of the spread of Shiite revolutionary zeal and began cracking down on Iraqi Shiite religious and political groups. At the same time, his security forces undertook a massive round-up of Iraqis of Persian descent; many were deported and their property was confiscated. The crackdown led to protests by leading clerics, including Ayatollah Muhammad Baqir al-Sadr. In June 1979, just as Sadr was about to visit the Ayatollah Khomeini in Iran, he was placed under house arrest. Shiites took to the streets of Najaf, Karbala, Kufa, and Baghdad in protest. Saddam's security forces came down hard on the protestors, arresting some 5,000, including leading members of the clergy. To Saddam, these protests justified his fear that a revolutionary Iran with a Shiite leadership posed a threat to his power and to the Iraqi regime itself.[22]

Alongside these iron-fist measures, Saddam took steps to placate Shiites and to present himself as a devout Muslim. He attempted to forge alliances amongst some of the clerical establishment and publicly prayed at Iraq's holiest shrines. Saddam toured Iraq's Shiite regions, announcing plans for economic development in the areas. He allocated some $80 million for the refurbishment of shrines and mosques and for the support of pilgrims to holy sites.[23]

In October 1979, Saddam gave an interview to a Paris-based Arabic newspaper in which he discussed the relationship between the Baath Party and Islam, asserting the Arabness of the Islamic faith. "We do not feel," he said, "that there is a divergence between the spirit of religion and the Baathist spirit.... Isn't the Koran one of the nation's most sacred sanctities...?"[24] Saddam then took direct aim at the Ayatollah Khomeini's very legitimacy as an Islamic leader and at the Iranian revolution's capacity to represent a broader Islamic political movement in the region. The Iranian revolution of 1979, Saddam asserted "is a non-Islamic revolution.... It can be a Persian, Afghan or Pakistani revolution, but it cannot be an Islamic revolution because a true Islamic revolution should

absorb the Arab ideology we have spoken about and remove any contra-
diction between it and this ideology."[25]

Undeterred, the Shiite protests continued, leading to harsher responses
by Saddam's security forces in the spring of 1980. Massive roundups and
executions were followed by an official announcement that membership
in the Shiite party, Dawa, was punishable by death. A Shiite organization then attempted to assassinate Tariq Aziz, an official close to Saddam
himself. In response, Saddam had Ayatollah Sadr and his sister arrested.
There are reports that the Ayatollah was forced to watch the rape and
execution of his sister; in a gruesome symbolic attack on his religious
status, his beard was allegedly set on fire before he was killed. Other leading clerics were placed under house arrest and tens of thousands of Shiites
with Iranian heritage were expelled and their property was confiscated.[26]

Upon hearing the news of Ayatollah Sadr's execution, an enraged
Ayatollah Khomeini said, "The war that the Iraqi Baath wants to ignite
is a war against Islam. As the Iranian army joined the people [in their
struggle against the Shah], oh Iraqi army, join your people.... The
people and army of Iraq must turn their backs on the Baath regime and
overthrow it ... because this regime is attacking Iran, attacking Islam and
the Quran...."[27] Saddam's response was sharp: "After all this, Khomeini
comes and calls on the Iraqi people ... to go out on the rooftops and
protest against their government. He said the Shah had gone and someone else had come. It turned out that it was another Shah, but this time
wearing a turban."[28] Saddam's antipathy against the new Iranian regime
grew, and he publicly stated, "the rule of the Shah was much better than
this mess."[29] By September, this intense war of words erupted into a long
and destructive war that would bring 1.5 million casualties, most of them
Iranians.

Saddam believed that by ratcheting up the rhetorical war with Iran's
new leaders, he stood to gain a lot. He could consolidate his regional
power, assume the mantle of Arab nationalism, and gain some strategically important territory. With the Iranian government mired in
postrevolutionary turmoil, Saddam gambled that he could win a quick
military victory that would garner him immense political capital within
Iraq and the Arab world. Many believed that Saddam had set his sights
on the Iranian province of Khuzistan, home to many ethnic Arabs and
rich in oil resources. Saddam gravely miscalculated his ability to achieve
a quick victory over Iran, and this action triggered what would be the longest conventional war in the twentieth century. "The Iraqi leadership's
belief that the incursion into Iran would be a walkover, leading to speedy
victory," wrote two leading scholars of the war, "stemmed not only from

faulty military intelligence, as well as a profound ignorance of history and of the nature of the foe, but also from an inflated sense of Iraq's capabilities."[30]

As his immediate justification, Saddam protested Iran's claim to sovereignty over some small islands in the Straits of Hormuz and complained that Iran had not fully complied with the 1975 Algiers Agreement delineating the two countries' borders along the Shatt-al-Arab—and had not handed over a small area of land to Iraq as promised. Saddam sent the Iranian government an ultimatum, to which they did not reply. In September 1980, Iraqi troops invaded Iran and occupied an area of about 150 square kilometers, claiming it as Iraqi territory. Soon thereafter, Saddam gave a speech before the Iraqi National Assembly during which he abrogated the 1975 Algiers Agreement with Iran. Within days of the speech, Iraqi forces invaded Iranian territory and bombed several Iranian airfields. The Iran-Iraq war had begun.

Saddam's increasingly Islamized revolutionary rhetoric and his ambition to assume the mantle of Arab nationalism together helped frame Iraq's war effort. As the war began, an official statement called on the Arab population to mobilize in this new "Qadisiyyat Saddam," as he called the war. Here, Saddam was referencing the seventh-century battle when the Sassanid rulers of the Persian Empire were defeated by the Arab Muslim armies.[31] Saddam's government issued a stamp, depicting the Arab warriors in the seventh century as Iraqi forces fighting under the banner of the twentieth-century Iraqi flag. Thus the history of Saddam's war was inscribed onto the landscape of early Islamic history. While Saddam Hussein wears a modern-day military uniform, his shadow is depicted wearing an early Islamic military helmet and cape. The star in the middle of the stamp was one of Saddam's symbols; each of the eight points of the star stood for a letter in his name as written in Arabic. "The power of pan-Arab and Iraqi nationalism made losers of those who bet that Iraqi Shi'a would turn against their own country in solidarity with their Iranian co-religionists," explained one Iraqi writer.[32]

In November 1980, Saddam again addressed the National Assembly on the war with Iran. Pointing out that Iranians were Persians and not Arabs, he questioned whether they could therefore be truly Muslim, declaring, "a person who attempts to humiliate the Arabs cannot be a Muslim.... The Quran is Arabic; the Prophet Muhammad was an Arab; the media of communication in heaven is Arabic; and the lessons given in the Quran are essentially derived from the human relations that prevailed in the Arab homeland.... Hence the efforts of some (people) to reverse the picture and attempt to make Tehran the homeland of the (Islamic)

Message. Had this been possible, the Almighty God would have chosen one of his Prophets from Tehran...."[33] The childhood lessons Saddam had learned from his uncle Khairallah had included a deep resentment of Persians; now the Ayatollah Khomeini's potential influence over Iraq's Shiites fueled Saddam's anti-Persian sentiments even further.

In the early 1980s, Iranian forces staved off the Iraqi invasion, pushing Saddam's forces into a defensive position and bombing key economic and military positions within Iraqi territory. By 1982, as the Israeli army invaded Lebanon, Saddam withdrew Iraqi troops from Iran. The Iranian army, in turn, took an increasingly aggressive stance, putting increasing pressure on the Iraqi forces. Emboldened, the Ayatollah Khomeini's conditions for a cease-fire included huge reparations by Iraq and the complete ouster of Saddam Hussein from office—terms that were clearly unacceptable to the Iraqis.[34] The military balance of power shifted in 1984, however. As Iran's military supplies diminished, Saddam was able to buy arms and other essential materials for his army from such countries as the Soviet Union, France, and Egypt. By 1987, Iraq was the largest importer of arms in the world.[35]

In the spring of 1985, Saddam again expanded the war by directing the Iraqi air forces to bomb civilian targets in 30 Iranian cities, including the capital city of Tehran, in an attempt to "terrorize and demoralize civilians" and by using chemical weapons against Iranian forces. "Hussein started a war," reported one journalist, "that he quickly discovered he couldn't win and soon thereafter found he couldn't end. And so once again he has gone back to the desperate expedients of using outlawed weapons on the battlefield and bringing death and destruction to the cities of Iran."[36] Iran retaliated by launching scuds on Baghdad and bombing several southern Iraqi cities. In January 1987, in a particularly brutal battle near Basra, some 25,000 Iranian and 10,000 Iraqi soldiers lost their lives.

The Iran-Iraq war was more than a war over territory, more than a war about oil, more than a war to prove military superiority—though it was all of those things. The Iran-Iraq war was also about personal political power, about which leader—Khomeini or Saddam—would become the most powerful leader in the region. Both leaders openly sought to overthrow the other. The war was also about ideology: would Saddam's Baathism or Khomeini's Islamism become the prevailing ideology of the region? Could Saddam's Baathism and Arab nationalism absorb enough Islamic ethos to appeal to the rising Islamist sentiment in the region? And could Khomeini's Islamism embrace enough nationalism to mobilize the Iranians to ward off the incursions onto Iranian territory? In some respects, the Iran-Iraq War was a war of wills—fueled by the intransigence of both leaders. This intransigence developed into a drawn-out war of attrition to some degree because of the interference of regional and global powers who became increasingly involved in the high-stakes conflict. Iraq's military superiority, due in part to the military and economic aid it received from the Arab world and some Western nations, was matched by Iran's larger army and its massive war mobilization effort.

By the end of February 1988, Iraq began a massive attack on Tehran; for two months, the city was attacked with hundreds of long-range scud missiles. Scuds were also launched against the Iranian holy city of Qum. The scuds generated a tremendous fear amongst Iranians, and there seemed to be a realistic threat that Saddam would use his missiles to attack the capital city with poison gas. Iran, in turn, entered into Iraqi Kurdistan. Saddam's response was one of the more tragic twists of this long and bitter war. Iraqi forces entered the town of Halabja, using chemical weapons against Kurdish civilians, killing as many as 5,000 men, women, and children; most were buried in a mass grave. Saddam Hussein's cousin, Ali Hassan Al-Majid, was the head of the Northern Bureau, established to control Kurdish areas; Al-Majid would later be dubbed "Chemical Ali," for having engineered this atrocity. The attack on Halabja further confirmed Iranian fears that Saddam would be willing to use chemical weapons and poison gas against major civilian centers within Iran.

In July 1988, Iran Air Flight 655, a commercial airline, was flying its regular route from the Iranian port city of Bandar Abbas to Dubai. As the plane flew over the Persian Gulf, it was shot down by the USS Vincennes. All 290 civilians on board were killed. Stationed in the Straits of Hormuz, the Vincennes was part of the American navy's efforts to counter Persian gunboats in the Gulf. The U.S. government reported that the crew of the Vincennes believed the civilian passenger plane was a jet fighter preparing for an attack. This tragedy coupled with increasing fears that Saddam may be preparing for a chemical weapons attack on Tehran, many believe, ultimately led the Iranian government to accept a UN-sponsored cease-fire.

In July 1988, Ayatollah Khomeini made a 90-minute speech that was broadcast on Iranian radio, announcing his decision to end the war. "I had promised," he declared, "to fight to the last drop of my blood and to my last breath.... Making this decision was deadlier that swallowing poison."[37] While Khomeini asserted that accepting the cease-fire was for the benefit of the Islamic Republic of Iran and his divine duty, he claimed "to me it would have been more bearable to accept death and martyrdom."[38] The United Nations Secretary General Javier Perez de Cuellar announced that Iran and Iraq were to sign a cease-fire ending the war on August 20, 1988 and then enter into peace negotiations in Geneva.

Though Saddam Hussein declared that the war had ended in a "spectacular Iraqi victory," world opinion was almost unanimous in seeing no clear winner in the war. Increasingly skeptical of Saddam's regional ambitions, some Gulf states who had once supported Iraq began to take steps to renew their diplomatic relations with Iran. Iraq, meanwhile, was saddled with an estimated debt of $60 billion, leaving its economy in tatters. Saddam hoped that the wealthy Arab states that had been his allies in the war would forgo their own loans and help him repay his debts to other states; few were willing to help resolve Iraq's financial crisis.[39] In the final analysis, the end of the Iran-Iraq war would not produce the regional political dynamics Saddam had hoped for in the fall of 1980. Saddam Hussein had not emerged as the undisputed leader of the Arab world.

SADDAM'S RELATIONS WITH THE UNITED STATES

During the Iran-Iraq War, Saddam Hussein's relations with the United States shifted. Iraq had cut ties with the United States after the 1967 war in denunciation of real and perceived American support for Israel. In the early 1980s, various analysts began calling for the United States to support Iraq's war effort based on a variety of justifications. Some arguments were strategic; given Iraq's oil reserves, its rising influence among the Gulf states, its position as a bulwark against the Islamic fundamentalism of the Iranian state, and its potential leadership role in the Arab world, these scholars argued, engagement with Iraq was increasingly important.[40]

A strong proponent of renewing U.S.-Iraq relations was Laurie Mylroie, a professor at Harvard University. She argued that the war had "altered Iraq's position in fundamental and enduring ways, with the result that American-Iraq cooperation offers a potential source of mutual benefit. Not to take up this offer means losing an important opportunity." Saddam's Baathist regime had brought stability to Iraq, Mylroie argued, and was "fervently secular and rationalistic. It derives from Western political traditions, and contrasts directly with the fundamentalist Islamic ideology espoused by Khomeini." Iraq's failures to win and even end the war, Mylroie argued, had replaced ideological fanaticism with a need for stability that could further ameliorate a renewal of U.S. relations. "...From an American perspective," she argued, "the more Saddam Husayn exercised control over the Ba'th party, including the ideologues, the better. Centralization of power permits the regime to deviate from unworkable principles and pursue its interests. Indeed, whatever else one thinks of the Iraqi president, he has shown a capacity to make strategic decisions and abide by them.... Iraq and the United States need each other."[41]

A few months after Mylroie published her article, a secret report by the CIA echoed some of her main points. The report predicted that after the war, Saddam would continue to try to be the leader of the Arab world, though "Saddam probably will try to promote his leadership goals through less radical means than Baghdad has employed in the past." Indeed, the CIA analysts predicted that the Iraqi leadership would become more moderate, asserting, "Although they will probably play a more aggressive regional role, we doubt that the leaders of post war Iraq will revert to the radicalism of the 1960s and mid-1970s that was characterized by strident attacks against the United States and efforts to overthrow Arab moderates. In addition to the maturity gained from 20 years of state leadership, Saddam and his lieutenants have found that many of their earlier revolutionary aims have not served the regime's national security objectives."[42]

Throughout the course of the Iran-Iraq War, U.S.-Iraqi relations had changed fundamentally. In March 1981, U.S. Secretary of State Alexander Haig spoke about Iraq before the Senate Foreign Relations Committee, noting Iraq's concern for "the behavior of Soviet imperialism in the Middle Eastern area."[43] The following month, Deputy Assistant Secretary of State Morris Draper visited Baghdad. An American diplomat in Baghdad cabled Washington in anticipation of the visit, "The atmosphere here is excellent following our decision not to sell arms to Iran, the increased Iraqi commerce and contacts with the U.S., mutual upgrading of diplomatic staffs and, most recently, hhe [sic] go ahead on five Boeing aircraft for Iraq.... We now have a greater convergence of interests with Iraq than at any time since the revolution of 1958."[44] In May, an American diplomat in Baghdad met with Tariq Aziz, Saddam's foreign policy spokesman. The two men confirmed their respective government's interest in building closer ties.[45] Early in 1982, the Reagan Administration removed Iraq from the United States' list of countries supporting international terrorism.

In the fall of 1982, a U.S. State Department official notified the U.S. Department of Commerce that officials in the Iraqi Ministry of Agriculture were interested in purchasing U.S. crop dusters; the purchases were expected to be carried out by June 1983.[46] Crop dusters are known to be used for disseminating chemical weapons, and by this time, Iran had been reporting on Iraqi use of chemical weapons. In November 1983, a U.S. State Department analyst reported to Secretary of State George Shultz, "We have recently received additional information confirming Iraqi use of chemical weapons. We also know that Iraq has acquired a CW [chemical weapons] production capability, primarily from Western firms, including possibly a U.S. foreign subsidiary." The analyst suggested bringing the matter up with Iraqis in the context of discussing improved relations. "It is important," he concluded, "however, that we approach Iraq very soon in order to maintain the credibility of the U.S. policy on CW, as well as to reduce or halt what now appears to be Iraq's almost daily use of CW."[47]

In October 1983, an analyst at the U.S. State Department issued a report on the possibility of an American "tilt" towards Iraq. Such a position had become desirable and tenable because of improved relations with Iraq and because of Iran's success in the war, which it was thought might bring about "Iraq's political collapse." The report set forth a number of options for the United States to follow, including allowing "U.S.-controlled [military] equipment to reach Iraq through third parties."[48] Shortly thereafter, Iran officially called for the United Nations to investigate its charges that Iraq was using chemical weapons in the war. Given the public nature of the announcement, U.S. officials contacted the Iraqi government directly, warning "... we believe the continued Iraqi use of CW will play into the hands of those who would wish to escalate tensions in the region.... We note that Iraq long ago acceded to the 1925 Geneva Protocol banning the use of CW."[49]

The U.S. government believed its warnings caused Saddam to stop the use of chemical weapons, but in February 1984, a United Nations investigation confirmed that chemical weapons had once again been used against Iranian forces. The United Nations Security Council condemned the use of chemical weapons in the Iran-Iraq war without directly naming Iraq. The U.S. Department of State issued a briefing paper on the subject stating, "Our efforts to curtail the flow of CW-related materials and to end the complicity of Western firms in the CW program of Iraq and Iran have met with some success. However, because of the dual purpose nature of many materials, we cannot stop all shipments of technical assistance that might be used for CW purposes short of a complete trade embargo on both nations."[50]

Seemingly undeterred, an Iraqi military spokesman announced, "The invaders should know that for every harmful insect there is an insecticide capable of annihilating it whatever their number and Iraq possesses this annihilation insecticide."[51] Following this statement, taken to be an admission of the use of chemical weapons, the U.S. government restated its warning to the Iraqi government through its representatives in Baghdad and Iraqi representatives in Washington, D.C. In March 1984, the U.S. government notified UN officials it would attempt to block any UN resolution condemning Iraq for the use of chemical weapons. At the same time, the United States issued a statement: "while condemning Iraq's resort to chemical weapons, the United States also calls on the government of Iran to accept the good offices offered by a number of countries and international organizations to put an end to the bloodshed."[52]

Meanwhile, diplomatic initiatives to advance U.S.-Iraqi relations had continued. In December 1983, Donald Rumsfeld traveled to Baghdad as an envoy of the U.S. president and met with Saddam Hussein. Rumsfeld was directed to tell Saddam that the U.S. government "would regard any major reversal of Iraq's fortune as a strategic defeat for the West."[53] On December 20, Rumsfeld held a 90-minute meeting with Saddam during which he delivered a letter from President Reagan to the Iraqi leader. During the meeting, Rumsfeld told Saddam that the U.S. government's "... understanding of the importance of balance in the world and the region was similar to Iraq's." Regarding the Iran-Iraq war, Rumsfeld told Saddam that the "US agreed it was not in [the] interest of [the] region or the West for conflict to create greater instability or for [the] outcome to be one which weakened Iraq's role or enhanced interests and ambitions of Iran."[54] Rumsfeld's visit with Saddam came amidst public revelations of Iraq's use of chemical weapons against Iran. The U.S. State Department had primed Rumsfeld to bring the matter up with Saddam; whether Rumsfeld expressed official U.S. concern in the meeting remains a matter of some controversy.

In the fall of 1984, the U.S. Defense Intelligence Agency produced a report on Iraq, noting "President Saddam Husayn will likely remain in power for the next two years. His control over the police and security organization remains pervasive, and opposition groups are in disarray.... The regime will continue its active campaign of coopting the opposition while ameliorating outstanding grievances and punishing as it deems appropriate."[55] The evidence is clear that during this period the United States had a firm understanding of the nature of Saddam Hussein's regime. Still, it was determined that U.S. strategic interests would be best served by establishing ties with Iraq. In March 1984, Donald Rumsfeld visited Iraq for a second time, meeting with Foreign Minister Tariq Aziz. In November 1984, the United States and Iraq officially renewed diplomatic relations, and both countries redesignated their "interest sections" in each other's capitals as full-fledged embassies under their respective flags.

From the original contacts made by Henry Kissinger, the U.S. government had been interested in the possibility of developing economic relations with Iraq. Haig had held a meeting in 1981 during which the possibility of American involvement in building the Iraqi metro system was discussed.[56] In early 1984, the Export-Import Bank of the United States issued a report determining Iraq to be a high credit risk because of the ongoing war and its heavy debt burden. Iraq had already incurred tens of billions of dollars in debt, mainly from Saudi Arabia and Kuwait, and was running an annual deficit estimated at $10 billion. The report listed some U.S. corporations who were positioned to do business with Iraq. These included Westinghouse and General Electric for power projects; Bechtel for the Baghdad Metro and an oil pipeline to Jordan; Bell Helicopter and Lockheed for helicopters; and Midland International and Halliburton for oil field equipment.[57] George Shultz, who as the U.S. Secretary of State from 1982 until 1989 was deeply involved in the process of renewing relations with Iraq, had a long history with Bechtel. From 1974–1982, he served as the president and director of Bechtel and, after leaving public office in 1989, he became a member of its board of directors.[58] By the summer of 1984, however, the Export-Import Bank seems to have reversed its assessment, providing nearly $500 million in loans to Iraq. By 1987, the United States "became Iraq's largest supplier of civilian goods," providing it with some $700 million in exports.[59]

The rapprochement between Iraq and the United States soon became strained. In the spring of 1987, Iraq attacked the Stark, an American naval ship in the Persian Gulf, killing 37 American sailors. Iraqi officials quickly apologized for the incident, declaring it a mistake. The incident, however, gave voice to critics of the U.S. administration's policy of tilting towards Iraq. Jim Hoagland, the *Washington Post* columnist who had been a longtime observer of Iraqi politics, wrote, "Because he is less fierce than he used to be, and because he has wrapped his brutal reign in a modernism that contrasts with the stifling theocracies that prevail elsewhere in the Persian Gulf, Saddam is now praised by our diplomats as pragmatic…. 'Pragmatic' has in fact become the current American buzzword for Saddam. It replaces 'ruthless,' the U.S. standby in the days when political rivals were hung from lampposts in the city square and Saddam openly challenged America's pretensions in the Middle East."[60]

Meanwhile, revelations in late 1986 about the Iran-Contra Affair, whereby members of the Reagan Administration had arranged for the sale of arms to Iran in exchange for funds used to back the Sandinistas in Nicaragua, angered the Iraqi regime. In July 1988, the U.S. government allowed a leader of the Kurdish opposition to travel to Washington to meet with several lower ranking U.S. State Department officials, further aggravating Saddam Hussein. At the same time, Iraqi officials complained loudly that the United States was providing strategically important military information to the Iranians.[61] As Iraq and Iran took steps to end their eight-year war, U.S. relations with Saddam's regime were strained at best.

THE GULF WAR

As early as 1988, the CIA had predicted that following the cessation of fighting between Iran and Iraq, Saddam would set his sights on some Kuwaiti territories. "Baghdad will probably try to gain control over Kuwait's Bubiyan and Warbah islands to increase its narrow access to the Gulf."[62] Saddam's increasingly hostile posture towards Kuwait was also a function of his financial troubles. Having declared victory over Iran in a war that he had proclaimed as having fought on behalf of the Arab nation, in particular the Gulf states, Saddam held that these same oil-rich states should now relieve him of tens of billions of dollars debt. No such assistance was forthcoming.

Saddam hosted an Arab summit in Baghdad in the spring of 1990, during which he accused Kuwait of "waging economic warfare against Iraq."[63] At the end of the summit, Saddam drove the leader of Kuwait to the airport and in a private conversation asked him for the two islands; the response was negative. In the following months, Saddam openly accused Kuwait and the United Arab Emirates (UAE) of circumventing production quotas established by the Organization of the Petroleum Exporting Countries (OPEC) and flooding the market with oil, thus damaging Iraq's economy by driving the price of its oil down. In a speech in July, Saddam declared, "The [oil production] policies of some Arab rulers are American."[64] He said the Kuwaitis had stabbed Iraq in the back "with a poison dagger" and even accused them of systematically stealing Iraqi oil over the past decade.[65] Saddam backed his words by sending some Republic Guard divisions to the Kuwaiti border. The dispute was not a simple squabble over oil prices. Given lingering disputes over the final demarcation of the two countries' borders, Kuwait's overproduction of oil was viewed by some as a way "to pressure Iraq into acknowledging that it has no further territorial claim."[66]

The United States had a two-pronged response to the growing dispute. On July 24, it dispatched two refueling tanker planes to the UAE and deployed some combat ships to the Persian Gulf. The Bush administration clearly stated that this was a sign of support for Kuwait and the UAE. A Pentagon spokesperson said, "We remain strongly committed to supporting the individual and collective self-defense of our friends in the gulf, with whom we have deep and longstanding ties."[67] On the other hand, on the following day, the American Ambassador to Iraq, April Glaspie, spoke privately with Saddam, telling him that the United States had no opinion regarding "your border disagreement with Kuwait." According to Tariq Aziz, Iraq's Foreign Minister, Saddam had originally intended a quick and limited military intervention into Iraq to take over the two disputed islands and an oil field. At the last minute, he decided that the Americans wouldn't mind if he took a larger swath of Kuwaiti land. This proved to be a monumental miscalculation.[68] On July 31, Iraqi and Kuwaiti representatives met in Jeddah, Saudi Arabia in an attempt to reconcile their differences. By then, Iraq had amassed nearly 100,000 troops along the Kuwaiti border. On August 1, the Iraqi representative walked out of the negotiations.

On August 2, the Iraqi Army invaded Kuwait. Iraqi tanks pressed into the capital city and troops seized the Emir of Kuwait's palace. Kuwaiti radio appealed to its two million citizens, "Your country is being subjected to a barbaric invasion. It is time to defend it."[69] On that very day, the United Nations Security Council passed Resolution 660 condemning the invasion and demanding an unconditional pullout; on August 6, UNSC Resolution 661 was passed, imposing economic sanctions on Iraq. President Bush declared, "There is no place for this sort of naked aggression in today's world."[70] A prominent journalist assessed the implications of Saddam's actions: "By seizing the desert sheikdom of Kuwait, Mr. Hussein betrayed and terrified his Arab brothers, destroyed the balance of power in the Persian Gulf, plunged the world's oil markets into chaos and challenged the assumption that the end of the cold war would bring peace to the world."[71]

On August 7, American troops were deployed into Saudi Arabia. Within six months, over half a million U.S. troops were stationed in Saudi Arabia. On August 10, Saddam gave a speech in which he spoke of a possible attack on Saudi Arabia, couching the war against Kuwait in Islamic and nationalist tones. "Arabs, Moslems, believers in God...," he declared, "This is your day to rise and spread quickly in order to defend Mecca, which is captive to the spears of the Americans and the Zionists.... Burn the soil under their feet. Burn the soil under the feet of the aggressors and invaders who want harm for your families in Iraq. Until the voice of right rises up in the Arab world, hit their interests wherever they are and rescue holy Mecca and the grave of the Prophet Mohammed in Medina."[72] Underlining his aspirations to present himself as a Muslim and Arab leader, Saddam had the Iraqi flag changed, adding the words *Allah-o-Akbar* [God is great] written in his own hand in the middle of the banner.

International condemnation of Iraq's invasion of Kuwait was unanimous. The Arab League and the United Nations condemned the invasion. On September 11, 1990, President Bush gave a speech on Iraq's invasion of Kuwait to a joint session of Congress. He said, "From the outset, acting hand in hand with others, we've sought to fashion the broadest possible international response to Iraq's aggression. The level of world cooperation and condemnation of Iraq is unprecedented. Armed forces from countries spanning four continents are there at the request of King Fahd of Saudi Arabia to deter and, if need be, to defend against attack. Muslims and non-Muslims, Arabs and non-Arabs, soldiers from many nations stand shoulder to shoulder, resolute against Saddam Hussein's ambitions." In November, the United Nations passed UNSC Resolution 678 authorizing the use of force to uphold all previous resolutions unless Iraq withdrew from Kuwait by January 15, 1991. The United States Congress, in turn, authorized President Bush to use military force pursuant to UNSC Resolution 678. Meanwhile, Iraq's parliament voted against a withdrawal from Kuwait and supported a war to maintain its occupation. The stage was set for a large-scale war between coalition forces from more than 30 countries and Iraq.

On January 15, 1991, President Bush met with his closest aides in the Oval Office of the White House. He signed a national security directive, authorizing an attack on Iraq unless there was a last-minute diplomatic breakthrough. He told the White House staff, "I have resolved all moral questions in my mind. This is black and white, good versus evil."[73] Operation Desert Storm began on January 16 with a massive air campaign by coalition forces. Allied forces consisted of hundreds of thousands of soldiers from 33 countries. On January 17, Iraqi state radio broadcast a speech by Saddam Hussein. "O great Iraqi people," Saddam declared, "sons of our great people, valiant men of our courageous armed forces.... The great duel, the mother of all battles, between the victorious right and the evil that will certainly be defeated has begun."[74]

For 40 days, coalition forces engaged in a massive air war, flying some 110,000 sorties and dropping 85,000 tons of explosives over Iraq. It was perhaps the heaviest bombardment of a country since the Second World War.[75] By February 24, the coalition forces began their ground offensive from Saudi Arabia. Code-named Operation Desert Saber, the ground war lasted 100 hours. The next day, Iraq agreed to a peace plan presented by Russia. By February 26, Iraqi troops began pulling out of Kuwait. Saddam

Hussein's army had suffered 150,000 casualties, and another 50,000 soldiers had been taken as prisoners of war by the coalition forces. On February 28 a cease-fire agreement was signed. UNSC Resolution 687 passed on April 3 setting forth the conditions for a permanent cease-fire.

Emboldened by the success of the coalition forces, the repressed social groups within Iraq rose up against Saddam. On February 15, President Bush had given a speech in which he had called on "the Iraqi military and the Iraqi people to take matters into their own hands—to force Saddam Hussein the dictator to step aside."[76] Many analysts suggest the possibility that repressed peoples in Iraq believed that American forces would support an internal rebellion and that President Bush's statements were meant to leave that impression. In March, the Shiites centered in southern Iraq rose up against Saddam's authority. Though they constituted a majority of Iraq's population, Saddam ensured that the Sunni minority had greater economic, social, and political power. By March 16, Saddam's forces had quashed the rebellion, killing some 30,000 Shiites. Another 70,000 fled to Iran.

Soon thereafter, the Kurdish nationalists centered in northern Iraq rose up against Saddam. In 1988, Saddam had used chemical weapons on the Kurdish town of Halabja; he also undertook a conventional war against Iraq's Kurdish population. By some estimates, as many as 100,000 Kurds were killed by Saddam's forces in the late 1980s. The Kurds now saw the end of the Gulf War as an opportunity to finally achieve a degree of autonomy. Their rebellion, however, was also ruthlessly repressed by Saddam. In massive numbers, Kurds began fleeing Iraq. Some fled across the border into Iran, where Iranian peasants with pick-up trucks and donkeys escorted them back to their villages. Other Kurds fled north toward Turkey, through the bitterly cold snowy mountains. International television crews, which had not covered scenes from the Shiite uprising in southern Iraq, filmed the desperate situation of Kurdish refugees. Human Rights Watch reported that some 100,000 Shiites and Kurds were displaced within Iraq, and another 70,000 became refugees in Saudi Arabia, Iran, and Turkey. "Saddam Hussein's record of brutally suppressing even mild dissent is well-known," the human rights organization reported. "When the March 1991 uprising confronted his regime with the most serious internal challenge it had ever faced, government forces responded with atrocities on a predictably massive scale."[77]

On April 5, President Bush decried "the terrible human tragedy unfolding in and around Iraq as a result of Saddam Hussein's brutal treatment of Iraqi citizens" and ordered that food and medicine be sent to the

Kurds. On April 16, he declared northern Iraq a "safe haven" in which American troops would protect the Kurds from Saddam's army. After some time, no-fly zones were established in northern and southern Iraq; the Iraqi military was not allowed to fly in these areas. Within northern Iraq, in the following decade, the Kurds would finally achieve a level of autonomy they had never known under Saddam Hussein's reign.

The UN passed UNSC Resolution 688 condemning "the repression of the Iraqi civilian population in many parts of Iraq, including most recently in the Kurdish-populated areas, which led to a massive flow of refugees towards and across international frontiers and to cross-border incursions which threaten international peace and security in the region....[78] It called for "an open dialogue ... to ensure that human and political rights of all Iraqi citizens are respected."

On April 3, the UNSC passed Resolution 687, demanding that Iraq reaffirm its "obligations under the Protocol for the Prohibition of the Use in War of Asphyxiating, Poisonous or Other Gases, and of Bacteriological Methods of Warfare, signed at Geneva on June 17 1925...." The resolution called for the formation of a special commission "which shall carry out immediate on-site inspection of Iraq's biological, chemical and missile capabilities....[79] The UN would establish the United Nations Special Commission (UNSCOM), a surveillance organization charged with ensuring Saddam's compliance with UN resolutions; in particular, UNSCOM would try to ensure that Saddam would destroy all weapons of mass destruction and cease all programs for producing biological, chemical, and nuclear weapons.

The United States decided that compliance with UN resolutions was not enough. Robert Gates, a deputy national security advisor, explained that as long as Saddam Hussein remained in power, the United States would impose sanctions on Iraq. "Iraqis will pay the price while [Saddam] remains in power," Gates said. "All possible sanctions will be maintained until he is gone."[80] The international community hoped the pressures of the sanctions would bring down Saddam's regime. At the same time, the United States decided to use covert strategies to overthrow Saddam Hussein. This policy, established by the Bush administration, would be continued after Bill Clinton became the president of the United States.

NOTES

1. Andrew Cockburn and Patrick Cockburn, *Saddam Hussein: An American Obsession* (London: Verso, 2002), p. 104.

2. Foreign Broadcast and Information Service (FBIS), Middle East and Africa (MEA), July 18, 1979, p. E1.

3. FBIS, MEA, July 18, 1979, p. E5.

4. Claudia Wright, "Iraq—New Power in the Middle East," *Foreign Affairs* (Winter 1979/80): 257–77.

5. As quoted in Amir Iskander, *Saddam Hussein: The Fighter, the Thinker, and the Man*, trans. Hassan Selim (Paris: Hachette Réalités, 1980), p. 399.

6. Ibid.

7. Footage of interview in film *Uncle Saddam* (2000) directed by Joel Soler.

8. Milton Viorst, "Iraq at War," *Foreign Affairs* (Winter 1986/7): 356.

9. Elaine Sciolino, "The Big Brother: Iraq Under Saddam Hussein," *The New York Times*, February 3, 1985.

10. FBIS, Latin America (LAT), December 20, 1978, p. Q2.

11. FBIS, MEA, March 7, 1979, p. E1.

12. Marvin Howe, "Some at Parley in Iraq Urge Tougher Stand," *The New York Times*, March 28, 1979.

13. Quoted in Howe, "Some at Parley in Iraq Urge Tougher Stand."

14. FBIS, MEA, March 23, 1979, p. E1.

15. Saddam Hussein, *Nidaluna wa Al-Siyasah Al-Dawaliyyah* [Our Struggle and Foreign Policy] (Beirut: Dar al-Tali` ah lil-Tiba` ah wa al-Nashr, 1978).

16. According to the Iraqi News Agency, by July 1979, the Iraqi regime had donated $17 million to Palestinian refugees "since the Zionist aggression against southern Lebanon last year."

17. Marvin Howe, "Iraq Now Has Powerful Claim to Leadership of Arab World," *The New York Times*, July 22, 1979.

18. Quoted in "Arabs Rebuff Iraq's Bid to Use Oil As a Weapon," *The New York Times*, November 21, 1979.

19. Joe Stork, "Iraq and the War in the Gulf," *Middle East Reports (MERIP)*, (June 1981): 18.

20. FBIS, MEA, July 5, 1979, p. E1.

21. Interview with *Alif Ba*, FBIS, MEA, February 15, 1979, p. E1.

22. Shahram Chubin and Charles Tripp, *Iran and Iraq at War* (Boulder, Colo.: Westview Press, 1988), pp. 25–26.

23. Dilip Hiro, *The Longest War: The Iran-Iraq Military Conflict* (London: Grafton Books, 1989), pp. 30–35.

24. FBIS, MEA, October 17, 1979, p. E10.

25. Interview with *Al-Mustaqbal*, FBIS, MEA, October 17, 1979, p. E4.

26. Tripp, Charles. *A History of Iraq* (Cambridge: University of Cambridge Press, 2000), pp. 220–30. In March 1999, Ayatollah Sadr's brother, Grand Ayatollah Muhammad Sadiq al-Sadr, was assassinated by Iraqi government agents. This led to another Shiite uprising, which was brutally suppressed by Saddam's regime. Human Rights Watch conducted a study on the case of the

Basra Massacre of 1999 after the fall of Saddam in 2003. The report can be accessed at http://hrw.org/campaigns/iraq/basra/.

27. As quoted in Hiro, *The Longest War*, p. 35.

28. Saddam Hussein on April 15, 1980, as quoted in *Iran and Iraq at War*, Chubin and Tripp, n.p.

29. Quoted in Youssef M. Ibrahim, "Khomeini Excites the Arab Masses, Pains Arab Rulers," *The New York Times*, November 25, 1979.

30. Chubin and Tripp, *Iran and Iraq at War*, p. 7.

31. Fouad Ajami, "The Arab Road," *Foreign Policy* (Summer 1982): 10.

32. Sinan Antoon, "Monumental Disrespect," *MERIP* (Fall 2003): 28.

33. Saddam Hussein, *President Saddam Hussein Addresses National Assembly on the War with Iran*, trans. N. A. Mudhaffer (Baghdad: Dar al-Ma'mun, 1981), pp. 8–10.

34. Simon Henderson, *Instant Empire: Saddam Hussein's Ambition for Iraq* (San Francisco: Mercury House, 1991), pp. 106–7.

35. Henderson, *Instant Empire*, p. 114.

36. "The Vicious War," *Los Angeles Times*, March 28, 1985.

37. Quoted in Edward Cody, "Khomeini Says Cease-Fire Decision His," *The Washington Post*, July 21, 1988.

38. Quoted in Dilip Hiro, "Why Iran Accepted Cease-Fire," *Toronto Star*, July 23, 1988.

39. Graham Fuller, "The Grief of Baghdad: It May Have Won the War, but It Could Easily Lose the Peace," *The Washington Post*, October 9, 1988; Daniel Drosdoff, "Iraq Wins Cease-Fire, but Loses Allies," *Chicago Sun-Times*, November 6, 1988.

40. For an example of this line of thinking, see Adeed I. Dawisha, "Iraq: The West's Opportunity," *Foreign Policy* (Winter 1980–1981): 134–53.

41. Laurie Mylroie, "The Baghdad Alternative," *Orbis* (Summer 1988): 339–54. Mylroie's views would shift, and she later postulated that Saddam was involved in the 1993 World Trade Center bombings, the bombing of U.S. embassies in Africa to the Oklahoma City bombing, and the September 11 attacks. See Peter Bergen, "Armchair Provocateur, Laurie Mylroie: The Neocons' Favorite Conspiracy Theorist," in *Washington Monthly*, December 2003, and Peter Bergen, "Did One Woman's Obsession Take America to War," *The Guardian*, Monday July 5, 2004.

42. U.S. Central Intelligence Agency, "Iraq's National Security Goals," December 1988, pp. iii, 11.

43. Stephen R. Shalom, "The United States and the Iran-Iraq War," *Z* (February 1990); accessed on Znet archives.

44. U.S. Interests Section in Iraq Cable from William L. Eagleton to the Department of State, April 4, 1981, National Security Archives (NSA).

45. U.S. Interests Section in Iraq Cable from William L. Eagleton to the Department of State, May 28, 1981, NSA.

46. U.S. Interests Section in Iraq Cable from William L. Eagleton to the Department of State, September 20, 1982, NSA.

47. U.S. Department of State, Bureau of Near Eastern and South Asian Affairs Information Memorandum from Jonathan T. Howe to George P. Shultz, November 1, 1983, NSA.

48. U.S. Department of State, Bureau of Near Eastern and South Asian Affairs Information Memorandum from Jonathan T. Howe to Lawrence S. Eagleburger, October 7, 1983, NSA.

49. U.S. Department of State, Bureau of Near Eastern and South Asian Affairs Information Memorandum from Jonathan T. Howe to Lawrence Eagleburger, November 21, 1983, NSA.

50. U.S. Department of State, Bureau of Politico-Military Affairs Briefing Paper, "Iraqi Illegal Use of Chemical Weapons," November 16, 1984, NSA.

51. Quoted in U.S. Interests Section in Iraq Cable from William L. Eagleton to the Department of State, February 22, 1984, NSA.

52. U.S. Department of State Cable from George P. Shultz to the Mission to the European Office of the United Nations and Other International Organizations, March 14, 1984, NSA.

53. U.S. Interests Section in Iraq Cable from William Eagleton to U.S. Embassy in Jordan, December 14, 1983, NSA.

54. U.S. Embassy in United Kingdom Cable from Charles H. Price to the Department of State, December 21, 1983, NSA.

55. U.S. Defense Intelligence Agency Intelligence Report, "Defense Estimative Brief: Prospects for Iran," September 25, 1984, NSA.

56. Department of State Cable from Alexander M. Haig to the Iraqi Interests Section, April 22, 1981, NSA. The meeting, Haig reported, "provided an opportunity for me to make a strong pitch for the U.S. company bidding on the metro project...."

57. Export-Import Bank of the United States, Memorandum to the Board of Directors Africa and Middle East Division, "Iraq: Country Review and Recommendations for Eximbank's Programs," February 21, 1984.

58. Hoover Institution, biography of George Shultz, http://www-hoover.stanford.edu/bios/shultz.html (accessed on December 12, 2004).

59. U.S. Central Intelligence Agency, "Iraq's National Security Goals," December 1988, p. iv.

60. Jim Hoagland, "The Shooting of the Stark," *The Washington Post*, May 29, 1987.

61. Youssef M. Ibrahim, "Iraq Says U.S. Supplied Iran with Data on Planned Raid," *The New York Times*, July 1, 1988.

62. U.S. Central Intelligence Agency, "Iraq's National Security Goals," December 1988, p. v.

63. Cockburn and Cockburn, *Saddam Hussein*, p. 84.

64. Quoted in Youssef M. Ibrahim, "Iraq Threatens Emirates and Kuwait on Oil Glut," *The New York Times*, July 18, 1990.

65. "Stay Iraq's Scimitar, Together," *The New York Times*, July 26, 1980.

66. Youssef M. Ibrahim, "Iraq Seeks Bigger Role in OPEC," The New York Times, June 28, 1990.

67. Quoted in Michael R. Gordon, "US Deploys Air and Sea Forces after Iraq Threatens 2 Neighbors," *The New York Times*, July 25, 1990.

68. Cockburn and Cockburn, *Saddam Hussein*, pp. 84–85.

69. Quoted in Michael R. Gordon, "Iraq Army Invades Capital of Kuwait in Fierce Fighting," *The New York Times*, August 2, 1990.

70. Quoted in R.W. Apple, Jr. "Naked Aggression," *The New York Times*, August 2, 1990.

71. Elaine Sciolino, "Arab of Vast Ambition: Saddam Hussein," *The New York Times*, August 5, 1990.

72. Quoted in Jerry M. Long, *Saddam's War of Words: Politics, Religion, and the Iraqi Invasion of Kuwait* (Austin: University of Texas Press, 2004), pp. 94–95.

73. Quoted in Elaine Sciolino, *The Outlaw State: Saddam Hussein's Quest for Power in the Gulf Crisis* (New York: John Wiley and Sons, 1991), p. 244.

74. As quoted in Efraim Karsh and Inari Rautsi, *Saddam Hussein: A Political Biography* (New York: Grove Press, 2002), p. 245.

75. Vivienne Walt, "Saddam Won't Die," January 18, 2001, http://www.salon.com.

76. Quoted in Cockburn and Cockburn, *Saddam Hussein*, p. 13.

77. "Endless Torment: The 1991 Uprising in Iraq and Its Aftermath," Human Rights Watch, June 1992, http://www.hrw.org.

78. Text of UNSC Resolution 688, April 5, 1991, http://www.un.org.

79. Text of UNSC Resolution 687, April 3, 1991, http://www.un.org.

80. Quoted in Jeremy Hardy, "Degraded Policy," *The Guardian*, November 18, 2000.

Saddam greets PLO Chairman Yasser Arafat at the Non-Aligned Summit
in Havana, Cuba in September 1979. [Photograph by Abbas. Courtesy of
Magnum Photos]

At the Islamic Summit in Taif,
Saudi Arabia in January 1981,
Saddam indulges one of his
favorite habits—smoking Cuban
cigars. [Photography by Abbas.
Courtesy of Magnum Photos]

One Iraqi complained to a journalist that there were more pictures of Saddam than people in Iraq; Saddam frequently sported a military beret and sunglasses. [Photograph by Steve McCurry. Courtesy of Magnum Photos]

Saddam's birthday was a national holiday, usually commenorated by offical stamps. [Iraqi stamp, collection of the author]

Saddam dubbed the Iran-Iraq War "Qadisiyyat Saddam," after the 7th century battle when the Persian Empire was defeated by the Arab Muslim armies. This stamp portrays medieval Arab warriors fighting under the banner of the 20th century Iraqi flag. [Iraqi stamp, collection of the author]

Most government offices and businesses in Iraq displayed a picture of Saddam; this photograph was damaged during the Iran-Iraq War. [Photograph by Steve McCurry. Courtesy of Magnum Photos]

In Iraq, even time was a marker of Saddam's power; his face was regularly reproduced on the faces of watches. [Photograph by Steve McCurry. Courtesy of Magnum Photos]

This giant picture of Saddam was erected outside the site office in Babylon, which oversaw the restoration and reconstruction of the ancient ruins—a project begun under Saddam's orders in the late 1970s. [Photograph by Stuart Franklin. Courtesy of Magnum Photos]

By the mid-1990s, the Guinness Book of World Records listed Saddam as the world's most frequently painted head of state. In 2002, the Saddam Art Center organized an exhibition of 80 portraits of Saddam Hussein. [Photograph by Thomas Dworzak. Courtesy of Magnum Photos]

The Martyr's Monument, a memorial honoring Iraqi soldiers killed in the Iran-Iraq War, is widely considered the most beautiful built during Saddam's reign. After the fall of Saddam, it was used as a military headquarter for the US army. [Photograph by Sinan Antoon, reproduced by his kind permission]

This stamp marks the fouth anniversary of Saddam's rise to the presidency of Iraq, a date that became a national holiday. [Iraqi stamp, collection of the author]

As coalition forces prepared to invade Iraq, Saddam called for a presidential election in 2002. He was the only candidate; his campaign posters (like this stamp) featured hearts. [Iraqi stamp, collection of the author]

Stickers of Saddam were printed to mark elections and the Eid; he liked to appear in both traditional Iraqi attire and expensive tailored suits. [Stickers, collection of author]

After the fall of Saddam's regime, US soldiers discovered this mural of Saddam's family in his son Uday's palace. [Photograph by Ilka Uimonen. Courtesy of Magnum Photos]

When a communications tower in Baghdad was destroyed in the 1991 Gulf War, Saddam had it rebuilt with a statue of himself standing guard. This 2003 photograph shows the tower still standing amidst devastation. [Photographs by Abbas. Courtesy of Magnum Photos]

Chapter 5

SADDAM AFTER
THE GULF WAR

THE SANCTIONS

Saddam Hussein emerged from the Gulf War defeated but not bowed, renewing his efforts to maintain his grip over power in Iraq. In the decade that followed, he would use his family connections and his wealth to circumvent various efforts to diminish his power and to overthrow his regime. Many Iraqis continued to have a mixed relationship with their leader. As one man explained to a journalist, "We love him and we fear him. Saddam gave Iraq a national identity. He is brave. He has distributed oil wealth equitably, bringing up what used to be a lower class to middle-class status. But there is this one-man, one-clan rule he has imposed and people are at the point where they are yearning for more freedom in Iraq."[1]

The Iraq over which Saddam now ruled had been fundamentally transformed by years of war. A thorough sanctions regime had been in place since August 1990. These sanctions were renewed and expanded by subsequent United Nations resolutions ending the Gulf War, which set in place a monitoring system tied to economic sanctions. Following the passage of UNSC Resolution 687, the United Nations Special Commission (UNSCOM) was established to ensure that Saddam's government destroyed all existing reserves of weapons of mass production and ceased the production of any new biological, chemical, and nuclear weapons and long-range missiles. For the UN, the sanctions were intended to bolster its efforts to monitor and destroy Saddam's illegal weapons programs. For the United States, however, the sanctions regime was also tied to a policy of regime change—though this linkage remained a matter of some controversy even within the U.S. administration.

These sanctions "created a set of conditions which virtually cut off Iraq from the world economy," noted the economist Abbas Alnasrawi. They included "a ban on all trade, an oil embargo, a freezing of Iraqi government financial assets, an arms embargo, suspension of international flights, and a ban on financial transactions."[2] The cumulative affect of the sanctions, following upon decades of misrule and years of destructive warfare, diminished the living standards of Iraq's middle class, relegating the poor to below subsistence levels. The Iraqi government set in place a system of food rationing, providing wheat flour, rice, vegetable oil, sugar, tea, and baby milk to the population. The Gulf War had destroyed a significant amount of Iraq's civilian infrastructure, and the sanctions prevented a complete economic recovery. Iraq now produced about a third of the electricity it had before the Gulf War, and power shortages became commonplace. This, in turn, affected water purification, irrigations systems, sewage systems, and hospitals.[3]

Amidst the growing deprivation of large numbers of Iraqis, Saddam doled out economic benefits to his loyalists, those who helped keep him in power. A 1994 edict provided the military, the security forces, and the police with special monthly allowances. Members of the Baath Party benefited from a more comprehensive food distribution network, while resources were distributed more widely in central Baghdad and Tikrit, regions with large populations of Saddam loyalists. Members of the regime's inner circle remained largely untouched by the negative effects of the sanctions.[4]

Ironically, though the sanctions were intended to check Saddam's power, they effectively rendered much of the population more dependent on the Iraqi government. Sarah Graham-Brown, who conducted an exhaustive study of the impact of the sanctions, wrote, "Despite reduced resources, the Government was able to perpetuate the population's dependence on state services, established over two decades, though this has not prevented the embargo from taking the greatest toll on those who are most vulnerable: children, old people and female-headed households."[5]

In 1989, Iraq's gross domestic product (GDP) per capita was $2,840; by 1997, it had dropped to $200.[6] The incomes of Iraq's civil servants, a large portion of the population, declined precipitously, as inflation skyrocketed. Airline pilots, teachers, doctors, nurses, and engineers found it impossible to support their families on their regular salaries. In 1993, a civil engineer who had become a taxi driver explained, "Now education is no use. As an engineer I would earn 30 dinars a month; now as a taxi driver I can earn 4,000 dinars. And I absolutely need 4,000."[7] Other Iraqis took to selling their possessions for cash with which they could feed their families. Auction houses were filled with furniture, appliances, and carpets of Iraqis looking to earn some cash for essentials. One colonel in the army told an American journalist, "I have nothing in my house. I have sold everything just to get rice or bread or–everything I have sold.... I am a colonel in the army, and you just imagine the condition of a simple man."[8]

The bookstores along Baghdad's al-Mutanabbi Street, named after the famed Iraqi poet, were filled with entire libraries that had been sold in exchange for sorely needed cash. Sidewalks along the street turned into a flea market, where all kinds of books—medical textbooks, poetry books, and paperback novels—were sold. One educated well-dressed man with sad eyes recited Arabic poetry and told an American video artist he was selling books by Lorca, Milton, and T. S. Eliot.[9]

The Baath Party had emphasized education, once winning awards from UNICEF for its literacy programs. The sanctions deeply affected Iraq's educational system. The condition of schools declined, and there were shortages of school supplies and books. The cost of sending children to school (clothes, transportation, supplies) became prohibitive for many Iraqis, and dropout rates increased. Some children began working as petty vendors to help supplement the family income.[10]

Indeed, while the intention of the economic sanctions was to influence the leadership of Iraq, their impact was felt most strongly by Iraq's children.[11] In 1995, the British medical journal *The Lancet* published an article by researchers at the Food and Agriculture Organization (FAO) estimating that the sanctions were responsible for the deaths of 567,000 Iraqi children. The American media picked up the story. When questioned about the figures, Madeleine Albright, then the American ambassador to the United Nations, responded famously, "The price is worth it." Subsequent studies showed those numbers to be inflated; one researcher at Columbia University found that the number of children who died as a result of the sanctions through 2000 was closer to 350,000.[12]

By 1996, the World Health Organization (WHO) reported, "The vast majority of the country's population has been on a semi-starvation diet for years."[13] In 1997, United Nations Children's Fund (UNICEF) issued a report on the impact of the sanctions. Nearly a million children, it stated, were chronically malnourished; in all over 30 percent of all Iraqi children under the age of five were malnourished, a more than 70 percent increase from 1991. "It is clear," said the UNICEF representative in Iraq, "that children are bearing the brunt of the current economic hardship."[14] Iraq's health system, once one of the most advanced in the Middle East, deteriorated under the sanctions. Hospitals reported an increase in diseases such as diabetes, cancer, kidney disease, pneumonia, diarrhea, whooping cough, and typhoid.[15]

In an attempt to alleviate the harsh impact of the sanctions on average Iraqis, the United Nations Security Council (UNSC) passed Resolution 986 in April 1995, which set in place an oil-for-food program, allowing Iraq to export oil in order to meet some of the immediate needs of its citizens. The resolution expressed "concern by the serious nutritional and health situation of the Iraqi population...."[16] Iraqi oil was once again sold on the world market in 1996, and essential supplies began arriving into Iraq in 1997.[17] Economists and humanitarian aid workers noted that while the oil-for-food program helped, it still did not solve the crisis. By the year 2000, the caloric intake of Iraqis was still at just 75 percent of what it had been in the late 1980s.[18]

Under such dire economic conditions, corruption rose sharply, as many Iraqis turned to theft, illegal trading, and bribery in order to earn a living.[19] Shortages of goods that could no longer be imported also increased smuggling, helping to foster a widespread system of corruption. Saddam's family were heavily involved in smuggling, increasing their wealth even further during the period of economic sanctions.

The sanctions regime effectively transformed Iraqi society. Once one of the wealthiest Arab countries, years of war followed by strict sanctions had destroyed Iraq's economy. The broader impact of the sanctions are more difficult to measure. Denis Halliday, who served as the head of the oil-for-food program from September 1997 until September 1998, wrote, "Sanctions have bitten deeply into the fabric of Iraqi society and norms, greatly straining traditional Iraqi and Islamic family values." Divorce rates soared, fewer couples could afford to get married, and more children were living in single-family homes. As many as two million educated Iraqis fled the country to find employment abroad. The sanctions impacted Iraqi women, as well; many who had once worked as civil servants quit their jobs that simply did not pay enough to work menial jobs in order to better support their families.[20]

SADDAM'S WEALTH

Though a broad swath of Iraqi people saw their living standards steadily declining as a result of the sanctions, Saddam and his family continued to amass a vast fortune. The exact amount of Saddam's wealth would remain a matter of some controversy, even after his fall from power some years later. In 1991, an investigator claimed that over the course of the previous decade, Saddam and his family had skimmed at least 10 billion dollars from Iraqi oil sales. Responding to the allegations that were aired on American television on the newsmagazine 60 Minutes, a U.S. Treasury Department official said that the department had collected the names of 100 individuals and companies around the world that were believed to be fronts for the Iraqi government.[21]

Saddam's old friends were involved in helping him arrange business contracts, and some of them became incredibly wealthy in the process. Nadhmi Auchi had once stood trial along with Saddam for the 1959 assassination attempt on Qasim, which became the hallmark of Saddam's political career. In the 1980s, Auchi carried out deals for the Iraqi regime, eventually moving to England. In his first big deal, Auchi negotiated the sale of Italian frigates to the Iraqi Ministry of Defense, making millions in commissions off of the deal. In 1987, he would be instrumental in helping to procure contracts for the building of a pipeline from Iraq to Saudi Arabia, making nearly 11 million pounds sterling as his commission. Auchi would become a billionaire, befriending royalty and politicians across Europe. Auchi was arrested in April 2003 in London on fraud charges involving one of his business deals [22]

Throughout the years of sanctions, Saddam's son Uday spearheaded a large and highly lucrative smuggling operation, focused on goods such as cigarettes, liquor, and luxury items.[23] Saddam's half-brother Barzan, who held an ambassadorial position in Geneva, Switzerland, was allegedly a chief handler of Saddam's wealth, helping to stash some of the funds in foreign bank accounts and investing large sums in international companies.[24] Saddam held, for example, 90 million dollars in shares of the French conglomerate Lagardère, which owns Hachette, a company that publishes magazines such as Elle and Car and Driver.[25] After the sanctions, in order to avoid the freezing of his assets, Saddam seems to have kept most of his wealth "outside of Iraq in such safe and liquid investments as bank deposits and government bonds—even U.S. Treasuries."[26]

Apparently, the sanctions did little to stymie Saddam's accumulation of personal wealth. In 1997, Forbes magazine estimated Saddam's worth at five billion dollars; by 2000, it had increased to seven billion.[27] By 2003, Forbes estimated that Saddam's wealth had dwindled to two billion. Still, as the magazine published its list of the world's billionaire kings, queens, and despots, Saddam was ranked seventh. He edged out Queen Elizabeth of England and Fidel Castro, his close friend and political inspiration.[28]

Even as the sanctions regime became entrenched, shifting the lifestyle of most Iraqis in fundamental ways, Saddam made a practice of publicly displaying his personal wealth. Wealth was a sign of power. He also spent large sums on his close allies. "The privileges of power are very costly," Edward Djerejian, a former American diplomat noted of Saddam's expenditures. "The substantial amounts of money that come in through the black market finance the elaborate security apparatus that surrounds him. And that means not only outfitting them militarily, but also taking care of people. That's one of the ways that he assures loyalty."[29]

After the end of the Gulf War, Saddam seems to have renewed his zeal for building palaces. By the end of the 1990s, some estimate he had built as many as 50 palaces. Between the end of the Gulf War and 1999, the U.S. Department of State estimated that Saddam spent two billion dollars on the construction of palaces.[30] These buildings had taken on renewed importance—as symbols of his power despite military defeat, as signs of his continued access to wealth despite the sanctions, and as sanctuaries in the face of constant threats of assassination and coup attempts. Each palace was outfitted with a bunker and a network of underground tunnels offering emergency exit routes; a contingent of specially trained Republican Guards carefully guarded each of his homes. The palaces were vast complexes; President Bill Clinton noted that one of Saddam's palaces was the size of the entire city of Washington, D.C.

Saddam commissioned special architects, craftsmen, and interior decorators to construct his palaces, like the Al-Azimiyah Palace and the Al-Salam Palace in Baghdad. Saddam carefully guarded the details of the buildings, and a circular was reportedly sent "to workers in the engineering department of the Presidential Office warning them that the harshest punishment will be inflicted on anyone who talks about the presidential sites, even to family members."[31] The buildings, often built along the banks of Iraq's rivers, melded Islamic and modernist architecture. They were surrounded with lush gardens, featuring man-made lakes filled with carp and elaborate waterfalls. Italian marble, carvings made of rare woods, gold plumbing fixtures, and huge crystal chandeliers filled the huge structures. The palaces were lavishly decorated with silk Persian carpets and furniture in the quasi-Louis XVI furniture favored by Middle Eastern bourgeoisie. Typically, the palaces contained a highly ornate throne on which Saddam would occasionally greet visitors.

Saddam's largesse extended to those loyal to him. For his birthday celebration in 1999, he commissioned the construction of a resort city, Saddamiat al-Tharthar, some 85 miles west of Baghdad. The project cost hundreds of millions of dollars to complete. A lakeside resort, the city contained stadiums, an amusement part, hospitals, parks, and 625 homes to be used exclusively by government officials. On his birthday, regular

Iraqi citizens were bussed to the resort city and allowed to stroll through its parks and lakeside promenades.[32]

THE UN, THE U.S., AND SADDAM

Though Saddam spent millions of dollars to demonstrate his power and to secure loyalty towards his regime, his hold on power after the Gulf War was challenged on various fronts. As part of the cease-fire to end the war, the United Nations had established UNSCOM to monitor Iraq's weapons of mass destruction. UNSCOM was assisted by the International Atomic Energy Agency (IAEA). UNSCOM faced continual obfuscation by the Saddam regime. Saddam charged those closest to him with the concealment of his weapons; that responsibility fell to a handful of members of his elite security organizations, including the Mukhabarat, the Special Republican Guards, and the Special Security Service. By 1997, one UNSCOM official explained the connectedness between Saddam's weapons concealment efforts and his own protection. "It is the Special Republican Guards," he explained, "we are interested in, the conceal-ment force. But they are also the protection force for Saddam. He can build new palaces, he can rebuild the weapons program, but he cannot replace the Special Guards, because they are the key loyal force. He does not have a replacement."[33]

Still, in the early years of the program, UNSCOM met with some suc-cess, finding and destroying stockpiles of forbidden weapons.[34] Between June 1991 and March 1993, UNSCOM and IAEA completed a total of 53 inspections.[35] In 1995, Iraq turned over masses of documents, causing a reassessment of UNSCOM's efforts in finding and destroying Iraq's ille-gal weapons. UNSCOM officials remained skeptical, asserting they did "not believe that Iraq has given a full and correct account of its biological weapons program."[36]

Following the end of the Gulf War, the United States continued a limited military engagement in Iraq. No-fly zones were established in the north, offering protection for Kurds, and in the south, to protect Shiite areas. The United States military undertook a number of bombing strikes against Iraqi targets between 1993 and 1998 in order to enforce the no-fly zones. In 1993, President Clinton authorized the bombing of an intelli-gence center in Baghdad after a failed Iraqi attempt to assassinate former President Bush.[37] In March 1997, Madeleine Albright, the U.S. ambas-sador to the United Nations, announced, "We do not agree with the nations who argue that if Iraq complies with its obligations concerning weapons of mass destruction, sanctions should be lifted."[38] The United

States, effectively, renewed its policy that sanctions were intended to bring about regime change and not just compliance with UN resolutions. "There could have been no clearer message to Saddam," two scholars of Iraq noted, "that he would have little to gain in further cooperation with the UN inspectors. Even had he been of a mind to yield the secrets of the weapons he had so tenaciously concealed since 1991, Albright had told the world that he would gain nothing by doing so."[39] The following month, an UNSCOM official reported to the UN, "Not much is unknown about Iraq's retained proscribed weapons capabilities. However, what is still not accounted for cannot be neglected."[40] Indeed, Saddam had much to lose by cooperating more fully with the weapons inspectors. If he had illegal weapons, he did not want them to be found. If he did not have illegal weapons, he did not want his enemies within and outside of Iraq to know of this, as it would render him vulnerable.

In October 1997, however, Saddam ordered all Americans on the UN monitoring team out of Iraq. Richard Butler, who at the time headed the UNSCOM program, protested by pulling out the entire monitoring team. Matters seemed to be coming to a head, and the Clinton administration considered military strikes against Saddam. The UN Secretary General Kofi Annan suggested he visit Baghdad, and the United States agreed. In 1998, Annan became the first major world leader to visit with Saddam since the end of the Gulf War. During their meeting, Annan smoked one of Saddam's famous cigars and the two agreed that UNSCOM would be allowed to inspect presidential sites, long suspected of being shelters for illegal weapons, accompanied by a team of diplomats.[41]

The Clinton administration, however, remained steadfast in its determination to find a way to remove Saddam from power short of a full-on military confrontation. Congress passed the Iraq Liberation Act (ILA) in October 1998. Although somewhat skeptical, President Clinton issued a statement noting, "This Act makes clear that it is the sense of the Congress that the United States should support those elements of the Iraqi opposition that advocate a very different future for Iraq than the bitter reality of internal repression and external aggression that the current regime in Baghdad now offers.... The United States looks forward to a democratically supported regime that would permit us to enter into a dialogue leading to the reintegration of Iraq into normal international life."[42] Congress gave the president authority to "draw down" up to the value of $97 million from Department of Defense stocks. Ultimately, the Clinton administration barely tapped into a few million dollars of this appropriation, though the administration did provide several million dollars in support to some Iraqi opposition groups. Additional funding was provided for Radio Free Iraq. The Clinton administration nominally supported the ILA but expressed concern about the mechanism of giving arms and material support to the Iraqi opposition, which included an array of groups often at odds with one another.[43]

The following month, President Clinton issued a statement about U.S. policy on Iraq noting that his administration would continue to work with UNSCOM to eliminate Iraq's weapons of mass destruction, enforce the sanctions and no-fly zones, and respond to any provocations by Iraq. "However," he added, "over the long term the best way to address that threat is through a government in Baghdad, a new government that is committed to represent and respect its people, not repress them; that is committed to peace in the region."[44] U.S. policy was shifting more towards regime change, though the mechanisms of this policy remained ambiguous, largely due to the lack of a clear and preferable alternative to Saddam's regime. As General Shalikashvili, who had once served as the chairman of the Joint Chiefs, explained, overthrowing dictators is "harder to do than to talk about." General Anthony Zinni cautioned against a hasty military action to overthrow Saddam, arguing, "I think a weakened, fragmented, chaotic Iraq, which could happen if this isn't done carefully, is more dangerous in the long run than a contained Saddam is now."[45]

By December 1998, matters once again came to a head. Saddam announced the end of all Iraqi cooperation with the inspectors. The Clinton administration set into place a long-planned military action called Operation Desert Fox. On December 16, 1998, Defense Secretary William Cohen spoke at a news briefing stating, "President Clinton's decision to strike Iraq has clear military goals. We want to degrade Saddam Hussein's ability to make and to use weapons of mass destruction. We want to diminish his ability to wage war against his neighbors. And we want to demonstrate the consequences of flouting international obligations."[46]

Operation Desert Fox continued over the course of four nights, with American and British bombs and missiles striking 100 Iraqi military targets. Secretary Cohen announced that the attacks were a result of Saddam's choosing "confrontation over cooperation" since the Gulf War. The Chairman of the Joint Chiefs of Staff General Shelton stated that the United States would continue to maintain a military presence in the region in order to "keep an eye on Saddam."[47] On December 19, President Clinton announced that the military campaign had achieved its goals. "We have inflicted significant damage," he stated, "on Saddam's weapons of mass destruction programs, on the command structures that direct and protect that capability, and on his military and security infrastructure."

He cautioned that as long as Saddam Hussein remained in power, he would continue to be a threat.[48] The bombing of Iraq destroyed missile sites, antiaircraft artillery, radar towers, and communications centers.[49]

Secretary of State Madeleine Albright explained that U.S. policy towards Iraq was one of "containment plus regime change."[50] In January 1999, Frank Ricciardone, a career diplomat in the State Department with extensive experience in the Middle East, was appointed as a special representative for transition in Iraq. U.S. efforts were intended, Ricciardone explained, to "create the environment and pressures in Iraq" that would lead to the overthrow of Saddam.[51] In subsequent months, American policy would be focused on trying to unite the Iraqi opposition and supplying them with "nonlethal aid."[52] While this unity seemed difficult to achieve, one U.S. official explained, "We think that it is important not to discount people who are willing to stand up against Saddam Hussein. It would be wrong for us to shut these people off as not worth our time."[53]

Throughout his two terms in office, President Clinton maintained a position of opposing Saddam Hussein through the administration of sanctions and limited military strikes. In 2000, during an interview with Amy Goodman on Pacifica Radio, he was asked about the effects of the sanctions on Iraq. "Remember," President Clinton said of Saddam, "this is the only guy, the only world leader today who has used chemical weapons on his own citizens. And the American people in my judgement should give him all the money he needs to take care of his kids. But we should do everything we can, and even if we are alone, to try to stop him from being in a position of murdering his kids again, and murdering other children in the Middle East. That's what I believe."[54]

SADDAM'S FAMILY

Throughout his presidency, Saddam relied heavily on his family to keep a tight reign on the Iraqi government. Many of his relatives and clansmen were given political offices, particularly in the sensitive areas such as the security forces, the secret service, and the military. But cracks began to appear in the veneer of family loyalty. As Saddam dealt with wars and attempts to overthrow him, he faced growing turmoil within his own family.

And Saddam had a new love in his life. Saddam was always particularly close to a man named Hanna Jajo, who was charged with tasting all of Saddam's food before he ate to ensure he would not be poisoned. It was Jajo who first introduced Saddam to a beautiful woman named Samira Shabandar, who at the time was married. Soon, Saddam arranged for her to be divorced. Much to the consternation of his wife Sajida and his children, Saddam took Samira as his second wife. A disgraced Sajida retreated to a quiet and reclusive life.

Saddam's oldest son, Uday, was particularly incensed by this humiliation of his mother. In October 1988, there was a huge party in Baghdad in honor of the Egyptian first lady. Uday appeared at the party drunk and enraged, killing Jajo. Hearing the news of his friend's death, a besotted and angry Saddam vowed to have Uday killed. A distraught Uday reportedly attempted suicide. Family members interceded, and Saddam decided to spare his son, sending him to Geneva instead to live with Saddam's half-brother Barzan. After a few months, Uday returned to Iraq and to his father's good graces.

Through the years, however, Uday developed a reputation as a heavy drinker and womanizer who regularly abused women. Like his father, he liked expensive cigars and scotch whiskey. He collected a fleet of dozens of luxury cars. As the head of Iraq's Olympic Committee and the Iraqi Football Association, Uday reportedly ordered the torture of some athletes who did not perform to his expectations. He ran two major Iraqi newspapers, which he often used to malign his enemies. By the mid-1990s, he headed up the notorious security group known as Saddam's Fedayeen. Throughout the sanctions, he operated a highly lucrative smuggling operation, accumulating more personal wealth.

To many, Uday came to symbolize all that was wrong with Saddam's regime. One evening in December 1996, Uday was headed to a party thrown by his cousin in the Mansour district, an affluent neighborhood of Baghdad. That night, someone else was driving his Porsche, and Uday was in the passenger's seat. As the car stopped at a red light, a group of men with machine guns sprayed it with bullets. The driver was killed instantly. Uday took eight bullets, but survived.[55] Iraqi television downplayed the incident, reporting, "He was the target of a cowardly attack, which led to a light wound."[56]

Qusay, Saddam's younger son, seemed somewhat different. He was more quiet and serious than Uday. Still, as the head of Iraq's Special Security Organization, Qusay was deeply involved in repressing Saddam's opponents. "Famous fathers," observed two scholars of Iraq, "often breed infamous sons."[57]

By the end of the 1990s, it appeared that Saddam was favoring Qusay as his potential political heir. In 2001, he was appointed to the powerful Iraqi Regional Command, the executive leadership of the Baath Party.[58] Uday and Qusay were often referred to as "Number 2" and "Number 3" by Iraqi government officials.[59] And the two brothers jockeyed for position to see which would be Number 2, which Number 3. As the eldest, Uday would traditionally inherit his father's position. In time, however, it seemed that it would be Qusay the younger son who was positioned to assume power after his father. Indeed, Qusay was declared "the caretaker" in case Saddam became ill or died.[60]

Saddam's sons were not the only members of his family to generate controversy. In May 1989, Saddam's cousin, Adnan Khairallah, died. Throughout his life, Saddam had been particularly close to Adnan, the son of his uncle Khairallah and the brother of his wife Sajida. Adnan Khairallah was the minister of defense, a sign that Saddam had the utmost trust in the man. During the Iran-Iraq War, Adnan had been instrumental in the war efforts. He became increasingly popular with Iraqis, who viewed him as a war hero. Adnan was returning to Baghdad from a visit to the northern region of Kurdistan when his helicopter crashed, killing all the passengers. The official explanation was that a sandstorm and mechanical failure had caused the crash. Most Iraqis, however, believed that Saddam had grown increasingly jealous of Adnan's popularity, viewing him as a potential threat to his own power. Rumors swirled that Saddam had arranged to have Adnan killed.[61] Whatever the facts may be, Saddam publicly mourned his fallen cousin, commissioning a huge tomb in his honor.

Saddam's sons-in-law were also increasingly powerful figures in his regime. Intermarriage between Saddam's children and his relatives was meant to further solidify the bonds of clan and family, though this strategy did not always prove fruitful. Uday married the daughter of Barzan, Saddam's half-brother. After reportedly beating her badly, that marriage ended in a matter of months. Rana, Saddam's daughter, married Saddam Kamel, the cousin who had portrayed Saddam in the film *The Long Days*. Her sister Raghad married his brother Hussein Kamel. Like Saddam, the Kamel brothers were originally from the small village of al-Awja outside of Tikrit.

Both men held positions in organizations that had become increasingly important to maintaining Saddam's power, helping to protect him and to deflect UNSCOM's probing inspections. Saddam Kamel worked in the secret services. Saddam appointed Hussein Kamel as the minister of defense industries and ultimately as minister of defense. Hussein Kamel had helped establish the Republican Guards and had worked to build up Iraq's weapons of mass destruction programs. But there were signs of problems. By the fall of 1991, Kamel was no longer Iraq's defense minister. His fall from power was ascribed by some to a bitter rivalry with Uday for power, control over resources, and Saddam's ear.[62] Saddam's cousin, Ali

Hassan al-Majid, became the new minister of defense; he had gained the ominous nickname "Chemical Ali" for his role in repressing and gassing the rebellious Kurds.[63]

Watban Ibrahim, Saddam's half-brother, had served as the minister of interior since 1991. Uday had long held a grudge against Watban and in the spring of 1995 publicly accused his ministry of security lapses. Soon thereafter, Saddam removed Watban from his post. Uday's disgruntlement with his uncle persisted, however. In August 1995, there was a huge party celebrating the end of the Iran-Iraq War, which Saddam marked as the anniversary of his victory. Uday appeared at the party, angry at his uncle Watban. It was late in the night, and Uday sprayed the guests with a hail of bullets from his sub-machine gun. Watban received a serious wound in the leg, and six young women were killed.

That same evening, the Kamel brothers, along with their wives and children, were driving through Iraq in a convoy of dark Mercedes cars. They were headed towards Jordan, where they planned to defect. Arriving at the al-Amra hotel in Amman, they phoned King Hussein of Jordan asking for political asylum. Through the years, King Hussein had retained close ties with Saddam, sometimes counseling him on personal matters and often allying with him in the political realm. By the mid-1990s, however, relations between Iraq and Jordan had cooled. By offering the Kamel brothers refuge in Jordan, King Hussein had severed his relationship with Saddam.[64] Shortly after the arrival of the defectors, King Hussein spoke with President Clinton, who extended full U.S. support and protection for Jordan. The defection of the Kamel brothers, members of Saddam's elite ruling clique, along with their wives, Saddam's daughters, was big news. The American press characterized it as "the hardest blow yet to the iron rule of President Hussein."[65] Hussein Kamel, in particular, was a "true insider" with first-hand information about Saddam's weapons of mass destruction.[66]

Within days of arriving in Amman, he gave a press conference. Flanked by bodyguards armed with automatic weapons, Kamel appeared serious in his tailored suit and full moustache. "We will work inside Iraq and the whole Arab world to topple the regime of Saddam," he told the gathering of international reporters. He called on the Republican Guards, the Iraqi Army, and all of Iraqi society to get ready to change Iraq into a modern society based on realism, which would have improved international relations.[67] But, in the final analysis, Kamel proved to be less than useful. As someone close to Saddam who had been heavily involved in repressing Iraqi Kurds and Shiites, he was not a credible opposition leader. One Arab official noted, "He is no leader of a revolt and he has no followers."[68] One American intelligence officer observed, "His plan was that he would return to Baghdad behind the U.S. Army and Air Force. End of Subject." For the U.S. administration, this was not a viable option. Kamel did speak with UNSCOM officials, providing startling new information on Saddam's weapons programs and his concealment efforts. He said that Saddam and his family were incensed by the sanctions and the inspections. "They are boiling with hatred," Kamel revealed.[69]

In Baghdad, the reaction was swift. Saddam dispatched Uday to Amman, where he claimed that Saddam's daughters had been kidnapped, and demanded their return. Uday was turned away. Saddam gave a speech denouncing the Kamel brothers, accusing them of stealing millions, and saying it would be better that they "die than live in humiliation." One Iraqi told a journalist, "Anybody who ever shook hands with Hussein Kamel has been arrested. They are cutting off all the branches of the tree connected to him, in the family and in the Government."[70]

The defection and the widespread media coverage it received were indications of a possible softening in Saddam's grip over Iraq. To reassert his power, Saddam called for a national referendum in the fall of 1995. There were no opponents running against Saddam in the elections. Iraqis were simply asked, "Do you agree that Saddam Hussein should be president of Iraq?" Billboards across Iraq brandished the slogan, "Yes, Yes, Yes to Saddam."[71] 99.96 percent of the Iraqi electorate reportedly voted in the affirmative.

Life in exile proved to be quite unappealing for the Kamel brothers. After the initial whirl, few paid attention to them. The Iraqi opposition rejected them as complicit with the Saddam regime. Intelligence officials no longer called for meetings. Even the Jordanian monarchy kept their distance. Meanwhile, Saddam's family sent conciliatory signals. Saddam phoned Hussein Kamel directly, asking him to return to Baghdad and assuring him he would be safe. Several months after defecting, the Kamel brothers packed their family up and drove in their Mercedes convoy back to Iraq. Across the border, they were met by Uday, who took Saddam's daughters and grandchildren with him. Iraqi television would shortly announce that the daughters were divorcing their husbands, who had forced them to go to Jordan against their will. The official announcement asserted, "They are refusing to stay married to men who betrayed the homeland, the trust and the lofty values of their noble families and kinfolk."[72] After their return to Iraq, Saddam's daughters would live secluded lives in Tikrit.

The Kamel brothers, meanwhile, returned home to Tikrit. Soon, a carload of automatic weapons was delivered to their house, signaling an impending fight, and providing them with a means of self-defense. This was Tikriti honor at work. The house was then surrounded by Republican Guards, led by Ali Hassan al-Majid. Saddam's sons, Uday and Qusay, stood by and watched. A fierce 13-hour gun battle ensued, leaving the Kamel brothers dead.[73] Saddam announced that he regretted the death of his sons-in-law, who had been killed by family matters to preserve their own honor without consulting him. "In the end," he said, "they cleansed their bodies of the shame by severing the rotten finger. Had their families asked my opinion, I would have forbidden them from killing . . . [but] good that they did not ask because when I forgive, I forgive."[74]

The Iraqi media called Kamel a Judas, noting, "Just as Judas—who physically resembled Jesus in Saddam's mind—betrayed the Messiah, so did Kamel—who resembles Saddam—commit an act of betrayal." Though Saddam had officially pardoned the Kamel brothers, their death was carried out as a bedouin rite of revenge by the al-Majid clan. The defection and its bloody resolution, then, were not presented as affairs of the state but as a personal familial affair.[75]

The defection of the Kamel brothers, resulting in part from a bitter feud with Uday, further exacerbated the rift in Saddam's family. His brother Barzan gave an interview with a major Arabic newspaper, in which he said of Uday, "If everyone knew their own size and ability, many problems would be avoided. The direction toward the inheritance of power in Iraq is unacceptable."[76] In December 1996, as Uday recovered from the assassination attempt on his life, Saddam summoned members of his family to the hospital. In anger and disgust, he accused them of violence and corruption. They were, he reminded them, completely beholden to him for all that they had. All the "power, influence, standing, which you are using in the ugliest way . . . we are not a monarchy, at least not yet."[77]

NOTES

1. Quoted in Youssef M. Ibrahim, "The Man Who Would be Feared," *The New York Times*, July 29, 1990.

2. Abbas Alnasrawi, *Iraq's Burdens: Oil, Sanctions and Underdevelopment* (Westport, Conn.: Greenwood Press, 2002), pp. 93–94.

3. Colin Rowat, "How Sanctions Hurt Iraq," *Middle East Report Online (MERIP)* (August 2, 2001), www.merip.org.

4. Alnasrawi, *Iraq's Burdens*, p. 100.

5. Sarah Graham-Brown, *Sanctioning Saddam: The Politics of Intervention in Iraq* (London: I.B. Tauris, 1999), p. 179.

6. "The Impact of Sanctions on Iraq," *MERIP* (Spring 1998), www.merip.org.

7. Quoted in Graham-Brown, *Sanctioning Saddam*, p. 183.

8. "Saddam's 29th Anniversary," *All Things Considered*, National Public Radio (NPR), July 17, 1999.

9. Paul Chan, film, "Baghdad in No Particular Order" (USA, 2003).

10. Graham-Brown, *Sanctioning Saddam*, p. 182.

11. Denis J. Halliday, "The Impact of the UN Sanctions on the People of Iraq," *Journal of Palestine Studies* (Winter 1999): 30.

12. David Cortright, "A Hard Look at Iraq Sanctions," *The Nation*, December 3, 2001, 20.

13. "The Impact of Sanctions on Iraq," *MERIP* (Spring 1998), www.merip.org.

14. "Nearly One Million Children Malnourished in Iraq," UNICEF, http://www.unicef.org/newsline (retrieved November 1, 2004).

15. Roger Norman, "Iraqi Sanctions, Human Rights and Humanitarian Law," *MERIP* (July–September 1996): 41.

16. Text of UNSC Resolution 986, April 14, 1995, http://www.un.org.

17. Alnasrawi, *Iraq's Burdens*, p. 89.

18. Food and Agriculture Organization (FAO) report cited in Alnasrawi, *Iraq's Burdens*, p. 97.

19. Graham-Brown, *Sanctioning Saddam*, p. 183.

20. Halliday, "The Impact of the UN Sanctions on the People of Iraq," pp. 33–34.

21. "Reports of Saddam's Wealth Provoke Denials, Questions," *San Francisco Chronicle*, March 26, 1991.

22. "Tycoon in Quiz over Ties to Labour," *The Observer*, April 6, 2003.

23. After the fall of Saddam, Paul Volcker headed an investigation into the United Nations' oil-for-food program. He questioned the reliability of rumors that Saddam had diverted billions of dollars from the oil-for-food program, noting that there was confusion between illegal funds acquired through smuggling and moneys obtained illegally under the UN program. See "Volcker Highlights Smuggling over Oil-for-Food in Iraq Inquiry," *The New York Times*, December 28, 2004.

24. Jack Kelley, "US Chases Regime Leaders," *USA Today*, April 17, 2003.

25. In 2003, a company official claimed that Saddam's shares had been frozen since 1990; see "Tracking Saddam's Billions," *BusinessWeek Online*, April 3, 2003.

26. Ibid.

27. "How Dictators Manage Their Billions," *Forbes*, June 22, 2000.

28. "Billionaires: Kings, Queens, and Despots," *Forbes*, March 17, 2003.

29. "How Dictators Manage Their Billions."

30. "Saddam Hussein's Iraq," a report prepared by the U.S. Department of State, September 1999.

31. Ibid.

32. Ibid.

33. Quoted in Andrew Cockburn and Patrick Cockburn, *Saddam Hussein: An American Obsession* (London: Verso, 2002), p. 268.

34. Phyllis Bennis, "U.S.-Iraq Conflict," *Foreign Policy in Focus*, November 1997, http://www.fpif.org.

35. Anthony H. Cordesman and Ahmed S. Hashim, *Iraq: Sanctions and Beyond* (Boulder, Colo.: Westview Press, 1997), p. 291.

36. Quoted in Cordesman and Hashim, *Iraq*, p. 327. The release of these documents followed the defection of Hussein Kamel, who once headed Iraq's weapons of mass destruction programs, to Jordan.

37. Tony Lang, "Moral Dilemmas of U.S. Policy Toward Iraq," February 2001, Carnegie Council on Ethics and International Affairs, http://www.carnegie council.org.

38. Quoted in Cockburn and Cockburn, *Saddam Hussein*, p. 263.

39. Ibid., p. 264.

40. Ibid., p. 265.

41. Ibid., p. 277.

42. "The Iraq Liberation Act," statement by the president, the White House, Office of the Press Secretary, October 31, 1998, http://www.library.cornell.edu/colldev/mideast/libera.htm.

43. Philip Sheldon, "House Votes $100 Million to Aid Foes of Baghdad," *The New York Times*, October 7, 1988.

44. "The Words That Broke the Suspense: From Clinton and the Iraqis," *The New York Times*, November 16, 1998.

45. Quoted in "Opponents Find That Ousting Hussein is Easier Said Than Done," *The New York Times*, November 16, 1998.

46. Secretary of Defense William S. Cohen, Department of Defense News Briefing, December 16, 1998, http://www.defenselink.mil.

47. Linda D. Kozaryn, "Four Nights; 100 Targets," American Forces Information Service, http://www.defenselink.mil.

48. Linda D. Kozaryn, "Clinton Says 'Mission Accomplished,'" American Forces Information Service, http://www.defenselink.mil.

49. Steven Lee Meyers, "Weeks of Bombing Leave Iraq's Power Structure Unshaken," *The New York Times*, March 7, 1999.

50. Quoted in Steven Erlanger, "What Now? Doubts about U.S. and U.N. Policy on Iraq Increase," *The New York Times*, December 21, 1988.

51. Quoted in Jane Perlez, "Albright Introduces a New Phrase to Promote Saddam's Ouster," *The New York Times*, January 29, 1999.

52. Jane Perlez, "Albright Says Hussein's Foes Are Building United Front," *The New York Times*, May 25, 1999.

53. Quoted in Alan Cowell, "A Lot of Pluribus, Not Much Unum," *The New York Times*, February 25, 2001.

54. "Bill Clinton on Sanctions Against Iraq: Amy Goodman Interviews Bill Clinton," *Democracy Now*, November 8, 2000, http://www.globalpolicy.org.

55. "Saddam's Grip Still Strong," *Morning Edition*, NPR, July 18, 1997.

56. Quoted in "Son of Iraqi Leader Is Target of an Assassination Attempt," *The New York Times*, December 13, 1996.

57. Cordesman and Hashim, *Iraq*, p. 31.

58. Heidi Kingstone, "Sibling Rivalry, Baghdad Style," *The Jerusalem Report*, June 18, 2001, p. 28.

59. Youssef M. Ibrahim, "Senior Army Aides to Iraq President Defect to Jordan," *The New York Times*, August 11, 1995.

60. Faleh A. Jabar, "Assessing the Iraqi Opposition," *MERIP Online* (March 23, 2001), http://www.merip.org.

61. Said K. Aburish, *Saddam Hussein: The Politics of Revenge* (London: Bloomsbury, 2000) p. 263.

62. Eric Schmitt, "The 'In' Iraqi Who Counted Himself Out," *The New York Times*, August 12, 1995.

63. By 1995, Saddam had appointed yet another minister of defense; Cordesman and Hashim, *Iraq*, pp. 22–24.

64. Cockburn and Cockburn, *Saddam Hussein*, pp. 191–210.

65. Ibrahim, "Senior Army Aides to Iraq President Defect to Jordan."

66. Cordesman and Hashim, *Iraq*, p. 25.

67. Quoted in Youssef M. Ibrahim, "Iraq Defector Says He Will Work to Topple Hussein," *The New York Times*, August 13, 1995.

68. Quoted in Youssef M. Ibrahim, "The Flight from Hussein's Camp," *The New York Times*, August 12, 1995.

69. Cockburn and Cockburn, *Saddam Hussein*, pp. 196–98.

70. Quoted in Youssef M. Ibrahim, "U.S. Bid to Topple Iraqi Falters," *The New York Times*, August 24, 1995.

71. Youssef M. Ibrahim, "Iraqis Go to Polls, Guess Who Will Win," *The New York Times*, October 15, 1995.

72. Quoted in Douglas Jehl, "Iraqi Defectors Killed 3 Days after Returning," *The New York Times*, February 24, 1996.

73. Cockburn and Cockburn, *Saddam Hussein*, pp. 203–10.

74. Quoted in Youssef M. Ibrahim, "Iraqi Offers Regrets in Killing of Defecting Sons-in-Laws," *The New York Times*, October May 10, 1996.

75. Cordesman and Hashim, *Iraq*, pp. 25–26.

76. *Al-Hayat* interview, as cited in "Saddam Hussein's Half Brother Criticizes Heir," *The New York Times*, August 31, 1995.

77. Cockburn and Cockburn, *Saddam Hussein*, p. 261.

Chapter 6

THE SPECTER OF SADDAM

THE UBIQUITY OF SADDAM'S IMAGE

Saddam Hussein's regime was a scopic regime; he used the power of imagery to control Iraqis, to turn them into his subjects. Early in his political career, as he helped oversee the public hangings of "enemies" of the Baathist state staged in Baghdad's Liberation Square, Saddam witnessed the political potential of public spectacle. Fear made an impression, left its mark on the body politic. Punishing political opponents in a public manner was an attempt to make the spectator—the Iraqi people—complicit in a macabre system of control. While an elaborate and ruthless security system was crucial to the maintenance of Saddam's brutal control, he carefully created an entire cultural apparatus of fear and power over the years. In Saddam's Iraq, public art, museums, novels, poetry, even urban form became extensions of the state, instruments of control, and manifestations of power. In some respects, Baghdad itself became a monument to the brutality of Saddam Hussein.

Everywhere in Iraq, one saw images of Saddam's power: his palaces were huge and lavish; his statues anchored public squares; his posters were plastered on every building. By the 1990s, the threat of coups and assassinations caused Saddam to retreat into the sanctity of his many palaces. Saddam had explained to an American researcher, "The man who leads the Iraqis must be of a quick and nimble pace so the others will not step on his heels, then his back, then step on his head and pass over him."[1] More and more, Saddam became a simulacrum—hidden from view while increasingly omnipresent. Iraqis flew out of Saddam International Airport, were treated in Saddam Hospital, and dined at the revolving restaurant atop the Saddam Tower of Challenge, built to replace a communication tower bombed by U.S. forces. Saddam's likeness was etched onto every banknote that Iraqis shopped with. Most Iraqi stamps paid visual homage to Saddam. He was etched onto the faces of watches and on calendars sold in Baghdad's markets. The anniversary of Saddam Hussein becoming president and his birthday were celebrated as Iraqi national holidays. By official decree, August 7 was to be marked each year as Saddam's victory in the Iran-Iraq War. Even time became a marker of Saddam's power.

Every day, Iraq's official newspapers carried a photograph of Saddam on the front page. Newspapers like *al-Thawra* regularly featured black-and-white political cartoons of Saddam. Often these drawings featured elements of the mythology Saddam wove together—Saddam at Babylon exchanging tributes with Nebuchadnezzar, Saddam astride his horse leading a troop of Babylonian soldiers into battle, Saddam surveying the warriors in the Battle of Qadisiyya. Sometimes, the drawings animated the Iraqi landscape itself, so that palm trees lobbed missiles at Iran's Ayatollah Khomeini, while the mountains of Iraqi Kurdistan morphed into armed guards fighting Iranians.[2]

Each night, the main story of the 8 o'clock evening news was about Saddam. But even before the nightly news program began, Iraqi television carried a video montage of Saddam, accompanied by songs eulogizing him. Saddam was shown wearing his black beret while dancing with the bedouin, puffing on his cigar; in his Arab headgear with a prominent smile shaking hands with Baghdadis in the streets; wearing camouflage while surveying a military parade; and kissing little girls who joyfully danced for him. One such video by the singer Haythem Yousef is set to an upbeat melody, portraying Saddam as the merciful father of all Iraqis: "Our father, indeed Saddam is our father. With him, there is no fear ... When he sits with us he fills the home with light." Another video shows Saddam awarding medals to his sons Uday and Qusay. The song lyrics celebrate his role as their father: "Indeed you the father of Uday, by the life of Uday and Qusay.... You are an inspiration to the nation, the miracle of this age; you are the conscience of the people; you are the bread and water."[3] In 1989, the head of Iraqi television decided to filter some of the songs that accompanied the nightly Saddam videos. He was promptly called to Saddam's office to explain himself. "Mr. President, we still broadcast the songs, but I have stopped some of them because they are so poorly written. They are rubbish." Saddam replied that he was not to act as a judge, admonishingly asking, "How can you prevent people from expressing their feelings toward me?" That day, all restrictions on the songs accompanying Saddam's nightly videos were lifted.[4]

Saddam was everyman and everywhere. By the mid-1990s, the Guinness Book of Records listed Saddam as the world's most frequently painted head of state.[5] Huge hand-painted murals of him dotted Iraq's public buildings. On the Ministry of Justice, Saddam was depicted in a judge's robes holding the scales of justice in one hand and a sword in the other. The Federation of Iraqi Women headquarters was graced with an image of Saddam embracing a bedouin woman. The Ministry of Agriculture boasted a picture of Saddam carrying a bowl of food. A caring Saddam touched the forehead of an ailing patient at the Ministry of Health. The Ministry of Transportation was adorned with a mural showing Saddam's face surrounded by trains, planes, and highways, while the Ministry of Oil's mural contained an image of Saddam amidst oil wells. Saddam chatted on the phone in the picture in front of the Ministry of Telecommunications. The Society of Photographers showed a casual Saddam taking a photograph. A billboard outside the Athletic Club showed Saddam in tribal headdress and sunglasses. The city of Baghdad became saturated with the image of Saddam Hussein.

"There are practically more pictures than people," one frustrated Iraqi told a journalist.[6] Iraqis saw pictures of Saddam as they conducted official affairs in government offices, as they prayed in mosques, as they shopped in stores, as they attended school, and as they sipped tea in the local café. Even Iraqis living in remote parts of the desert or the marshland affixed pictures of Saddam on their homes for good measure. It was as if Saddam's picture became the political version of the "evil eye" Arabs traditionally keep in their homes to ward off ill thoughts and deeds.

ART AS A WEAPON

Though Saddam's wars brought death, destruction, debt, and countless hardships to Iraq, he interpreted them as victories. To Saddam, they provided an opportunity to construct a certain image of himself—and by extension all of Iraq. Even as the wars still raged on, Saddam was busy planning and commissioning elaborate war monuments. An entire coterie of architects, engineers, construction workers, designers, and artists was deployed to transform Iraqi public space into a tableau memorializing Saddam Hussein. In the process, the very meaning of Iraqi art became transformed; increasingly, its intrinsic aesthetics gave way to authoritarian tropes in the service of the state and its leader. In the spring of 2002,

Iraq's minister of culture, Hamad Youssef Hamadi, called Iraqi art "a weapon in the hands of the people."[7]

Indeed Saddam's very hands became the stuff of which his most vulgar monument, the Victory Arch, was made. In the mid-1980s, while tens of thousands of Iraqi and Iranian soldiers and civilians were caught amidst the brutal violence of the Iran-Iraq War, Saddam sketched out a plan for a victory arch to commemorate what he would call a victory at the end of the war. The Iraqi artist Muhammad Ghani oversaw the project to completion. The 40-ton monument extends across a thoroughfare on the military parade ground in Baghdad. A giant forearm, based on an exact replica of Saddam's arms, rises from each side of the passageway through which Iraqi soldiers would parade. Each hand holds a giant sword made from the guns of dead Iraqi soldiers. The two swords come together, forming an arch. Collectively, the swords weigh 24 tons and were created in an Iraqi foundry established explicitly to craft them. The base of the arms are surrounded by nets holding the helmets of 5,000 Iranian soldiers, some riddled with bullet holes.

"Iraqis live in a world where Saddam's iron fists literally reside over them," wrote an architectural critic.[8] The arms of the 40-ton monument were created by Morris Singer, a fine arts foundry in England that had created the famous lions in Trafalgar Square. Based on a cast of Saddam's arms, they include a thumbprint of Saddam's to ensure their authenticity. Years later, the foundry's director Chris Boverhoff told journalists, "The project was awarded at a time when Iraq was a valued ally of the West, and when British companies were being encouraged to support and develop work in the region. We are of course pleased to be associated with such a fine piece of work and we are justly proud of the craftsmanship that went into it, but like right-thinking people the world over we deplore the regime that Saddam created and presided over."[9]

Saddam announced the building of the monument in the shape of an arch made of two swords in a 1985 speech. "We have chosen that Iraqis will pass under the fluttering flag protected by their swords which have cut through the necks of the aggressors. And so we have willed it an arch to victory, and a symbol of Qadisiyya."[10] The intermingling of Saddam's war with Iran and the historic Arab-Islamic battle against ancient Persia was to be permanently memorialized in this monument. Saddam's self-declared victory, unacknowledged by any other international entity, would be cast in the form of what he called "one of the largest works of art in the world."[11] The monument became, in essence, a physical manifestation of Saddam Hussein's mythology, his reconstruction of reality into a truth in the service of his own power. To complete the fiction, on the day of the monument's inauguration in 1989, Saddam rode beneath the crossed swords atop a white steed. This was clearly an allusion to Hussein, the Prophet Muhammad's grandson, who is deeply revered by Shiites. Known for riding a white horse, Hussein fell in battle in Karbala, an Iraqi city that is holy to all Muslims, especially Shiites.

The arduous eight-year war with Iran would provide Saddam with the opportunity to commission several other war memorials. The Monument of the Unknown Soldier, completed in 1982, is perhaps the strangest example of Saddam architecture. The Iraqi architect turned oppositionist intellectual, Kanan Makiya, refers to it as "the tilted behemoth, which looks like a flying saucer...."[12] It was designed by Khalid al-Rahal and is meant to replicate a traditional shield carried by Iraqi warriors as it fell to the ground, dropping from the clutches of a dying soldier. A museum beneath the monument exhibits the sword belonging to the commander of the Arab forces in the Battle of Qadisiyya alongside a machine gun of Saddam's.

In Basra, the southern port city that felt the full brunt of the war's savagery, Saddam commissioned yet another war memorial that was completed in 1989. Created by various Iraqi artists based on actual photographs of Iraqi soldiers, a series of 80 statues flank the corniche alongside the Shatt al-Arab waterway. Each statue-soldier points an accusing finger in the direction of Iran.

Ismail al-Turk designed the Martyr's Monument, the war memorial widely considered to be the most beautiful and moving built during Saddam's reign. Completed in 1982, the structure is "aimed to capture in stone and cement the moment of martyrdom itself," wrote the Iraqi writer Sinan Antoon. "Its giant blue dome, whose color and shape are reminiscent of the traditional dome of the mosque, is split open, clearing the way for the soldier's soul to rise to the heavens. As if to represent his soul, an Iraqi flag rendered in sculpture ascends from the underground level of the monument...."[13] A wall surrounding the underground level of the monument lists the names of the hundreds of thousands of Iraqi soldiers who lost their lives in the Iran-Iraq War. The monument was built by the Mitsubishi Corporation on a design by the firm of Ove Arup and Partners, who built the famous Opera House in Sydney, Australia. It cost a quarter of a billion dollars. Its design was inspired, according to the official pamphlet issued on its inauguration, by "principles of the glorification of the 'Martyr.'"[14]

Saddam would fight other wars that would provide impetus for yet more Iraqi war memorials. An American missile destroyed one of Baghdad's telecommunications towers. Saddam ordered that the pieces of the missile be collected, melted down, and "cast into agonized portraits of the leaders of the anti-Iraq coalition."[15] The grimacing images of President George H. W. Bush and British Prime Minister Margaret Thatcher surround a statue of Saddam Hussein wearing his signature black beret and military uniform. The ubiquitous gun sits in a holster on his side and his arm is raised in victory. Any defeat could be recast into a dogged triumph at the request of Saddam.

In 1991, during the Gulf War, an American bomb landed on the Amiriya air-raid shelter, killing 400 Iraqis, most of them women and children. To memorialize this event, Saddam turned to Dr. Ala Bashir, his personal plastic surgeon and perhaps his favorite Iraqi artist. Through the years, Bashir had been commissioned to create several monuments throughout Baghdad. The Amiriya monument he designed has been described as a "gruesome, Medusa-like bronze of an androgynous human face grimacing in pain." Standing in a traffic circle in southern Baghdad, the structure consists of two joined blocks of limestone, one piece of which echoes the shape of a woman's back. Initially called The Union, the sculpture was renamed The Union between the Leader and His People.[16]

Perhaps Saddam's most ambitious design project was not, in fact, a war memorial. As early as 1978, he began a massive plan to restore—or rather to reconstruct—ancient Babylon. The temple of Ishtar, Nebuchadnezzar's southern fortress, the amphitheater built by ancient Greeks, Ishtar's gate, and the Ziggurat were the focus of the multi-phase reconstruction project.[17] Massive walls with gates fashioned in a style imagined to be authentically Babylonian were erected, surrounding the original site of Babylon. Nebuchadnezzar had memorialized himself by having his name inscribed onto some of the bricks in the original Babylonian structure. True to form, walls erected on behest of Saddam Hussein contain bricks marked with his name. Saddam built a palace for himself on a hilltop overlooking the site of ancient Babylon.

Archaeology was a special interest to Saddam, allowing him an opportunity to connect his modern-day reign to the ancient history of Iraq. "Antiques are the most precious relics the Iraqis possess," he told a group of Iraqi archaeologists, "showing the world that our country, which today is undergoing an extraordinary renaissance, is the [legitimate] offspring of previous civilizations which offered up a great contribution to humanity."[18]

Indeed, Saddam's monumental fetishism was not mere vanity, though that no doubt played a part in his insistence on the constant reiteration of his likeness throughout Iraq. Saddam sought to create a visual manifestation of a revolutionary civilization. His cultural production was an attempt to create an experiential alternative to Western civilization and to an Iraqi past that was disconnected from his Baathist regime. Saddam understood that Iraqis could not remain fully immersed in past cultures or engaged with a Westernized modernity—and still be complicit participants in the Baathist revolution and subjects to Saddam's control. "Such thought and behaviour would mean we are non-revolutionary," Saddam explained, "as we would be offering no innovative addition to life, and our role would be restricted to the automatic transferral [sic] of ideas and experiences of other people."[19]

For Saddam, the visual impulse stemmed from an essential human need. "Throughout history, man has constantly strived for what is beyond his vision. However, we sometimes find that this aspiration causes him to adopt from the visible itself, a condition which almost seems to exist outside his will and outside the practical realm of his sense. From the stone idol which he himself makes, he creates a god, even though the material for this idol is part of the earth on the surface of which he stands and works," he explained. Saddam's monuments to himself were his attempt at turning the earth on which Iraqis stood into idols, gods. This process was an inevitable development for a man who was sated with materiality and fully in control of his surroundings. "The human need to aspire outside and beyond the visible often intensifies when his control of mankind or knowledge of the visible increases, or when his enjoyment of it has reached the point where 'all' his material needs as a human being have been satisfied, and he has begun to feel suffocated or 'empty' as a result of this material saturation," he concluded.[20]

Elaborating on this discussion by Saddam Hussein, Kanan Makiya wrote, "Whether or not the world was created in seven days, being creative was henceforth indissolubly bound up with human expression, self-realization, and the freedom to act upon that world with a view to reshaping it. The application of this attribute to politics and culture was the great achievement of the French Revolution. From these origins came the secular notions of artistic creation that we all now use and the view of politics as art which Saddam Husain was expounding to his biographer."[21]

SADDAM'S MUSEUM

If building monuments became an obsession for Saddam—an attempt to build himself, literally and figuratively, into the historical landscape of Iraq—it would make sense that he would commission a museum devoted to his own life. The Triumph Leader Museum, a two-story structure erected in the center of Baghdad in the mid-1990s, turned Saddam's life into a virtual exhibition.[22] The center of a round building featured a glass clock tower with a pendulum that held four gold Kalashnikov rifles. The clock beeped out a melody written in honor of Saddam on the hour, every hour.

The museum's exhibitions unfolded with a room filled with photographs of Saddam. Each stage of Saddam's life, from his early childhood in Al-Awja to his presidency, were reconstructed in the photographic display. Images of Saddam with the French President George Pompidou, the Soviet leader Leonid Brezhnev, the Yugoslavian statesman Marshall Tito, and Cuba's Fidel Castro testified to his political history. The museum exhibited personal items used by Saddam like cigar holders, sunglasses, and walking sticks. Visitors to the museum could view an old Chevrolet station wagon with bullet holes. It was, allegedly, the very car that Prime Minister Qasim was riding in when Saddam attempted to assassinate him in 1959.

A central feature of the museum was an elaborate display of the gifts that Iraqi professional groups and numerous heads of state gave to Saddam. The gifts from foreign dignitaries recalled the years of the Iran-Iraq War when Saddam was courted by many Western allies as a bulwark against the Islamic regime in Tehran. The seal of the state of California was presented to Saddam in a red velvet box in 1984. There was a football signed by the New York Giants football team.

The centerpiece of the collection, however, was not on display but placed in special storage elsewhere. These were a pair of gold riding spurs given to Saddam in the early 1980s by U.S. President Ronald Reagan; the gift was an acknowledgement of the two men's shared love of riding. As relations between the United States and Iraq soured, the museum's displays were edited. Saddam's letters to President Reagan and pictures of him meeting with American officials were carefully removed.

Leaders from the Third World also granted Saddam gifts and honors, which were carefully displayed in the museum. There were the handguns and the rifle presented to him by King Hussein of Jordan and the Kalashnikov from Libya's Muammar Qaddafi. Fidel Castro had presented him with a cut glass bowl, while Yasser Arafat gave Saddam a replica of the Al-Aqsa Mosque in Jerusalem. Venezuela's leader Hugo Chavez sent him Latin American music. In 1998, the Indo-Iraq Friendship Society gave him their "man of the century" award, celebrating him as a revolutionary and a statesman who had "infused new life and hope in his people."

The museum's tour guides, often from Saddam's hometown of Tikrit, narrated the exhibition, embellishing the life and interests of the Iraqi leader. Pointing out an elaborate chess set, one tour guide explained, "The President is an excellent player, but he doesn't have time." But other items on display testified to another special interest of Saddam's. Guns, daggers, swords, scepters, artillery shells, and mortars cast in gold rounded out the museum's collection.

SADDAM ART AND SADDAM'S ART COLLECTION

In the summer of 1993, the Saddam Art Center in Baghdad celebrated the confluence of Saddam's 56th birthday and the 25th anniversary of the coup that brought him to power with an exhibition of forty portraits of the leader.[23] In Baathist Iraq, painting Saddam became its own profession, Saddam art its own genre. One Iraqi artist opened a small business devoted to selling pictures of Saddam he drew using his own blood.[24] Saddam's drive to construct a revolutionary art, with himself as the central subject, produced an entire artistic market economy. One sculptor, Khalid Farhan, was said to produce a statue of Saddam every six months over a 10-year period.[25] Some painters could produce—and sell—as many as 200 paintings of Saddam. Mejdi Ahmed, an artist who painted abstract modern canvases, made his living from painting Saddam portraits. Throughout the 1990s, he painted 30 in all. "It pays well," he explained. "Many are in government offices."[26]

What becomes of artists and art in a totalitarian regime bent on deploying culture as a means of control? Baathist Iraq might have been fertile ground for resistance art. In societies where the public sphere is diminished, where the state controls the media and the universities, it is often the filmmakers, the photographers, the painters, and the sculptors who construct images of alternative realities, who open up creative spaces for political criticism. But in Iraq, Saddam's personal fixation on visual culture seems to have usurped the social space where art and politics meet.

When looking back on the work of artists who produced Saddam art, it is hard to judge artistic motivations. Artists are made of flesh; they may be valorized or demonized, but they remain subject to the human condition. How free were Iraq's artists to resist Saddam's decrees to produce the anachronistic art he demanded in the service of himself and his state? It's hard to know what choices an artist had to make when he tamed his paint strokes, when he turned to total abstraction, or when he produced picture after picture of Saddam—in order to evade the harsh consequences of social criticism and political defiance in Baathist Iraq. It is harder still to measure the impact of the sanctions throughout the 1990s on Iraqi artistic production. The sanctions curtailed travel and the importation of foreign publications, deepening the cultural isolation of Iraqi artists. The harsh economic environment surely increased their dependence on funds made available by the government for the production of Saddam art. Even those artists who spoke to scholars and journalists in glowing terms about Saddam may have been conditioned by the system of rewards and punishment at play. Shakir Khalid painted some of the famous murals of Saddam. "I have met with Saddam Hussein," he boasted to a Western journalist in 2003. "You may see in Saddam Hussein features like cheerfulness, trust, fidelity, strength and absolute belief." One of Khalid's massive paintings showed Saddam in army fatigues astride his white horse charging from Babylon to Jerusalem's Dome of the Rock. "Artists are not forced to draw Saddam Hussein art," he explained, "but it's only natural to draw a country's leader for patriotic occasions. You need to do patriotic art and Saddam Hussein is a symbol of the country."[27]

If Saddam promoted a public art focused on his likeness, his personal art collection reflected a different aesthetic impulse. The canvases he chose to decorate his personal living quarters tended towards the fantastic and the erotic. A favorite artist was the American painter Rowena Morrill, whose fantasy images feature highly muscular men and voluptuous women doing battle with snakes, dragons, and stone demons. Morrill's early childhood in Japan inspired many of her paintings, often created for the covers of paperback sword-and-sorcery novels.[28] "I loved those wonderful Japanese ghost stories," she told the BBC. Shocked to discover that Saddam had collected her art, she told reporters, "I was utterly stunned. I can't say that I take anything coming from a quarter like that as a compliment. However, I certainly think that—if in fact he was looking at my works and thinking anything—I'm curious."[29]

Much was made by the press about Saddam's proclivity towards fantastical canvases. Nothing in these paintings suggested an intrinsically Iraqi or Islamic sensibility. "There's not much that is culturally embedded about his taste in paintings," wrote The Guardian's art critic. "These [paintings] have the iconography of psychotic porn. They're certainly not Islamic."[30] But one can see how these battle scenes where beautiful naked men and women use their cut bodies and elegant swords to fight off fantastical demons might appeal to Saddam. As he felt increasingly embattled, his self-perception may have been reflected in the imagery of these paintings. In this regard, these paintings may have been extensions of another kind of Saddam art—the fantastical victorious warrior he may have thought or willed himself to be.

SADDAM AS AUTHOR

In the aftermath of the Gulf War, as Saddam retreated more and more from public life, he turned to books. Given his penchant for reading, it is not altogether surprising that Saddam would eventually turn to writing novels. Saddam had already demonstrated a belief in the political potential of narrative. As he took over the reigns of power in Iraq, he had commissioned *The Long Days*, a fictionalized account of his role in the assassination attempt on Qasim in 1958 and his daring escape to Syria. The book had also been produced as a feature-length film starring Saddam Kamel as the hero. Now, it was time for Saddam to rise to the challenge of writing political novels himself. There is, of course, a long precedence of authorship by authoritarian leaders. Napoleon, Hitler, and Mao all left behind poetry and prose—a genre that has been dubbed "dictator literature" or "dic lit" for short.[31]

Zabiba and the King, Saddam's debut novel, appeared in 2000. It was published anonymously. Whether Saddam actually wrote the book became a matter of some conjecture. Saad Hadi, a journalist involved with Saddam's writing efforts, said, "He'd sit in his state room and recount simple tales, while his aides recorded his every word." Iraqi novelists would then be called upon to improve on Saddam's stories. The wife of one such author, Sami al-Anizi, claimed that her husband contributed to *Zabiba and the King*. One morning, she recounted, he was called and given the task of producing a final version of *Zabiba and the King* based on Saddam's notes. Two months later, as he completed his work on the book, he collapsed in his home and died. His wife believes that Sami al-Anizi was poisoned in order to help maintain the fiction that the novel was entirely penned by Saddam himself.[32] U.S. intelligence officers believed that even if Saddam did not personally write the book, he was deeply involved in its production. The CIA, England's MI6, and Israel's Mossad all reportedly studied it carefully for "insight into Saddam's political thinking."[33] Many Iraqis seemed to believe the book was actually written by Saddam. An Iraqi businessman explained, "The King speaks to Zabibah in the way Hussein might address a member of his Revolutionary Command Council. The language is as torturous as his speeches, and the subject matter is very egotistical."[34]

Saddam's first contribution to the dictator literature genre mingles a Harlequin romance ethos with war fiction. The tradition of bedouin storytelling is added to the mix, as Saddam begins the story as a tale told by a wise old bedouin woman. Iraq's defeat to coalition forces in the Gulf War forms the backdrop of the book. In the prologue, Saddam wrote, "I am Iraq, the only one in the whole Earth, declaring firmly, for all to hear: 'you, Brutality and Lawlessness, stay where you are or retreat! ... Let all the cowards, compromisers, and traitors get out. We shall not capitulate!'"[35]

Interestingly, the beacon of the Arab Socialist movement chose the character of a king to represent himself. But Saddam's king is a sad and lonely king, who grew up in a troubled family. He lives in isolation, bunkered down in a heavily fortified palace. Security strictures permit few windows to let in the sunshine and little outdoor space, so the king becomes increasingly morose and detached from nature. His many wives and concubines offer him little by way of meaningful love and understanding; indeed some participate in palace subterfuge, working with scurrilous courtiers to poison him.

On a rare outing outside the palace grounds, the king meets Zabiba, a poor commoner. Entranced by this beautiful but simple and honest woman, the king begins to spend more and more time with her, despite the fact that she is married. On his command, Zabiba begins making visits to the palace, where she meets with the king in his private quarters. Zabiba is the embodiment of the Iraqi people. "I am the daughter of my people," Zabiba declares. The growing love between Zabiba and the king is meant to symbolize the abiding tie between Saddam and all Iraqis. "I fell in love with you, Zabiba, so that in you and through you I could love the people," the king tells her.

Much of the novel is taken up with long conversations between the two. The king explains the difficulties and burdens of power, and she encourages him to be more just, caring, and connected to the people of his land. "I am the king of a great country. I love when the people are free and I love to express myself sometimes by having a good laugh with the common folk, though I don't want to do that all the time," the king says. Zabiba responds, "If you speak naturally with the common people, they come back to their human state, but if you treat them as if they were puppets, they could rebel."

In an extended conversation, Zabiba and the king discuss the question of the foreign occupation of Arab lands and the shortcomings of other Arab leaders. At the time that Saddam wrote the book, U.S. forces remained stationed in Saudi Arabia. "Isn't the presence of foreign powers on the land of the state contrary to noble ideals? Don't you see that many kings around us invite foreigners? Even now they are still on their lands. Don't you think that it casts a shadow on them and their nations?" the king asks Zabiba. She replies, "Truly, foreign presence whether by invasion or invitation, influences the worldview and traditions of the people. And it destroys the freedom of the will of its king, contradicting the notion of a free state, and the sons of that country are not free in it."

Another question that deeply concerns the king was that of succession. Given his own troubled childhood, which was fraught with familial conflict and the convoluted constellation of his own wives, concubines, and offspring, the king has some misgivings about who will succeed him as king. Here, too, Zabiba counsels him not to rely on his advisors but to interact directly with the people. With this insight from the people, the king will be able to find a just solution to the succession quandary—dispatching with the practice of inherited power altogether. Rather than making succession a birthright, Zabiba urges the king to give power to those who are sincere and capable. The novel's focus on the question of succession may well have reflected Saddam's growing concern with the turmoil in his own family and with mounting evidence that his oldest son, Uday, was hardly fit for leadership.

After some time, Zabiba tires of visiting the king with whom she is now deeply in love and then returning to her husband with whom she must continue conjugal relations. Zabiba's marriage was an arranged one, and her husband is a tyrannical uncaring man who regularly beats her. Eventually, she and the king decide to marry, and he begins to arrange for her to be granted a divorce. Shortly after arriving at this decision, Zabiba mounts the white horse that the king had given her and begins riding back towards her modest home, content that soon she will be free of life with her wretched husband. Along the way, however, she is accosted by a hooded man. Gallantly fighting him off to the best of her ability, Zabiba finally gives in under the weight of his kicks and punches. He gags her and rips her clothes off. He then rapes her. At one point, she frees her mouth from the gag and bites into his neck, causing him to bleed profusely. He finally runs off, leaving her in a humiliated mound in the countryside. Her faithful horse, the treasured gift from the king, stands nearby and comes to her. Comforted by its familiarity, she finds the strength to ride him the rest of the distance to her home. There, she finds her husband washing blood from a wound in his neck. She realizes that it was he who had raped her.

Zabiba's rape at the hands of her husband occurs on January 17, which not coincidentally is the date that the Gulf War began. Zabiba's husband, then, is meant to stand for the coalition forces and the United States in particular. In the book, Saddam wrote, "Violence always brings a horrendous amount of pain, independently of whether it is a man who rapes a woman, an army of enemies invading a nation, or a law being violated by those who spurn it. But it is even worse when one is betrayed to the point of humiliation, whether by a country or a human being."

The only consolation Zabiba has is in knowing that she has bravely resisted her attacker—and that the king has promised to avenge this act of violence. Upon hearing her story, he tells Zabiba, "The king will wage war so that the heroes become heroes, so that the banner of truth flies high over the land, and so that the people have somebody who will be worthy of becoming its conscience and who will defend it.... May all evil plotters be vanquished!"

The king and Zabiba wage war against their enemy. By now, Zabiba has become a beloved hero of the people, who see her as the embodiment of all that is good in Iraq. Though the enemy goes down in defeat, Zabiba is killed in battle. She is mourned by all. Following her advice, the king establishes his people's council, but they become mired in factionalism and rivalry. When they get word that the king has passed away, they are inspired by his example to govern with wisdom.

Within two years, Iraq's bookstores were filled with Saddam's second novel, *The Fortified Castle*. Another love story set against the backdrop of war, it tells the story of an Iraqi soldier after the Gulf War who falls in love with a Kurd from the northern regions. A third novel followed. Entitled *Men and the City*, it told the story of Saddam's family and the Baath Party. Saddam's final novel, *Be Gone Demons!*, appeared just as U.S. President George W. Bush was preparing to invade Iraq in 2003.

The content of the novels—their mingling of romance and war stories, of fact and fiction—reveal something of Saddam. Taken together, they reflect a sense of embitterment, betrayal, and defiance. They suggest a man who sees himself as pained and victimized but also brave and heroic. Aware of his estrangement from "the people," Saddam seems like a man somewhat trapped within the complex of security and luxury in which he had become ensconced. The constant reiteration of his bedouin childhood, his emotional connection with the common folk, his reverence for the people seem to suggest a fixation with the increasingly unbridgeable divide between him, the Leader, and the Iraqi people. This need to mingle with the people, to be reminded of where he came from, was reflected in Saddam's often spontaneous walkabouts in Baghdad, even during times of war. His car would stop, and he would grin broadly as he was embraced by regular Iraqis. The need for that affection, that approval, that respect from commoners seeps through Saddam's novels.

The manner in which the books were published and promoted also reflected Saddam's tendency to mix the personal and the political, to conflate his own interests with that of the state. *Zabiba and the King* was issued in a million copies, an inordinately large run given the population of Iraq; clearly the book was intended for a pan-Arab audience. It was reissued in 2002 on January 17, to commemorate the anniversary of the "Mother of All Battles." A spokesperson for the publisher reissuing the book said the timing was meant to "consecrate the meaning of steadfastness and resistance in the face of the unjust embargo and wicked aggression."[36]

The distribution of Saddam's second novel was even more ambitious. Two million copies of *The Fortified Castle* were issued. The Ministry of Interior handled the distribution of the book, setting sales quotas for each province of Iraq. Iraq's civil servants, teachers, soldiers, and Baath Party members were all expected to purchase a copy of the book, priced at about two dollars. Uday alone bought 250,000 copies to distribute to employees in the various organizations he headed.[37] The Iraqi press reported that all revenues from the books would be distributed to the poor and needy.

Advertisements for the books ran regularly on Iraqi radio and television and in state newspapers. In the summer of 2001, Mizahim al-Baiati reported that he was supervising the script for a 20-part television serial based on *Zabiba and the King*. The series was to be produced by Iraqi satellite television.[38] The Iraqi theater director, Sadun Albedi, boasted to journalists in 2002 that the theatrical adaptation of the book was a huge success. "I insist," Albedi said, "that it is one of the best play production[s] in the history of modern theater in Iraq, yes. We are going to perform this in many Arabic countries, yes."[39] The Iraqi cultural apparatus was fully deployed to promote Saddam's contributions to dictator literature.

THE CULTURE OF RESISTANCE

Throughout his reign, Saddam created a vast network of cultural production focused singularly on embellishing, demonstrating, and celebrating his power. The ubiquity of Saddam was meant to eradicate the distinctions between the state and its leader, to constantly remind each Iraqi that the state watched over them. Beyond its central role in the machinations of control, Saddam art was also an essential cog in one of Saddam's loftier ambitions—that of creating an alternative revolutionary

Arab culture. Indeed, an overarching characteristic of Saddam's regime was its dependence on visual culture as an instrument of power.

This fixation left little space for a spontaneous, indigenous cultural life to grow and develop in Iraq. Indeed, as Saddam's power grew, Baghdad's stature as a cultural center of Arab life diminished. As Anthony Shadid, an author and journalist with an intimate and deep knowledge of Iraq, noted, in the 1970s, Baghdad flourished as a site of secular cosmopolitanism. A generation ago, wrote Shadid, "Palestinian students received scholarships to study in Iraq and Arab writers and artists fled the anarchy of Lebanon's civil war to bring their intellectual force to a flowering Baghdad, making 1970s Iraq, for those on the 'correct' side of politics, a time as nostalgic as the romanticized city of Abbassid glory." Under Saddam, this rich cultural landscape gave way to "the sycophancy of much of the country's sanctioned intellectual life."[40]

Still, despite his best efforts, Saddam was unable to hermetically seal the minds of Iraqis; cultural hegemony, even in authoritarian regimes, is never complete. During his 1999 visit to Baghdad, Shadid found a flourishing theater scene focused on satirical drama. Throughout the 1990s, some 20 theater houses had been opened in the Iraqi capital. Iraqis quoted lines from the popular plays, which were often sold out for weeks. A *Party for a Respectful Person*, which had a three-year run, featured a mid-level Iraqi bureaucrat whose work was defined by favoritism. Other plays, often set in Iraq's past, depicted prison life with its commensurate system of interrogation and torture. After the Gulf War, Kuwaitis became a favorite target of Iraq's satirists, though the jokes about that shiekhdom's corruption could easily be understood as a parable for Iraq's own circumstances. Uncharacteristically, Saddam's government gave a fair amount of leeway to Iraq's dramatists. Perhaps even they recognized the need to release some of the tensions of everyday life in post-war Iraq. One playwright explained to Shadid, "Iraqis feel they are suffocating with the sanctions, and the theater gives them the lungs they can breathe with."[41]

As Saddam's regime became a likely target for military engagement by the administration of President George W. Bush, satirical theater continued to thrive in Baghdad. In the winter of 2003, the National Theater on al-Fatah Square presented a comedy entitled, *The Tramp*. By then, the theater had become a refuge for Baghdadis, for whom theater going had become a regular family outing. Kasim al-Mallak, the National Theater's director, said, "In my experience, people always come here when there is a war. It is usually a comedy." A woman in the audience explained, "Under these circumstances, we have to laugh."[42] Faced with political authoritarianism, economic hardship, and increasing uncertainty about the future,

Iraqis turned to humor and wit. Comedic theater became a space for communal relief—and perhaps resistance. "In a country like Iraq," one filmmaker explained, "comedy and tragedy are never very far apart."[43]

This comedic strategy of cultural resistance was also used in Iraqi Kurdistan, which after the Gulf War gained a fair amount of autonomy. Under U.S. military protection, Kurds began to create a political life that was increasingly independent of Saddam's centralized authority. Hassan Rashid, a leading Iraqi comedian, took advantage of the greater freedom in Kurdistan to make a satirical film about Saddam. Goran Faili, an Iraqi actor who resembled Saddam, starred in the leading role. In preparation for his role, Faili spent months studying footage of Saddam, mimicking his slow walk, and practicing his Tikriti accent. His costume for the film was a military beret, camouflage, and sunglasses. Fifty Kurdish guerillas were hired to play Iraqi soldiers.

In one scene, extras danced for Saddam in the same vein as the nightly music videos shown on Iraqi television every day. Another scene showed Saddam making a long speech to his cabinet, threatening to have all of them beheaded. In the ultimate insult, the slogan of the Baath Party, "Unity, Freedom, and Socialism" was depicted as graffiti in a bathroom. The highly popular film was shown on Kurdish television. Word of the film got back to Saddam, who was hardly amused. Watching a bootlegged copy of the film, he called on his security forces to kill the entire cast of the production. The would-be assassins were caught by Kurdish authorities, but leading actor Faili went into hiding for several years.[44]

Theorists have suggested that the public sphere serves a critical role in shaping democratic societies. It is ultimately journalists, filmmakers, artists, and writers who help construct this critical space between the state and the people where political criticism, debate, and dialogue can take place. Throughout his reign, Saddam effectively inhibited the Iraqi public sphere by usurping so much of that country's cultural production for his own purposes. Saddam art became the prevalent cultural ethos of Iraq. Time will tell whether a nascent culture of resistance, a burgeoning public sphere was able to exist underground and behind closed doors, hidden from the omnipresent Baathist state.

Saddam relied on representations of himself woven into the everyday life of Iraqis as a way to remind them that he was the *al-qa'id al-darurah*, or the indispensable leader.[45] As he withdrew into the quiet safety of his palaces, public displays of his likeness became even more prevalent throughout Iraq. But, ultimately, when the time came to prove to Iraqis that he was still their Glorious Leader, the Lion of Babylon, the Man of the Long Days, Saddam stepped out of the shadows and turned himself into the ultimate display of power. In the winter of 2001, with rumors swirling through Baghdad that Saddam had suffered a crippling stroke, he appeared at a military parade, held his rifle up in one hand and shot it in the air for five straight hours. According to the official count, President Saddam Hussein fired off 140 shots.[46]

NOTES

1. Quoted in Robert Ruby, "Hussein's Personality Cult Dominates Daily Life in Iraq," *Toronto Star*, August 7, 1988.

2. See examples of the political art in Amatzia Baram, *Culture, History and Ideology in the Formation of Ba'thist Iraq, 1968–89* (New York: St. Martin's Press, 1991).

3. Translations from "The Survival of Saddam," *Frontline*, http://www.pbs.org/wghb/pages/frontline/.

4. The exchange is recounted in Mark Bowden, "Tales of the Tyrant," *Atlantic Monthly*, May 2002.

5. Calvin Trillin, "Saddam: Can't Color Him Humble," *The Seattle Post-Intelligencer*, August 24, 1993.

6. Quoted in Elizabeth Neuffer, "Hussein Grows As Icon As Potential War Looms," *Boston Globe*, January 6, 2003.

7. Quoted in Hugh Pope, "Saddam Can Count on Vivid Support from Iraq's Artists," *Wall Street Journal*, May 31, 2002.

8. Edward McBride, "Monuments to Self: Baghdad's Grand Projects in the Age of Saddam Hussein," *Metropolis*, June 1999, http://www.metropolismag.com.

9. Quoted in "UK Firm May Have a Hand in Saddam's Fall," *The Telegraph*, August 4, 2003. Saddam's thumbprint, which was used for the project, had remained in the foundry's safe; after the fall of Saddam, it was sent to the British government to be used to authenticate Saddam Hussein's identity when he was captured.

10. Quoted in Kanan Makiya, *The Monument: Art and Vulgarity in Saddam Hussein's Iraq* (London: I. B. Tauris, 2004; originally published 1991), p. 3.

11. Quoted from invitation card to inauguration of the monument, in Makiya, *The Monument*, p. 1.

12. Makiya, *The Monument*, p. 26.

13. Sinan Antoon, "Monumental Disrespect," *Middle East Report (MERIP)* (Fall 2003): 28.

14. Makiya, *The Monument*, p. 23.

15. Edward McBride, "Monuments to Self."

16. Jon Lee Anderson, "Letter from Baghdad: Saddam's Ear," *The New Yorker*, May 5, 2003, http://www.newyorker.com.

17. Baram, *Culture, History and Ideology in the Formation of Ba'thist Iraq*, p.46.

18. Quoted in Baram, *Culture, History and Ideology in the Formation of Ba'thist Iraq*, p. 41.

19. Interview with Saddam Hussein, Amir Iskander, *Saddam Hussein: the Fighter, the Thinker, and the Man*, trans. Hassan Selim (Paris: Hachette Réalités, 1980), p. 359.

20. Ibid.

21. Makiya, *The Monument*, p. 35.

22. Information on the museum was taken from Rory McCarthy, "Saddam Makes an Exhibition of Himself," *The Guardian*, January 10, 2003; Jeremy Scahill, "American Gifts to Saddam MIA in Baghdad," IraqJournal.org, October 23, 2002, http://www.iraqjournal.org/journals/021023.html; Mike Shuster, "Saddam Hussein Museum—His Excellency's Personal Stuff," *Weekend Edition*, National Public Radio (NPR), September 21, 1996.

23. Paul Lewis, "In Iraq, a 'One-man Show' Acquires New Meaning," *The New York Times*, August 10, 1993.

24. Makiya, *The Monument*, p. 103.

25. Elizabeth Neuffer, "Hussein Grows as Icon as Potential War Looms."

26. Vivienne Walt, "Saddam Won't Die," January 18, 2001, http://www.salon.com.

27. Quoted in Bill Glauber, "Hussein Is Rarely Seen, but Always in View," *Knight Ridder Tribune Business News*, January 23, 2003.

28. Franklin Harris, "Don't Laugh at Saddam's Art Collection," *The Decatur Daily*, April 24, 2003.

29. Quoted in "Saddam's Favourite Artist," *BBC News World Edition*, May 14, 2003, http://news.bbc.co.uk.

30. Jonathan Jones, "Look at the Size of Those Missiles," *The Guardian*, April 15, 2003.

31. Jo Tatchell, "Heroes and Villains, *The Guardian*, July 6, 2004.

32. "Saddam the Great Dictator of Fairy Tales," *The Telegraph*, July 12, 2003.

33. Waiel Faleh, "'Saddam's Novel' Set To Become TV Series," *Columbian*, June 12, 2002; Jo Tatchell, "Heroes and Villains."

34. Quoted in Michael Theodoulou, "New Iraqi Literary King Is Not-Quite Anonymous," *The Christian Science Monitor*, December 11, 2001.

35. Anonymous, *Zabibah wa-al-malik* (al-Jizah: Dar 'Ashtar, 2002). Quotes from *Zabiba and the King* are taken from the English translation: Saddam Hussein, *Zabiba and the King*, ed. Robert Lawrence (College Station, Tex.: Virtualbookworm.com Publishing, 2004).

36. "New Edition of Saddam Novel Published in Iraq," Iraq News Agency, as presented on *BBC Monitoring Middle East*, January 18, 2002.

37. "Iraqis Must Buy Two Million Copies of Saddam's Novel," *Middle East Online*, Feb. 19, 2002, http://www.middle-east-online.com.

38. Faleh, "'Saddam's Novel' Set to Become TV Series."

39. "Saddam Hussein Determined to Leave His Mark on Iraq," NPR, *Morning Edition*, August 13, 2002.

40. Anthony Shadid, "Daring Theater Offers Respite from Baghdad's Misery," *MERIP* (Summer 1999): 13.

41. Ibid.

42. Quoted in Patrick Graham, "Iraqis in Stitches at Thought of War," *The Observer*, February 23, 2003.

43. Quoted in Luke Harding, "The Joke's on Saddam," *The Guardian*, March 14, 2003.

44. Ibid.

45. The nomenclature comes from Kenneth M. Pollack, *The Threatening Storm: The Case for Invading Iraq* (New York: Random House, 2002), p. 149.

46. Statistic from *Harpers Weekly Review*, January 9, 2001, http://www.harpers.org/weeklyreview.html.

Chapter 7

THE FALL OF SADDAM

UNFINISHED BUSINESS

On March 1, 1991, President George Bush gave a press conference at the White House. Asked about the end of the Gulf War, he replied, "... To be honest, with you ... I haven't yet felt this wonderfully euphoric feeling that many of the American people feel. You mention World War II. There was a definitive end to that conflict and now we have Saddam Hussein still there." George Bush had experienced war first-hand as a navy pilot in the Pacific theater during the Second World War; for him, that was the definitive war, one with a clear ending. The Gulf War proved to have a "ragged ending," one that led to unforeseen consequences like Saddam's brutal suppression of rebellions by the Shiites and the Kurds, continued U.S. military presence in the region, and years of sanctions and weapons inspections.

Despite a humiliating defeat at the hands of coalition forces, Saddam's regime did not fall from power as some analysts in the U.S. government had predicted. Indeed, he had proved resilient, surviving assassination and coup attempts. It was later revealed that Prime Minister Yitzhak Rabin had approved a 1992 plot to use Israeli soldiers to assassinate Saddam at the funeral of his uncle Khairallah. During a training mission in the Israeli desert in November 1992, a unit accidentally shot a real missile at the Israeli soldiers who were stand-ins for Saddam and his bodyguards, killing five of them. The plan was then abandoned.[1]

In the summer of 1996, the Clinton White House ordered the CIA to organize and implement a coup to overthrow Saddam. Having infiltrated a group of Iraqis they presumed were amongst the military elite closest to Saddam, the CIA provided them with mobile phones with direct lines to the CIA. Having long prepared for various coup scenarios, Saddam's intelligence uncovered the plot. His agents arrested hundreds of Iraqis believed to be involved in the CIA plot, torturing and executing some of them. In the process, they found one of the CIA's mobile phones. An agent of Saddam's placed a call. When an American agent answered, he was told that their men were dead and they should pack up and go home.[2]

American policy towards Saddam remained one of containment and regime change, though the practical means for the latter remained unclear. By 1998, a group of politicians and analysts wrote a letter to President Clinton calling for the use of military force to overthrow Saddam Hussein. The group had formed an organization in 1997 called the Project for the New American Century. In their letter to the president, they argued, "The only acceptable strategy is one that eliminates the possibility that Iraq will be able to use or threaten to use weapons of mass destruction. In the near term, this means a willingness to undertake military action as diplomacy is clearly failing. In the long term, it means removing Saddam Hussein and his regime from power. That now needs to be the aim of American foreign policy. We urge you to articulate this aim, and to turn your Administration's attention to implementing a strategy for removing Saddam's regime from power."[3] While President Clinton did not fully support these policies, another U.S. president would.

When George W. Bush became president following the 2000 elections, 11 of the 18 signatories to the letter would become officials of the American government, including Donald Rumsfeld who became secretary of defense and Paul Wolfowitz who became the second in command at the Pentagon. They represented a group of politicians who had believed that ending the Gulf War in 1991 without removing Saddam from power was a grave mistake. Known as "neocons," they viewed U.S. policy towards Iraq as part of a larger change in America's role in the post-Cold War era. Early in the Bush presidency, however, there were few overt indications that U.S. policy towards Iraq was bound to change significantly.

The terrorist attacks of September 11, 2001, however, precipitated a change in U.S. policy towards Iraq. In statements made after the attacks, the president said the United States would pursue terrorists and those who harbored and assisted them, including states. On September 14, President Bush met with his war cabinet at Camp David; the question of Iraq and its potential role in the war on terrorism was broached. On October 11,

President Bush gave a primetime news conference. The journalist Helen Thomas asked the President about news that some of his advisors were urging him "to go after Iraq." George Bush replied, "This is a long war against terrorist activity.... There's no question that the leader of Iraq is an evil man. After all, he gassed his own people. We know he's been developing weapons of mass destruction, and I think it's in his advantage to allow inspectors back in his country to make sure that he's conforming to the agreement he made after he was soundly trounced in the Gulf War. And so we're watching him carefully."[4]

Even as the United States engaged in a war against Afghanistan to target the Taliban regime that had supported Al-Qaeda, the group that had spearheaded the September 11 attacks, it seemed increasingly likely that an attack against Iraq was a serious possibility. As Kenneth M. Pollock, a former CIA analyst and a National Security Council official with expertise on Iraq, explained, the attacks strengthened the position of the neocons within the administration. "It does seem clear," Pollock said, "that after September 11 this group seized upon the events of September 11 to resurrect their policy of going after Saddam Hussein and of regime change in Iraq."[5]

A GRAVE AND GROWING DANGER

On the evening of January 29, 2002, President Bush delivered the State of the Union address. In his speech, the president celebrated a victory over terrorism in Afghanistan noting, "The American flag flies again over our embassy in Kabul." He cautioned, however, that "our war on terror is well begun, but it is only begun." Those in his administration who had argued for an expanded and prolonged war on terrorism that would include a stance against states harboring and supporting terrorists had apparently prevailed, and regime change in Iraq was central to this agenda. "Iraq continues to flaunt its hostility toward America and to support terror," the president asserted. "The Iraqi regime has plotted to develop anthrax, and nerve gas, and nuclear weapons for over a decade.... States like these, and their terrorist allies, constitute an axis of evil, arming to threaten the peace of the world. By seeking weapons of mass destruction, these regimes pose a grave and growing danger.... I will not wait on events, while dangers gather. I will not stand by as peril draws closer and closer. The United States of America will not permit the world's most dangerous regimes to threaten us with the world's most destructive weapons."[6]

In the months following the president's speech, the prospect of a military attack on Iraq to oust Saddam grew, with the administration focusing increasingly on the threat posed by Saddam's weapons of mass destruction. In August 2002, Vice President Cheney spoke via secure telephone lines to a group of Iraqi dissidents opposing Saddam Hussein. Following that meeting, Cheney argued for an assertive military posture against Iraq. "The risk of inaction," he said, "(is) far greater than the risk of action. What we must not do in the face of a mortal threat is to give into wishful thinking or willful blindness."[7] The following month, Cheney told a CNN reporter that Saddam had worked on expanding his weapons of mass destruction programs since the end of the weapons inspections in 1998. "He's been free—and we know he has—to continue to improve his chemical weapons capability. We know he has worked to and has succeeded in improving his biological weapons capability. And we're confident he has also begun, once again, to acquire a nuclear weapon." Cheney continued by asserting, "We have to deal with the emerging threat. The question is how best to do it." He called for the support of the international community in the confrontation with Saddam Hussein, which he viewed through the lens of the September 11 attacks. "We have to be concerned now," Cheney noted, "about the possibility that we're vulnerable to an attack the likes of which we did not experience prior to last September 11—with a far more deadly weapon. We have to worry about the possible marriage, if you will, of a rogue state like Saddam Hussein's Iraq with a terrorist organization like al Qaeda."[8]

To mark the first anniversary of the September 11 attacks, President Bush delivered a speech to the United Nations General Assembly in New York. Again, a connection was made between those terrorist attacks and Iraq. "In the attacks on America a year ago, we saw the destructive intentions of our enemies," he said. "This threat hides within many nations, including my own. In cells and camps, terrorists are plotting further destruction, and building new bases for their war against civilization. And our greatest fear is that terrorists will find a shortcut to their mad ambitions when an outlaw regime supplies them with the technologies to kill on a massive scale. In one place—in one regime—we find all these dangers, in their most lethal and aggressive forms. . . ." This place, in President Bush's view, was Saddam Hussein's Iraq. "The history, the logic, and the facts lead to one conclusion: Saddam Hussein's regime is a grave and gathering danger."[9]

Two days later, President Bush gave a radio address focused primarily on the threat posed by Iraq. "Today this regime is likely to maintain stockpiles of chemical and biological agents, and is improving and expanding facilities capable of producing chemical and biological weapons," Bush said. "Today Saddam Hussein has the scientists and the infrastructure for a nuclear weapons program, and has illicitly sought to purchase the equipment needed to enrich uranium for a nuclear weapon."[10] Later in September, President Bush spoke to reporters from Houston, Texas. He continued to argue that Saddam Hussein posed a national security threat to the United States, recalling the assassination attempt on his father in 1993 that had been linked to the Iraqi regime. "After all," the President said, "this is the guy who tried to kill my dad."[11]

Throughout the fall of 2002, President Bush and top officials of his administration continued to contend that Saddam Hussein's regime was linked to terrorist groups, possessed weapons of mass destruction, and posed a grave and growing danger to the United States. Increasingly, their statements underlined the urgency of taking immediate military action to prevent potentially lethal attacks on the United States. Vice President Dick Cheney appeared on "Meet the Press," where he accused Saddam of working to develop nuclear weapons and to stockpile chemical and biological arms. "Increasingly, we believe that the United States may well become the target of those activities," Cheney said. "And what we've seen recently [that] has raised our level of concern to the current state of unrest ... is that he now is trying, through his illicit procurement network, to acquire the equipment he needs to be able to enrich uranium—specifically aluminum tubes." Cheney concluded, "We're at the point where we think time is not on our side." When asked about the evidence the administration had to support these assertions, National Security Advisor Condoleezza Rice told CNN, "there will always be some uncertainty.... We don't want the smoking gun to be a mushroom cloud."[12] The administration was in effect arguing that the threat posed by Saddam was so grave that taking time to thoroughly assess the realities of that threat was too dangerous a prospect.

DEBATING A WAR ON SADDAM

Beyond the circle of administration officials that continued their efforts to focus attention on Saddam's alleged threatening weapons programs, there was little unanimity about the best way to deal with the situation at hand. The options were to use the UN's diplomatic capacities to curb a possible threat and allow UN inspections to ferret out any possible weapons of mass destruction that Saddam was storing and producing, to build a large international coalition like the one that defeated Iraq in the Gulf War of 1991 in preparation for a military attack, or to launch a preemptive war against Iraq in the near future.

Top officials in the U.S. administration were not of one mind on the best possible option to pursue. Donald Rumsfeld, Dick Cheney, and Condoleezza Rice advocated a war to root out Saddam's weapons program, which they were convinced posed an imminent threat to the United States. In December 2002, Paul Wolfowitz gave a speech in which he stated, "Disarming Iraq's arsenal of terror is a crucial part of winning the war on terror." Richard Perle, the chairman of the Defense Policy Board based in the Pentagon, supported a war, noting that Saddam also posed a threat to Israel, an important ally of the United States. Colin Powell, the secretary of state, who had been one of the military officials directing the Gulf War of 1991, long advocated working through the UN and allowing inspectors time to find possible weapons systems. As fall turned to winter, however, Powell's position seemed to grow closer towards a support for a war.[13]

Several former government officials who had served under the first President Bush and had led the United States' war efforts against Saddam in 1991, expressed serious reservations about going to war against Iraq at this juncture. Brent Scowcroft, who served as the national security advisor, spoke out in the press in support of a strong diplomatic initiative focused on the UN and suggested Saddam was not targeting the United States. "There is scant evidence to tie Saddam to terrorist organizations, and even less to the Sept. 11 attacks," he wrote in an editorial in *The Wall Street Journal*. "Indeed Saddam's goals have little in common with the terrorists who threaten us, and there is little incentive for him to make common cause with them."[14] Lawrence Eagleburger, who was secretary of state under the first President Bush, said that in case of a war that ousted Saddam, the United States would have to stay invested in Iraq for an extensive period. "If we get him out of office," he predicted, "we'll probably have to stay there in Iraq for some period of time."[15]

Retired Ambassador Edward Peck, who had served as chief of the U.S. Interests Section in Baghdad from 1977 until 1980, wrote that the cornerstone of U.S. policy towards Iraq since its invasion of Kuwait had been to get rid of Saddam. "The basic errors in this approach are that overthrowing Saddam does not accord with our principles, particularly if it involves hundreds of thousands of lives, and that success would not necessarily be in our interests. No one has given the United States the right to determine who rules Iraq."[16] Warren Christopher, who had served as secretary of state from 1993 until 1997, wrote in an editorial in *The New York Times*, "Unless the president has been provided intelligence about Iraq's capacities that he has not shared or even hinted at in his public statements, the threats from North Korea and from international terrorism are more imminent than those posed by Iraq. No doubt the world would be better off without Saddam Hussein reigning in Iraq, but we must recognize that the effort of removing him right now may well distract us from dealing with graver threats."[17]

Two leading journalists who had covered Saddam Hussein for decades, since his years as an aide to President Bakr, offered very different opinions on the Bush administration's approach. Jim Hoagland of *The Washington Post* wrote, "Saddam Hussein has for 11 years periodically sent out his aides to promise disarmament while he has consistently shown the Iraqi public in deed that his weapons of mass destruction will have to be pried from his cold, dead fingers. He seems to have finally encountered an American president willing to take him at his deed."[18] Meanwhile, in the French newspaper *Le Monde Diplomatique*, Eric Rouleau wrote of the concerted efforts of the Bush administration to affect public opinion. "But the high doses of misinformation seems not to have produced the desired effect," Rouleau observed. "Against all expectations, the war plan has spawned many questions and much opposition—more than any before. Never have the European countries (pubic opinion, as well as most governments) expressed such reservations about their American ally. Never have the Arab states been as united (at least publicly) in condemning an initiative which is, after all, aimed at getting rid of a man most of them fear or despise."[19]

Scholars who had devoted years to studying the Middle East in general and Iraq in particular were not a particularly strong voice in the public debate on how to deal with Saddam in the months before the war. On campuses across the United States, however, debate was heated; students and professors alike organized teach-ins, film series, symposia, and demonstrations. A handful of scholars and analysts did voice their views in more public forums, attempting to impart their knowledge to the administration and the public at this critical juncture. Kenneth M. Pollack, who left his position at the National Security Council with the change in administration to become the director of research at the Saban Center for Middle East Policy at the Brookings Institution, published a highly influential book entitled *The Threatening Storm: The Case for Invading Iraq* in 2002. Pollock became a frequent commentator on Iraq in the American media. In his book, Pollock argued, "Unfortunately, the only prudent and realistic course of action left to the United States is to mount a full-scale invasion of Iraq to smash the Iraqi armed forces, depose Saddam's regime, and rid the country of weapons of mass destruction." Considering other policy options available to the U.S. administration, Pollock concluded, "It is the regime change approach that is most likely to win the ready support of those among the Iraqi armed forces and populace who are looking to overthrow Saddam."[20]

Edward Said, a professor at Columbia University, wrote an essay for the *London Review of Books* that was published days after his death on September 25, 2002. A leading public intellectual, Said had become an important interlocutor between the United States and the Arab world. In his essay, Said discounted claims that an Iraq weakened by decades of war and sanctions could be a threat to U.S. freedom and security. Said continued, "I am not even going to bother to add my condemnations of Saddam Hussein: I shall take for granted that he deserves to be ousted and punished. Worst of all, he is a threat to his own people." But Said underlined the potential dangers of a policy of regime change through military intervention; he pointed out that alleged connections between a secular Iraq and the "insanely theocratic al-Qaeda" were baseless. In Said's view, the outcome of the war was too unclear, undefined, and potentially dangerous.[21] This view was supported by Toby Dodge, a British political scientist who had closely studied Iraq for a decade. "The removal of Saddam Hussein, if possible," Dodge cautioned, "could cause greater regional instability than his continued rule."[22]

Some politicians from the Democratic and Republican Parties also spoke up against a war that would be launched quickly and without international support. Charles Rangel, a Democratic congressman from New York, said, "As a combat veteran of the Korean conflict, I have no use for dictators. Saddam Hussein—whatever threat he poses—should be dealt with firmly, under the banner of the United Nations and with the full cooperation of our allies. The United States should not insist on going it alone."[23] Democratic Senator Robert Byrd of Virginia was also a strong voice against the Bush administration's push towards war. At a hearing of the Senate Armed Services Committee in September 2002, he asked Defense Secretary Rumsfeld about an article in *Newsweek*. Senator Byrd quoted the article's discussion of U.S. policy towards Saddam, "America helped make a monster. What to do with him—and what happens after he is gone—has haunted us for a quarter century." He also noted that a former head of the Center for Disease Control had written a letter in 1995 to a senator pointing out that "the U.S. Government provided nearly two dozen viral and bacterial samples to Iraqi scientists in 1985—samples that included the plague, botulism, and anthrax, among other deadly diseases." Senator Byrd asserted, "The American people need to know whether the United States is in large part responsible for the very Iraqi weapons of mass destruction which the administration now seeks to destroy. We may very well have created the monster that we seek to eliminate. The Senate deserves to know the whole story. The American people deserve to know the whole story."[24]

In October 2002, the U.S. Congress passed an Iraq war resolution. The Senate voted 77 to 23 in favor, while the House voted 296 to 133 in favor. The resolution required that the president notify congress before or within 48 hours of the start of military action that all diplomatic efforts to enforce UN resolutions had failed. President Bush said, "The Congress has spoken clearly to the international community and the United Nations Security Council. Saddam Hussein and his outlaw regime pose a grave threat to the region, the world, and the United States. Inaction is not an option, disarmament is a must." Though the vote was largely supportive, debate on the resolution was at times contentious, with some lawmakers arguing that the resolution's language was too broad and its passage too soon.[25] Even some who voted for the resolution spoke out against the war. Senator Chuck Hagel, a Republican who had served in Vietnam, frequently spoke out against the Bush policy. In December, following a trip to the Middle East, Hagel spoke before the Council of Foreign Relations, noting, "We are pushing our friends and allies in these regions into a box, with no good alternatives, by pressing for a call to arms in the absence of an imminent and urgent threat to our security. This is the reality of our situation. In the Middle East and elsewhere, no one questions our power, but many question our purpose. We cannot be viewed by the world as in a rush to wage war."[26]

As President Bush's calls for military action intensified, some diplomatic initiatives were undertaken. On November 8, the UN Security Council passed Resolution 1441 with the aim of disarming Iraq of any possible weapons of mass destruction. If Saddam refused to do so, he would face serious consequences. By the end of November, UN weapons inspectors returned to Iraq for the first time in four years. The Swedish diplomat Hans Blix, who led the weapons inspections, would call them the most far-ranging and effective inspections of Iraq to date.

Although the UN Security Council called on Saddam to disarm, debates about how to best achieve that goal polarized the international community. Prime Minister Tony Blair of England proved to be President Bush's strongest ally in support of a war against Saddam. Blair argued that Saddam had to be disarmed. "Unless the world takes a stand on this issue of WMD [weapons of mass destruction]," he argued, "we will rue the consequences of our weakness." The British Foreign Secretary Jack Straw elaborated on England's position, clearly stating that the removal of Iraq's WMDs was the main purpose of the war: "Our primary objective is to rid Iraq of its weapons of mass destruction and their associated programmes and means of delivery, including prohibited ballistic missiles, as set out in UNSCRs [United Nations Security Council Resolutions]. This would reduce Iraq's ability to threaten its neighbours and the region, and prevent Iraq from using WMD against its own people."[27]

The leaders of Spain and Italy also joined this alliance, which called for the use of military force to disarm Saddam. On the other hand, the leaders of Germany, France, Russia, and China favored disarming Saddam using peaceful means, working through the auspices of the UN. In the months leading up to the war, they continually called for supporting the inspections process being coordinated by the International Atomic Energy Authority (IAEA) and the UN.

"I WILL ALWAYS LOVE YOU"

While the Bush administration continued to make its case for war against Iraq, and pundits, politicians, and scholars debated the merits of that position, Saddam Hussein was busy campaigning. On October 15, 2002, his government held elections, and Iraqis headed to the polls. Iraqis could vote yes or no to another seven-year term for Saddam as Iraq's president. No other candidate ran for the office. Saddam's campaign theme was Whitney Houston's ballad, "I Will Always Love You," which played repeatedly on Iraqi television and radio. His motto was "Everyone loves Saddam," and his campaign posters featured heart designs. Polling stations served tea and sweets. Voters were regaled by Iraqi children singing patriotic songs. According to Izzat Ibrahim al-Duri, the vice chairman of Iraq's Revolutionary Command Council, all 11,445,638 eligible Iraqi voters cast a yes vote for Saddam. In the previous election, Saddam had secured 99.96 percent of the vote; this time, he had managed a clean 100 percent. The White House spokesperson scoffed, "Not a very serious day, not a very serious vote and nobody places credibility on it."[28]

Having secured another term as Iraq's president, Saddam took steps towards preventing a military invasion of Iraq led by U.S. forces. In November, he had allowed weapons inspectors to return to Iraq. In December, Saddam delivered a declaration to the United Nations denying that Iraq had any weapons of mass destruction. The United Nations said the information he presented was incomplete, while the United States called it untrue. In January 2003, Hans Blix, the Swedish diplomat who served as the chief UN weapons inspector, observed, "We have now been there for some two months and been covering the country in ever wider sweeps and we haven't found any smoking guns."[29] In the midst of holding high-level meetings with Iraqi officials in Baghdad, Blix told reporters, "We do not think that war is inevitable. We think that the inspections process that we are conducting is the peaceful alternative." At the same time, Mohammed el-Baradei, head of the International Atomic Energy Authority, was meeting with Saddam's top scientific advisors. "We are having constructive meetings," al-Baradei said.[30]

In order to mobilize the Iraqi people, Saddam gave numerous speeches. On January 6, the anniversary of the establishment of the Iraqi army, Saddam gave a defiant speech that was broadcast on Iraqi television. He urged the Iraqi people to resistance, noting "If anyone attempts to intimidate you, the people of Iraq, repel him and tell him he is a small midget while we belong to a nation of glorious Faith, a great nation and an ancient people...." In case of a war, Saddam ensured the Iraqi people of a victory: "Our chests are filled with the great conviction in our victory, whose fruit will be in our hands and whose banners will be all over our heads as a great people in a glorious nation, God willing. Shame, and more shame, with defeat will go to your opponent."[31]

Later that same month, Saddam spoke on the anniversary of the start of the Gulf War of 1991, which he called "the Grand Confrontation" during which the Iraqi army "defeated all evil troops of more than thirty states." Saddam's rambling and convoluted speech was woven throughout with references to Iraq's ancient civilization and to Islam. He likened the current forces that were being mounted against his regime to those of the Mongol armies of Hulegu who attacked Baghdad in 1258. He called on Iraqis to muster their strength to defeat "the Mongols of this age." He also tied the military threats against his regime to the Israeli-Palestinian conflict. "The entire nation will rise up in defence of its right to life, of its role and of anything it holds sacred," Saddam asserted. "Long Live Iraq with its brave jihadist army.... Glory and heaven be for the martyrs of Iraq, Palestine, and the nation.... Allah is greatest."[32]

Despite Saddam's defiance, pressures for him to surrender power mounted. In early January, the U.S. and British military began deploying troops to the Middle East. In an attempt at mediation, Saudi officials offered to secure amnesty for Saddam and other top Iraqi officials if they agreed to leave Iraq. "If to avoid a war," Donald Rumsfeld told reporters during a televised interview, "I would recommend that some provision be made so that the senior leadership of that country and their families be provided haven in some other country."[33] Such an option apparently had no appeal to Saddam.

In late February, Saddam granted an exclusive interview to the American journalist Dan Rather, who traveled to Baghdad, where he spoke with the Iraqi leader for an hour. In the interview, which had high ratings when it aired on CBS, Saddam said that Iraq had accepted UN resolution 1441 because "Iraq was empty, was void of any such weapons...." Saddam expressed a desire to prevent the war from happening. "Nobody can sort of take Iraq apart," he said. "That is not the fair will of Allah, and it's not fair to the people of Iraq who are facing the difficulties in resolve and through serious work and through creativity." Reminding the viewers that Iraq was the cradle of civilization, Saddam asserted that its long history would allow it to withstand and survive a military threat, even one from "a huge power."

When asked about 1991, Saddam pointed out Iraq had never taken aggressive action against the United States itself. Once again, he argued that Iraq was not defeated in that war. Iraq made the decision to withdraw from Kuwait, he explained, and "the Iraq Army was not defeated." Saddam disputed the notion that Iraq posed a threat to the United States, asking "What did Iraq threaten the United States with? Iraq has not committed any aggressive [action] against the United States.... Neither an official nor anybody in Iraq says that the United States is our enemy or that we must fight the United States."[34]

Offered the opportunity to speak directly to the American people, Saddam said that he wished that the Iraqi people and the American people could "live in peace." He then challenged President Bush to a debate that would be shown on satellite television. "This is something proposed in earnest," Saddam said. "This is proposed out of my respect for the public opinion of the United States."[35] President Bush had no intention of participating in such a debate; instead his administration continued to mount a public defense of their call for military action against Saddam's regime.

SADDAM'S IRAQ: THE NEXUS OF POISON AND TERROR?

UNSC Resolution 1441 had called on the weapons inspectors to update the Security Council on their progress within 60 days. On January 27, Hans Blix noted "access has been provided to all sites we have wanted to inspect and with one exception it has been prompt.... Our inspections have included universities, military bases, presidential sites and private residences." Blix did object to allegations by Iraqi officials that the inspectors were tied to intelligence collecting. His staff now included some 250 members from 60 countries. Together, they had "conducted about 300 inspections to more than 230 sites." Blix called for greater cooperation by Saddam's regime regarding finding relevant items, activities, and documents and with permitting private interviews with personnel involved in Iraq's weapons programs.[36]

On the same day that Blix updated the UN, U.S. Secretary of State Colin Powell spoke to the World Economic Forum in Washington, D.C. Powell contended that Saddam Hussein had links with al-Qaeda. For a long time, Powell had been an advocate for diplomacy within the administration. If a war was to be undertaken, Powell felt, it should be after exhausting other options and with the support of the UN and an international coalition. In February 2003, Powell appeared before the UN Security Council and in a closely watched presentation argued the United States' case against Iraq. Because of his well-known reservations against a hasty and largely unilateral war and because of his personal credibility, Powell's arguments carried much weight in the international community and in the United States domestic arena. Powell told the UN Security Council, "The facts on Iraq's behavior demonstrate that Saddam Hussein and his regime have made no effort—no effort—to disarm as required by the international community. Indeed, the facts and Iraq's behavior show that Saddam Hussein and his regime are concealing their efforts to produce more weapons of mass destruction."

Arguing that Saddam had failed to comply with UN resolutions calling for the eradication of its weapons of mass destruction, Powell further asserted the possibility of cooperation between Saddam and Osama Bin Laden. "They say Saddam Hussein's secular tyranny and al Qaeda's religious tyranny do not mix," Powell said. "I am not comforted by this thought. Ambition and hatred are enough to bring Iraq and al Qaeda together, enough so al Qaeda could learn how to build more sophisticated bombs and learn how to forge documents, and enough so that al Qaeda could turn to Iraq for help in acquiring expertise on weapons of mass destruction." For decades, Saddam had supported terrorism, Powell noted, "And this support continues. The nexus of poisons and terror is new. The nexus of terror and Iraq is old. The combination is lethal." Leaving Saddam in power with weapons of mass destruction was "not an option.... We must not shrink from whatever is ahead of us." In his presentation, Powell used tape recordings and satellite photographs as supportive evidence for his claims that the United States had "irrefutable and undeniable" proof that Saddam possessed weapons of mass destruction.[37]

The man many thought of as a bulwark against war was now making the case for President Bush's position—and doing so quite persuasively in a very public forum. Nevertheless, public opinion remained largely divided. On February 16, anti-war demonstrations were held in 300 cities in 60 countries. Millions of people took to the streets in Amsterdam, Athens, Barcelona, Berlin, Rome, Sydney, Mexico City, Istanbul, Bangkok, Hong Kong, Tokyo, and other international cities. In the United States, rallies were held in major cities such as New York and Chicago, but also in smaller towns like Gainesville, Georgia; Macomb, Illinois; and Juneau, Alaska. At the rally in New York, Archbishop Desmund Tutu of South Africa, a Nobel Peace Prize winner, said, "We are members of one family, God's family, the human family.... Any war, before you have exhausted all possible peaceful means, is immoral." Considered the largest ever demonstration in history, an estimated 7.5 million people participated in the worldwide protests. When asked about the impact of such a massive demonstration on the political decision-making process, President Bush replied, "Size of protest, it's like deciding, 'Well, I'm going to decide policy based up on a focus group,' The role of a leader is to decide policy based upon the security—in this case—security of the people."[38]

On March 2, Arab League members gathered in Sharm al-Sheikh in Egypt to discuss the Iraqi situation. They rejected any military aggression against Iraq. The Arab leaders called for the UN inspectors to be given more time to continue their work and pressed Saddam to cooperate more fully with the inspections. During the summit, the United Arab Emirates publicly called on Saddam Hussein to step down as the leader of Iraq.

On March 5, France, Russia, and Germany issued a joint declaration noting, "Our common objective remains the full and effective disarmament of Iraq, in compliance with resolution 1441. We consider that this objective can be achieved by the peaceful means of the inspections." They called on Iraq to cooperate with inspectors and to disarm fully. From their perspective, the best way to achieve peace in the Middle East was not to focus exclusively on Iraq but to work towards a comprehensive peace settlement involving the Arab-Israeli conflict as well. In the declaration, the three members of the UN Security Council stressed that they would not support a UN resolution authorizing a war. It was clear that if there was to be a war, it would not receive the support of the UN or a broad international coalition.[39]

A MOMENT OF TRUTH

U.S. President Bush, British Prime Minister Blair, and Spanish Prime Minister Jose Maria Aznar gathered in the Azores on March 16, 2003. They announced that March 17 was "a moment of truth for the world."

President Bush clearly set forth their case for war. "The dictator of Iraq and his weapons of mass destruction," he said, "are a threat to the security of free nations. He is a danger to his neighbors. He's a sponsor of terrorism. He's an obstacle to progress in the Middle East. For decades he has been the cruel, cruel oppressor of the Iraq people." Prime Minister Blair addressed those who continued to support action through the UN. Blair explained the situation as an impasse. "But the truth is that without a credible ultimatum authorizing force in the event of non-compliance," Blair argued, "then more discussion is just more delay, with Saddam remaining armed with weapons of mass destruction and continuing a brutal, murderous regime in Iraq."[40]

Protestors, foreign leaders, and UN officials continued to call for more time for the inspections process to continue looking for WMDs and to express strong opposition to a war that they did not consider the last viable option. When France, Germany, and Russia declared that they would block any UN resolution authorizing war, however, the Bush administration saw little incentive to continue pursuing diplomatic initiatives. War seemed imminent.

In President Bush's view, diplomacy favored Saddam. Speaking from the White House on March 17, he said, "The Iraqi regime has used diplomacy as a ploy to gain time and advantage." Once again, President Bush clearly stated his reasons for going to war: "Intelligence gathered by this and other governments leaves no doubt that the Iraq regime continues to possess and conceal some of the most lethal weapons ever devised.... The regime has a history of reckless aggression in the Middle East. It has a deep hatred of America and our friends. And it has aided, trained, and harbored terrorists, including operatives of al Qaeda." There was, according to the President, evidence that Saddam had weapons of mass destruction and that he had aided al-Qaeda. President Bush gave Saddam a deadline for leaving Iraq. "All the decades of deceit and cruelty have now reached an end," he said. "Saddam Hussein and his sons must leave Iraq within 48 hours. Their refusal to do so will result in military conflict, commenced at a time of our choosing." President Bush's deadline not only applied to Saddam, but in effect put an end to weapons inspections. He cautioned, "For their own safety, all foreign nationals—including journalists and inspectors—should leave Iraq immediately."[41]

UN weapons inspectors were forced to abandon their work and leave Iraq. Speaking to reporters, a clearly frustrated Blix said that he believed the inspections were progressing well and should not have been stopped. Saddam's regime had given "more cooperation on substance," Blix said. "They showered us with letters trying to explain this and that. But ...

when we analyse it, we find relatively little new material in it." The presence of U.S. forces in the region, better intelligence, and complete support from the UN Security Council had strengthened the inspections process, he said. Following leads given to them by U.S. intelligence, Blix's team found no evidence that Iraq possessed weapons of mass destruction. "I must regret," Blix said after three and a half months of intensive inspections, "we have not found the results in so many cases.... We certainly have not found any smoking guns."[42]

At 10 p.m. on the evening of March 19, 2003, President Bush addressed the nation from his desk in the Oval Office. "My fellow citizens," he said, "at this hour, American and coalition forces are in the early stages of military operations to disarm Iraq, free its people and to defend the world from grave danger. On my orders, coalition forces have begun striking selected targets of military importance to undermine Saddam Hussein's ability to wage war."[43]

On March 24, Saddam appeared on Iraqi television. "These forces have pushed into our land," he said, "and wherever they encroach they are trapped in our land, leaving the desert behind them, and find Iraqi citizens surrounding them and shooting at them.... Oh brave fighters, hit your enemy with all your strength.... Hit them so that good and its people may reign and evil evicted back to its place."[44] In the early days of the war, Iraq's Information Minister, Mohammed Saeed al-Sahaf, frequently appeared before the press, offering his unique spin on events. On April 1, he read a speech by Saddam. "Strike at them, fight them," Saddam urged the Iraqi people. "They are aggressors, evil, accursed by God, the exalted. You shall be victorious and they shall be vanquished."[45]

As coalition troops pressed into Iraqi territory, Saddam remained convinced that Baghdad would be impenetrable. After a heavy night of bombardment, on April 3 U.S. forces reached Saddam International Airport, some 10 miles from Baghdad. The following day, Saddam told Iraqis in a speech that the enemy "will not be able to storm Baghdad, because there are believers who are willing to sacrifice their lives for God and the nation, so every Iraqi family be assured and have no fear."[46] Amidst rumors that he may have been killed, Saddam was shown on Iraqi television greeting Iraqis along the streets of Baghdad.

On April 7, U.S. forces entered Baghdad. "Battling through sometimes fierce Iraqi resistance, heavily armed U.S. troops pushed into the heart of Baghdad with tanks and armored personnel carriers today and seized two of President Saddam Hussein's opulent palaces along the Tigris River," Anthony Shadid of *The Washington Post* reported.[47] Television reports showed American marines relaxing in Saddam's palace along the Tigris, which served as a headquarters for U.S. forces. Other sites associated with Saddam Hussein's regime would soon be taken over by the occupying forces. Abu Ghraib, west of Baghdad, would serve as a prison for the coalition forces; the Martyr's Memorial honoring Iraqi soldiers killed in the Iran-Iraq War would become a U.S. military headquarters.[48] British soldiers had secured Basra, a major port city in the south of Iraq. On April 8, three journalists were killed by coalition forces. Fighter jets struck missiles at the headquarters of Al-Jazeera and Al-Arabiya networks. Shells also struck the Palestine Hotel, where many in the international media stayed while covering the war from Baghdad.

On April 9, Baghdad fell. "Swept aside by US troops who drove through the streets of Baghdad," Shadid reported, "President Saddam Hussein's government collapsed today, ending three decades of ruthless Baath Party rule that sought to make Iraq the champion of a modern Arab world but left a legacy of fear, poverty, and bitterness."[49] The fall of Baghdad was marked by a scene akin to street theater. A small crowd appeared in the square in front of the Palestine Hotel, which had come under fire just the day before. In full view of the cameras of the world press staying in the hotel, a group of Iraqi boys and men started to drag down a statue of Saddam. Soon a group of American soldiers riding a tank appeared. One soldier reached up and draped an American flag over the statue. The soldiers helped topple the statue, a moment that came to symbolize the fall of Saddam Hussein.

AFTER THE FALL

The war in Iraq continued, but Saddam Hussein's whereabouts remained a mystery. On April 18, Abu Dhabi television showed a man bearing a remarkable resemblance to Saddam dressed in military fatigues walking through the Azimiyah district of Baghdad. A tape recording of Saddam speaking was broadcast. Saddam defiantly assured Iraqis, "We are confident that victory at the end will be ours. . . ." Throughout the spring and summer, as coalition forces tried to find Saddam, he managed to remain well hidden. On July 4, the United States announced a $25 million reward for information leading to the capture of Saddam. Countering rumors of his death, Saddam periodically released audio- and videotaped messages that were broadcast on Arab and international news networks. Intelligence sources authenticated these tapes. From hiding, Saddam called on Iraqis to fight the coalition forces, criticized the newly formed Iraqi governing council, and insisted that "the war is not finished."[50]

At the end of July, two of Saddam's daughters, Raghad and Rana, were given asylum in Jordan. His whereabouts still unknown, Saddam mourned the death of his two sons, Uday and Qusay. They were killed in a gun battle in a villa in Mosul, a town in Iraqi Kurdistan. In a taped message, Saddam said his sons were martyrs, but added "If Saddam Hussein had 100 sons, he would have offered them on the same path which is the path of jihad."[51] Pictures of the men's bullet-ridden bodies were released to prove that they were indeed dead. On August 2, they were buried in a small cemetery near Al-Awja, the village where Saddam Hussein was born. Gusts of dusty wind enveloped some 150 tribesmen and relatives gathered at the cemetery, as they watched the two coffins draped in the Iraqi flag buried. A large force of American troops guarded against possible protests from a close distance.[52]

Though Saddam Hussein was no longer the ruler of Iraq and his Baath Party had been officially disbanded, the fate of Iraq remained unclear. As spring turned to summer, scenes of massive looting gave way to a fierce insurgency targeted against coalition forces and the Iraqi Governing Council. The coalition forces had issued a deck of 55 cards, identifying the top officials of Saddam's regime that they were hoping to capture. Saddam was the Ace of Spades. Leading Baathists were arrested and questioned, while the Iraq Survey Group (ISG) conducted an exhaustive search of Iraq to find the stores of illegal weapons that Saddam had allegedly concealed from UN inspectors.

Gradually, a picture began to emerge—of Saddam's last months in power and of the evidence used by President Bush to justify the war on Iraq. The U.S. Senate issued a report on prewar intelligence on Iraq, noting that warnings about Saddam's weapons of mass destruction and ties to Al Qaeda were unfounded. David Kay, who headed the ISG, announced that no weapons of mass destruction would be found in Iraq. Producing a 1,000-page report, the ISG concluded that Saddam had the intent to acquire weapons of mass destruction but did not have the actual weapons. Speaking at the Council of Foreign Relations in the fall of 2004, Donald Rumsfeld said there was "no strong evidence" that linked Saddam's Iraq to al-Qaeda.[53]

Apparently, Saddam had guarded the fact that he didn't have weapons of mass destruction as assiduously as he had once concealed his actual weapons. According to a top Iraqi officials, Saddam's ego and a fear of being perceived as weak prevented him from admitting that he had long been in compliance with UN resolutions to disarm. This reluctance was followed, according to Tariq Aziz who had been Saddam's deputy prime minister, by a series of miscalculations. "A few weeks before the attacks,"

Aziz said during his debriefing sessions after surrendering to American forces, "Saddam thought that the US would not use ground forces.... He was overconfident. He was clever, but his calculations were poor. It wasn't that he wasn't receiving the information. It was right there on television, but he didn't understand international relations." The former minister of defense said that they understood that the goal of the war was to end the regime, but Saddam remained convinced that Iraqis would take to the streets, fighting to prevent the fall of Baghdad. In the last few years of his reign, according to his top advisors, Saddam focused almost exclusively on keeping his regime in power by securing his dynasty. Increasingly, he listened to the advice of his son Qusay, who told Saddam "We are 10 times more powerful than in 1991." [54]

Ultimately, it would appear that the very things that helped Saddam achieve such control over Iraqis—his penchant for secrecy, his unwillingness to share real power, his confidence in his ability to rise above any obstacles—proved to be his downfall. The report issued by the ISG portrayed Saddam as Santiago, the main character in Ernest Hemingway's novel *The Old Man and the Sea*. Saddam had read the book years ago while he was in a Baghdad prison. The ISG report observed, "Saddam tended to characterize, in a very Hemingway-esque way, his life as a relentless struggle against overwhelming odds, but carried out with courage, perseverance and dignity. Much like Santiago, ultimately left with only the marlin's skeleton as the trophy of his success, to Saddam even a hollow victory was by his reckoning a real one."[55]

THE RED DAWN: THE CAPTURE OF SADDAM

On the evening of Saturday, December 12, 600 American soldiers from the Fourth Infantry Division from Fort Hood, Texas undertook Operation Red Dawn. The title came from the Hollywood film *The Red Dawn*, starring Patrick Swayze and Charlie Sheen, which portrayed a Soviet invasion of the United States. Close allies of Saddam who had been captured near Tikrit had given information on his probable whereabouts. For nearly nine months, Saddam had evaded Task Force 121, the elite unit charged with finding "high value targets," those individual most sought after by the American military. The soldiers participating in Operation Red Dawn converged on two sites dubbed Wolverine 1 and Wolverine 2. Unmanned drones and helicopters filmed the operation as it unfolded and was closely watched by top U.S. military and intelligence officials.

Saddam was found hiding in an old farmhouse near Al-Dawr, a village south of Tikrit. Standing outside the farmhouse, one could spot the flickering lights of Saddam's palace built along the river in his hometown. Saddam was found cowering in a spiderhole in the ground measuring eight by six feet. The hole was lit with a single light and had a fan to allow for air circulation. With him, Saddam had a pistol. He was wearing black pants, a white t-shirt, and a black shirt. In the small two room house, American soldiers found two AK-47s, $750,000 in cash, some clothes, and books. In the makeshift kitchen, they found piles of garbage and dirty dishes. For food, Saddam had some rotting fruit, Turkish Delight, Mars candy bars, and cans of Spam. There was no cell phone or any other kind of communications equipment in the house.

An Iraqi taxi, which Saddam used to travel between various hiding places, was parked outside. For months, Saddam had traveled between 20 to 30 safe houses in the vicinity of Tikrit. A network of family and clan protected him and helped him keep abreast of events. Before they were killed, Saddam would meet from time to time with his sons. Interestingly, Saddam's days in hiding echoed his earlier escape along the Tigris and into Syria in 1959, as depicted in the film and novel *The Long Days*.[56]

As Operation Red Dawn unfolded, neither Saddam nor the two guards who were watching over the farmhouse offered any resistance. The hundreds of heavily armed American soldiers did not fire a single shot as they captured Saddam. Unlike his sons, who in the Tikriti tradition confronted their captors with a fierce gun battle in which they lost their lives, Saddam gave himself up without a fight. Commentaries in the Arab press wrote of a sense of humiliation and bitterness that Saddam was captured without resisting and that the Iraqi people were not the ones that ultimately caught him. "The image that former president Saddam Hussein gave during his arrest by American occupation forces is a painful and shocking image," said the editor of a major Egyptian newspaper. "It's an image no Arab wished [from] the president of one of the most important Arab states. Many Arabs and Iraqis hoped that Iraqis themselves would end his reign." Many editorials echoed the sentiment that "History would have been different if the Americans had taken a body and not a prisoner." Despite widespread hatred for Saddam, his passivity in the face of capture was felt as a kind of betrayal by some. One Arab commentator wrote, "What we saw was the televised unveiling of a 30-year-old lie. A leader surrendered without fighting, the Arab street is stunned, and the Arab media appear to be in a state of shock."[57] When he was captured, Saddam appeared disheveled, dazed, and confused. As American soldiers pulled the Ace of Spades from his spiderhole, he said quietly, "I am Saddam Hussein. I'm the President of Iraq, and I want to negotiate."

NOTES

1. Greg Myre, "92 Israeli Plan to Kill Hussein is Reported," *The New York Times*, December 17, 2003.

2. "Gunning For Saddam," *Frontline* (2001, 60 mins), Public Broadcasting Service (PBS).

3. "An Open Letter to President Clinton: 'Remove Saddam from Power,'" January 26, 1998, reprinted in *The Iraq War Reader,* ed. Micah L. Sifry and Christopher Cerf (New York: Touchstone Books, 2003), pp. 199–201.

4. "Bush: We're Watching 'Evil' Saddam Carefully," Friday October 12, 2001, NewsMax.com.

5. "The Long Road to War," Interview with *Frontline* (2003, 120 mins), PBS.

6. The President's State of the Union Address, January 29, 2002, http://www.whitehouse.gov.

7. Tim Reid, "Attack on Saddam Cannot Wait, says Cheney," *The London Times*, August 27, 2002.

8. "Cheney: Saddam Working on Nuclear Weapons," September 10, 2002, http://www.cnn.com.

9. Remarks by the president in Address to the United Nations General Assembly, September 12, 2002, http://www.whitehouse.gov.

10. Radio address by the president to the nation, September 14, 2002, http://www.whitehouse.gov.

11. "Bush Calls Saddam 'the Guy Who Tried to Kill My Dad," September 27, 2002, http://www.cnn.com.

12. "Top Bush Officials Push Case against Saddam," September 8, 2002, http://www.cnn.com.

13. "Prominent Policymakers and Where They Stand," *San Francisco Chronicle*, March 20, 2003.

14. Brent Scowcroft, "Don't Attack Saddam," *The Wall Street Journal,* August 15, 2002. See also Brent Scowcroft, "An Effort to Match in the Middle East," *The Washington Post,* November 21, 2002.

15. Edward Epstein, "Pundits Already at War on Iraq," *San Francisco Chronicle*, September 3, 2002.

16. Edward Peck, "Doing It All Wrong in the Middle East: Iraq," *Mediterranean Quarterly,* 2001: 13–26.

17. Warren Christopher, "Iraq Belongs on the Back Burner," *The New York Times*, December 31, 2002.

18. Jim Hoagland, "Brinksmanship in Baghdad," *The Washington Post,* September 20, 2002.

19. Eric Rouleau, "Countdown to War," *Le Monde diplomatique*, February 2003.

20. Kenneth M. Pollock, *The Threatening Storm: The Case for Invading Iraq* (New York: Random House, 2002), pp. 335, 337.

21. Edward Said, "'We' Know Who 'We' Are," *London Review of Books*, October 17, 2002.

22. Toby Dodge, "Iraq and the Bush Doctrine," *The Guardian*, March 24, 2002.

23. Charles B. Rangel, "Iraq War: Tough Talk on the Golf Course Won't Do," *New York Amsterdam News*, September 12, 2002.

24. Senator Robert Byrd, "How Saddam Happened," Congressional Record: September 20, 2002 (Senate), Page S8987-S8998, Federation of American Scientists Web site, http://www.fas.org/irp/congress/2002_cr/s092002.html.

25. "Senate Approves Iraq War Resolution," October 11, 2002, http://www.cnn.com.

26. Quoted in R.C. Longworth, "The Ball is Rolling toward Iraq War," *Chicago Tribune*, December 22, 2002.

27. Blair and Straw quotes in "Blair Underlines Support for Bush," *The Guardian*, January 7, 2003.

28. "Saddam Wins 100% of Vote," *BBC News World Edition*, October 16, 2002, http://www.bbc.co.uk; "Iraq Election," *All Things Considered*, National Public Radio (NPR), October 15, 2002.

29. Quoted in "Iraq Chronology: 2003," *Four Corners*, Australian Broadcasting Corporation, http://www.abc.net.au.

30. Richard Norton-Taylor and Helena Smith, "US Offers Immunity to Saddam," *The Guardian*, January 20, 2003.

31. Translation from "Full Text: Saddam Hussein's Speech," *The Guardian*, January 6, 2003.

32. Translation from "Full Text: Saddam Hussein's Speech," *The Guardian*, January 17, 2003.

33. Norton-Taylor and Smith, "US Offers Immunity to Saddam."

34. "Transcript: Saddam Hussein Interview," February 26, 2003, http://www.cbsnews.com.

35. Ibid.

36. Hans Blix, "Security Council, 27 January, 2003: An Update on Inspection," http://www.un.org/Depts/unmovic/Bx27.htm.

37. Transcript of Powell's UN Presentation, February 6, 2003, http://www.cnn.com.

38. "Cities Jammed in Worldwide Protest of War in Iraq," February 16, 2003, http://www.cnn.com; "President Bush Not Swayed by Anti-War Protests," February 18, 2003, PBS, *Online News Hour*, http://www.pbs.org.

39. "Full Text of the Joint Declaration," *The Guardian*, March 6, 2003.

40. "Full Text: Azores Press Conference," *The Guardian*, March 17, 2003.

41. Remarks by the president in address to the nation, March 17, 2003, http://www.whitehouse.gov.

42. Elizabeh Neuffer, "Blix Doubts Iraq Will Use Bioweapons," *Boston Globe*, March 19, 2003; Gary Younge and Oliver Burkeman, "War in the Gulf: Blix Says He Wanted More Time for Inspections," *The Guardian*, March 20, 2003.

43. "President Bush Addresses the Nation," March 19, 2003, http://www.whitehouse.gov.

44. Extracts from the speech, "The Enemy is Trapped in the Sacred Land of Iraq," *The Guardian*, March 24, 2003.

45. Text of speech, "Strike at Them, Fight Them," *The Guardian*, April 1, 2003.

46. Excerpts of speech, *The Guardian*, April 4, 2003.

47. Shadid, who would win a Pulitzer Prize for his reporting of the war in Iraq, was the only American print journalist reporting from Baghdad who spoke Arabic. Anthony Shadid and Rajiv Chandrasekaran, "US Forces Seize 2 Hussein Palaces as Armor Reaches Heart of Baghdad," *The Washington Post*, April 8, 2003.

48. See Sinan Antoon, "Monumental Disrespect," *Middle East Report* (Fall 2003).

49. Anthony Shadid, "Hussein's Baghdad Falls," *The Washington Post*, April 10, 2003.

50. "US: Bodies Identified as Uday and Qusay," *The Guardian*, July 23, 2003.

51. Quoted in Jamie Wilson and Jonathan Steele, "Saddam Praises Dead Sons As US 'Closes In' on Former Iraqi Dictator," *The Guardian*, July 30, 2003.

52. Jamie Wilson, "Tribe Gathers to Bury Saddam's Sons," *The Observer*, August 3, 2003.

53. John H. Cushman, Jr., ""Panel Describes Long Weakening of Hussein Army," *The New York Times*, July 11, 2004; "Rumsfeld's Missing Link," *The Guardian*, October 6, 2004; "Analysis: Iraq Survey Group Draft Report Concludes Saddam Hussein Had the Intent of Reviving Weapons Programs, but Had No Stockpiles," *All Things Considered*, NPR, September 17, 2004; Mark Oliver, "Iraq had no WMD—Inspectors," *The Guardian*, October 6, 2004.

54. Peter Beaumont, "Facing Defeat, Saddam Clung to His Fantasies," *The Observer*, October 10, 2004.

55. Quoted in Beaumont, "Facing Defeat, Saddam Clung to His Fantasies."

56. John F. Burns and Eric Schmitt, "As a Fugitive, Hussein Stayed Close to Home," *The New York Times*, December 21, 2003.

57. Editorials from *Al-Ahram*, *Al-Hayat*, and *Asharq al-Awsat* newspapers quoted in "Newspapers Mirror Arab Humiliation at Saddam's Capture," December 15, 2003, http://www.aljazeerah.info and Samia Nakhoul, "Surrender Widely Seen As a Total Humiliation," *The Washington Post*, December 16, 2003.

BIBLIOGRAPHY

BOOKS AND SCHOLARLY ARTICLES

Aburish, Said K. *Saddam Hussein: The Politics of Revenge*. London: Bloomsbury, 2000.

Aflaq, Michel. "Baathism." In *The Saddam Hussein Reader*, ed. Turi Munthe. New York: Thunder's Mouth Press, 2002.

Ajami, Fouad. "The Arab Road." *Foreign Policy* (Summer 1982): 3–25.

———. "The End of Pan-Arabism." *Foreign Affairs* (Winter 1978/79): 355–73.

Alnasrawi, Abbas. *Iraq's Burdens: Oil, Sanctions and Underdevelopment*. Westport, Conn.: Greenwood Press, 2002.

Antoon, Sinan. "Monumental Disrespect." *Middle East Report* (Fall 2003).

Attiyah, Ghassan. *Iraq: 1908–1921: A Socio-Political Study*. Beirut: The Arab Institute for Research and Publishing, 1973.

Baram, Amatzia. *Culture, History and Ideology in the Formation of Ba'thist Iraq, 1968–89*. New York: St. Martin's Press, 1991.

———. "The Ruling Political Elite in Bathi Iraq, 1968–1986: The Changing Features of a Collective Profile." *International Journal of Middle East Studies* (November 1989): 447–93.

Batatu, Hanna. "Iraq's Underground Shi'i Movements," *Middle East Reports* (January 1982): 3–9.

———. *The Old Social Classes and the Revolutionary Movements of Iraq*. Princeton, N.J.: Princeton University Press, 1978.

Bell, Gertrude, ed. *The Letters of Gertrude Bell*. Vol. 2. New York: Boni and Liveright, 1927.

Bennis, Phyllis. "U.S.-Iraq Conflict." *Foreign Policy in Focus* (November 1997). http://www.fpif.org.

Chubin, Shahram, and Charles Tripp. *Iran and Iraq at War*. Boulder, Colo:: Westview Press, 1988.

Cockburn, Andrew, and Patrick Cockburn. *Saddam Hussein: An American Obsession*. London: Verso, 2002.

Cordesman, Anthony H., and Ahmed S. Hashin. *Iraq: Sanctions and Beyond*. Boulder, Colo:: Westview Press, 1997.

Coughlin, Con. *Saddam: King of Terror*. New York: Ecco, 2002.

Dann, Uriel. *Iraq under Qassem: A Political History, 1958–1963*. Jerusalem: Israel Universities Press, 1969.

Darwish, Adel. "Saddam Hussein: The Godfather of Baghdad." http://www.mid-eastnews.com/iraq003.html (retrieved May 9, 2004).

Davidson, Nigel. "The Termination of the Iraq Mandate." *International Affairs* (January 1933): 60–78.

Dawisha, Adeed I. "Iraq: The West's Opportunity." *Foreign Policy* (Winter 1980–81): 134–53.

Dodge, Toby. *Inventing Iraq: The Failure of Nation Building and a History Denied*. New York: Columbia University Press, 2003.

Elwell-Sutton, A. S. "The Tigris Above Baghdad." *Geographical Journal* 60, no. 1 (July 1922): 20–40.

Farouk-Sluglett, Marion, and Peter Sluglett. *Iraq Since 1958: From Revolution to Dictatorship,* revised edition. London: I. B. Tauris, 2001.

———. "The Historiography of Modern Iraq." *The American Historical Review* (December 1991): 1408–21.

Fromkin, David. *A Peace to End All Peace*. New York: Henry Holt and Company, 1989.

Galvani, John. "The Baathi Revolution in Iraq." *Middle East Report* (September–October 1972).

Graham-Brown, Sarah. *Sanctioning Saddam: The Politics of Intervention in Iraq*. London: I. B. Tauris, 1999.

Haas, Ernst B. "The Reconciliation of Conflicting Colonial Policy Aims: Acceptance of the League of Nations Mandate System." *International Organization* 6, no. 4 (November 1952): 521–36.

Halliday, Denis J. "The Impact of the UN Sanctions on the People of Iraq." *Journal of Palestine Studies* (Winter 1999): 29–37.

Helms, Christine Moss. *Iraq: Eastern Flank of the Arab World*. Washington, D.C.: The Brookings Institution, 1984.

Henderson, Simon. *Instant Empire: Saddam Hussein's Ambition for Iraq*. San Francisco: Mercury House, 1991.

Hiro, Dilip. *The Longest War: The Iran-Iraq Military Conflict*. London: Grafton Books, 1989.

Hoover Institution, biography of George Shultz. http://www-hoover.stanford. edu/bios/shultz.html (retrieved December 12, 2004).

Hussein, Saddam. *Nidaluna wa Al-Siyasah Al-Dawaliyyah* [Our Struggle and Foreign Policy]. Beirut: Dar al-Tali` ah lil-Tiba` ah wa al-Nashr, 1978.

———. *One Common Trench? Or Two Opposite Ones*. Baghdad; Arab Baath Socialist Party, 1977.

———. "Reservations about Rabat." *Journal of Palestine Studies* (Winter 1975): 141–42.

———. *Revolution and National Education*, trans. N. A. Mudhaffer. Baghdad: Dar al-Ma'mun for Translation and Publishing, 1981.

———. *The Revolution and the Young*, trans. K. Kishtainy. Baghdad: Translation and Foreign Language House, 1981.

———. *The Revolution and Woman in Iraq*, trans. K. Kishtainy. Baghdad: Translation and Foreign Language House, 1981.

———. *Saddam Hussein on Current Events in Iraq*, trans. K. Kishtainy. London: Longmann, 1977.

———. *Social and Foreign Affairs in Iraq*, trans. K. Kishtany. London: Croom Helm, 1979.

———. *Al-thawrah wa al-tarbiyah al-wataniyyah* [The Revolution and National Education]. Baghdad: Maktab Al-Wataniyyah, 1977.

———. (Anonymous), *Zabibah wa-al-malik*. al-Jizah : Dar 'Ashtar, 2002. English translation: Saddam Hussein, *Zabiba and the King*, ed. Robert Lawrence. College Station, Tex.: Virtualbookworm.com Publishing, 2004.

"The Impact of Sanctions on Iraq." *Middle East Reports* (Spring 1998). http:// www.merip.org.

"Iraq Coup Attempt," *Middle East Reports* (August 1973): 15–16.

Iskander, Amir. *Saddam Hussein: The Fighter, the Thinker, and the Man*, trans. Hassan Selim. Paris: Hachette Réalités, 1980.

Jabar, Faleh A. "Assessing the Iraqi Opposition." *Middle East Report Online* (March 23, 2001). http://www.merip.org.

Karsh, Efraim, and Inari Rautsi. *Saddam Hussein: A Political Biography*, 2nd revised edition. New York: Grove Press, 2002.

Kedourie, Elie. *The Chatham House Version and Other Middle-Eastern Studies*. New York: Praeger Publishers, 1970.

Khadduri, Majid. *Socialist Iraq: A Study in Iraqi Politics Since 1968*. Washington, D.C.: The Middle East Institute, 1978.

Klieman, Aaron S. *Foundations of British Policy in the Arab World: The Cairo Conference of 1921*. Baltimore, Md.: Johns Hopkins Press, 1970.

Lang, Tony. "Moral Dilemmas of U.S. Policy Toward Iraq." Carnegie Council on Ethics and International Affairs, February 2001. http://www.carnegiecouncil.org.

Long, Jerry M. *Saddam's War of Words: Politics, Religion, and the Iraqi Invasion of Kuwait.* Austin: University of Texas Press, 2004.

Makiya, Kanan. *The Monument: Art and Vulgarity in Saddam Hussein's Iraq.* London, I. B. Tauris: 2004; originally published 1991.

———. *Republic of Fear: The Politics of Modern Iraq,* updated edition. Berkeley: University of California Press, 1998.

Marr, Phebe. *The Modern History of Iraq.* Boulder, Colo.: Westview Press, 1985.

McBride, Edward. "Monuments to Self: Baghdad's Grand Projects in the Age of Saddam Hussein." *Metropolis* (June 1999). http://www.metropolismag.com.

McDowall, David. *A Modern History of the Kurds,* revised edition. London: I. B. Tauris, 1997.

Mu'allah, 'Abd al-Amir. *The Long Days,* trans. Mohieddin Ismail. London: Ithaca Press, 1979.

———. *Nahr Yashuqqu Majrah* [A River Carves Its Own Path]. Baghdad: Dar al-Shu'un al-Thaqafiyyah al-`Ammah, 1995.

Mylroie, Laurie. "The Baghdad Alternative." *Orbis* (Summer 1988): 339–54.

Noblock, Tim, ed. *Iraq: The Contemporary State.* New York: St. Martin's Press, 1982.

Norman, Roger. "Iraqi Sanctions, Human Rights and Humanitarian Law." *Middle East Reports* (July–September 1996).

Peck, Edward. "Doing It All Wrong in the Middle East: Iraq." *Mediterranean Quarterly* (2001): 13–26.

Penrose, Edith, and E. F. Penrose. *Iraq: International Relations and National Development.* London: Ernest Benn, 1978.

Pollack, Kenneth M. *The Threatening Storm: The Case for Invading Iraq.* New York: Random House, 2002.

Post, Jerrold M., ed. *The Psychological Assessment of Political Leaders.* Ann Arbor: University of Michigan Press, 2003.

Rondot, Philippe. "Saddam Hussein al-Takriti." *Maghreb/Machrek* 83 (1979): 24–29.

Rowat, Colin. "How Sanctions Hurt Iraq." *Middle East Report Online* (August 2, 2001). http://www.merip.org.

Sciolino, Elaine. *The Outlaw State: Saddam Hussein's Quest for Power in the Gulf Crisis.* New York: John Wiley and Sons, 1991.

Shadid, Anthony. "Daring Theater Offers respite from Baghdad's Misery." *Middle East Report* (Summer 1999): 13–14.

Shalom, Stephen R. "The United States and the Iran-Iraq War." Z (February 1990), accessed on Znet archives.

Shohat, Ella. "Rupture and Return: Zionist Discourse and the Study of Arab Jews." *Social Text* (Summer 2003): 49–74.

Simon, Reeva S. *Iraq between the Two World Wars: The Creation and Implementation of a Nationalist Ideology.* New York: Columbia University Press, 1986.

Simons, Geoff. *Iraq: From Sumer to Saddam.* New York: St. Martin's Press, 1996, originally published 1994.

Sluglett, Peter. *Britain in Iraq, 1914–1932.* London: Ithaca Press, 1976.

El-Solh, Raghid. *Britain's Two Wars with Iraq: 1941/1991.* Reading, UK: Ithaca Press, 1996.

Sousa, Alya. "The Eradication of Illiteracy in Iraq." In *Iraq: The Contemporary State,* ed. Tim Noblock. New York: St. Martin's Press, 1982.

Stark, Freya. *Baghdad Sketches.* London: John Murray, 1946; originally published 1937.

Stork, Joe. "Iraq and the War in the Gulf." *Middle East Reports* (June 1981): 3–18.

———. "State Power and Economic Structure: Class Determination and State Formation in Contemporary Iraq." In *Iraq: The Contemporary State,* ed. Tim Noblock. New York: St. Martin's Press, 1982, pp. 27–46.

Tripp, Charles. *A History of Iraq.* Cambridge: Cambridge University Press, 2000.

Viorst, Milton. "Iraq at War." *Foreign Affairs* (Winter 1986/7): 349–65.

Wilson, Arnold T. "The Middle East." *Journal of the British Institute of International Affairs* (March 1926): 96–110.

Wilson, Sir Arnold. *Loyalties: Mesopotamia.* Vol 2. London: Oxford University Press, 1936; originally published 1931.

Wright, Claudia. "Implications of the Iraq-Iran War." *Foreign Affairs* (Winter 1980/81): 275–303.

———. "Iraq—New Power in the Middle East." *Foreign Affairs* (Winter 1979/80): 257–77.

Wright, Frank Lloyd. "Frank Lloyd Wright Designs for Baghdad." *Architectural Forum* (May 1958): 89–101.

Wright, Quincy. "The Government of Iraq." *The American Political Science Review* (November 1926): 743–69.

ARTICLES IN THE POPULAR MEDIA: NEWSPAPERS, MAGAZINES, RADIO, AND THE INTERNET

"Analysis: Iraq Survey Group Draft Report Concludes Saddam Hussein Had the Intent of Reviving Weapons Programs, but Had No Stockpiles," *All Things Considered*. National Public Radio, September 17, 2004.

Anderson, Jon Lee. "Letter from Baghdad: Saddam's Ear." *The New Yorker*, May 5, 2003. http://www.newyorker.com.

Apple, R. W., Jr. "Naked Aggression." *The New York Times*, August 2, 1990.

"Arabs Rebuff Iraq's Bid to Use Oil As a Weapon." *The New York Times*, November 21, 1979.

"Baghdad Parade Mourns Soldiers." *The New York Times*, December 6, 1968.

Beaumont, Peter. "Facing Defeat, Saddam Clung to His Fantasies." *The Observer*, October 10, 2004.

Belair, Felix. "Director of CIA Briefs President." *The New York Times*, April 12, 1969.

Bergen, Peter. "Armchair Provocateur, Laurie Mylroie: The Neocons' Favorite Conspiracy Theorist." *Washington Monthly*, December 2003.

————, "Did One Woman's Obsession Take America to War." *The Guardian*, July 5, 2004.

"Billionaires: Kings, Queens, and Despots." *Forbes*, March 17, 2003.

"Blair Underlines Support for Bush." *The Guardian*, January 7, 2003.

Blix, Hans. "Security Council, 27 January, 2003: An Update on Inspection." http://www.un.org/Depts/unmovic/Bx27.htm.

Bowden, Mark. "Tales of the Tyrant." *Atlantic Monthly*, May 2002.

Brady, Thomas F. "Party Rivalries Plague the Iraqis," *The New York Times*, October 27, 1968.

Burns, John F., and Eric Schmitt. "As a Fugitive, Hussein Stayed Close to Home." *The New York Times*, December 21, 2003.

"Bush Calls Saddam 'the Guy Who Tried to Kill My Dad.'" September 27, 2002. http://www.cnn.com.

"Bush: We're Watching 'Evil' Saddam Carefully." Friday October 12, 2001. http://NewsMax.com.

Candler, Edmund. "British Welcome in Baghdad." *The Guardian*, March 16, 1917.

"Cheney: Saddam Working on Nuclear Weapons." September 10, 2002. http://www.cnn.com.

Christopher, Warren. "Iraq Belongs on the Back Burner," *The New York Times*, December 31, 2002.

"Cities Jammed in Worldwide Protest of War in Iraq." February 16, 2003. http://www.cnn.com.

Cody, Edward. "Khomeini Says Cease-Fire Decision His." *The Washington Post*, July 21, 1988.

Cooley, John K. "Militancy Growing in Iraq?" *The Christian Science Monitor*, January 28, 1969.

———. "Iraq Inner Circle." *The Christian Science Monitor*, February 6, 1969.

Cortright, David. "A Hard Look at Iraq Sanctions." *The Nation*, December 3, 2001.

Cowell, Alan. "A Lot of Pluribus, Not Much Unum." *The New York Times*, February 25, 2001.

Cushman, John H., Jr. "Panel Describes Long Weakening of Hussein Army." *The New York Times*, July 11, 2004.

Dodge, Toby. "Iraq and the Bush Doctrine." *The Guardian*, March 24, 2002.

Drosdoff, Daniel. "Iraq Wins Cease-Fire, but Loses Allies." *Chicago Sun-Times*, November 6, 1988.

"Endless Torment: The 1991 Uprising in Iraq and Its Aftermath." *Human Rights Watch*, June 1992. http://www.hrw.org.

Epstein, Edward. "Pundits Already at War on Iraq." *San Francisco Chronicle*, September 3, 2002.

Erlanger, Steven. "What Now? Doubts about U.S. and U.N. Policy on Iraq Increase." *The New York Times*, December 21, 1988.

Evans, Rowland, and Robert Novak. "US-Iraqi Relations: Warming Trend?" *The Washington Post*, November 9, 1973.

Faleh, Waiel. "'Saddam's Novel' Set to Become TV Series." *Columbian*, June 12, 2002.

Feron, James. "Air Strikes in Jordan." *The New York Times*, December 3, 1968.

———. "Iraqis in Jordan Complicate the Struggle with Israel." *The New York Times*, December 8, 1968.

———. "Strange Mideast War." *The New York Times*, December 6, 1968.

Fuller, Graham. "The Grief of Baghdad: It May Have Won the War; but It Could Easily Lose the Peace." *The Washington Post*, October 9, 1988.

Glauber, Bill. "Hussein Is Rarely Seen, but Always in View." *Knight Ridder Tribune Business News*, January 23, 2003.

Gordon, Michael R. "Iraq Army Invades Capital of Kuwait in Fierce Fighting." *The New York Times*, August 2, 1990.

———, "US Deploys Air and Sea Forces after Iraq Threatens 2 Neighbors." *The New York Times*, July 25, 1990.

Graham, Patrick. "Iraqis in Stitches at Thought of War." *The Observer*, February 23, 2003.

"Gunning For Saddam." *Frontline* (2001, 60 mins), Public Broadcasting Service.

Hadi, Saad, "Baghdad's Forgotten Glory." *Al-Ahram Weekly On-line*, April 17–23, 2003.

Harding, Luke. "The Joke's on Saddam." *The Guardian*, March 14, 2003.

Hardy, Jeremy. "Degraded Policy." *The Guardian*, November 18, 2000.

Harper's Weekly Review, http://www.harpers.org/weekly review.html.

Harris, Franklin. "Don't Laugh at Saddam's Art Collection." *The Decatur Daily*, April 24, 2003.

Hiro, Dilip. "Why Iran Accepted Cease-Fire." *Toronto Star*, July 23, 1988.

Hirst, David. "Baathists Now Put Iraq First." *The Guardian*, July 19, 1968.

Hoagland, Jim. "Brinksmanship in Baghdad." *The Washington Post*, September 20, 2002.

————. "Saddam, Iraq's Suave Strongman." *The Washington Post*, May 11, 1975.

————. "The Shooting of the Stark." *The Washington Post*, May 29, 1987.

"How Dictators Manage Their Billions." *Forbes*, June 22, 2000.

Howe, Marvin. "Iraq Now Has Powerful Claim to Leadership of Arab World." *The New York Times*, July 22, 1979.

Ibrahim, Youssef M. "The Flight from Hussein's Camp." *The New York Times*, August 12, 1995.

————. "Iraq Defector Says He Will Work to Topple Hussein." *The New York Times*, August 13, 1995.

————. "Iraqi Offers Regrets in Killing of Defecting Sons-in-Law." *The New York Times*, May 10, 1996.

————. "Iraqis Go to Polls, Guess Who Will Win." *The New York Times*, October 15, 1995.

————. "Iraq Says U.S. Supplied Iran with Data on Planned Raid." *The New York Times*, July 1, 1988.

————. "Iraq Seeks Bigger Role in OPEC." *The New York Times*, June 28, 1990.

————. "Iraq Threatens Emirates and Kuwait on Oil Glut." *The New York Times*, July 18, 1990.

————. "Khomeini Excites the Arab Masses, Pains Arab Rulers." *The New York Times*, November 25, 1979.

————. "The Man Who Would Be Feared." *The New York Times*, July 29, 1990.

————. "Senior Army Aides to Iraq President Defect to Jordan." *The New York Times*, August 11, 1995.

————. "U.S. Bid to Topple Iraqi Falters." *The New York Times*, August 24, 1995.

"Iraq Chronology: 2003." *Four Corners*. Australian Broadcasting Corporation. http://www.abc.net.au.

"Iraq Election." *All Things Considered*. National Public Radio, October 15, 2002.

"Iraqi Head Gets Full Power." *Christian Science Monitor,* July 16, 1973.

"Iraqis Must Buy Two Million Copies of Saddam's Novel." *Middle East Online,* Feb. 19, 2002. http://www.middle-east-online.com.

"Iraq Killing." *The Washington Post,* July 7, 1973.

"Iraq's New Chief of State." *The New York Times,* July 25, 1968.

Jehl, Douglas. "Iraqi Defectors Killed 3 Days after Returning." *The New York Times,* February 24, 1996.

Jones, Jonathan. "Look at the Size of Those Missiles." *The Guardian,* April 15, 2003.

"Junta Rules Iraq in Rightist Coup." *The New York Times,* July 18, 1968.

Kelley, Jack. "US Chases Regime Leaders." *USA Today,* April 17, 2003.

Kingstone, Heidi. "Sibling Rivalry, Baghdad Style." *The Jerusalem Report,* June 18, 2001.

de Onis, Juan. "Iraq Says He'd Welcome Better Relations with US." *The New York Times,* July 15, 1973.

Rouleau, Eric. "Les nouveaux dirigeants irakiens mettent l'accent sur leur volonté de consolider les relations entre Bagdad et Paris." *Le Monde,* August 7, 1968.

Ruby, Robert. "Hussein's Personality Cult Dominates Daily Life in Iraq." *Toronto Star,* August 7, 1988.

"Rumsfeld's Missing Link." *The Guardian,* October 6, 2004.

"Saddam Hussein Determined to Leave His Mark on Iraq." *Morning Edition,* National Public Radio, August 13, 2002.

"Saddam Hussein's Half Brother Criticizes Heir." *The New York Times,* August 31, 1995.

"Saddam's Favourite Artist." *BBC News World Edition,* May 14, 2003. http://news.bbc.co.uk.

"Saddam's Grip Still Strong." *Morning Edition.* National Public Radio, July 18, 1997.

"Saddam the Great Dictator of Fairy Tales." *The Telegraph,* July 12, 2003.

"Saddam Wins 100% of Vote." *BBC News World Edition,* October 16, 2002. http://www.bbc.co.uk.

Said, Edward. "'We' Know Who 'We' Are." *London Review of Books,* October 17, 2002.

Sale, Richard. "Exclusive: Saddam Key in Early CIA Plot." UPI Intelligence Correspondent, publisher. April 10, 2003. http://www.upi.com/view.cfm?StoryID=20030410–070214–6557r (retrieved July 13, 2004).

Scahill, Jeremy. "American Gifts to Saddam MIA in Baghdad." IraqJournal.org, October 23, 2002, http://www.iraqjournal.org/journals/021023.html.

Schmidt, Dana Adams. "CIA Head Warns of Danger in Iraq." *The New York Times,* April 29, 1959.

———. "Tension Runs High in Baghdad on Eve of New Political Trial." *The New York Times*, February 28, 1970.

Schmitt, Eric. "The 'In' Iraqi Who Counted Himself Out." *The New York Times*, August 12, 1995.

Sciolino, Elaine. "Arab of Vast Ambition: Saddam Hussein." *The New York Times*, August 5, 1990.

———. "The Big Brother: Iraq under Saddam Hussein." *The New York Times*, February 3, 1985.

"Scores Reported Held after Iraqi Assassination." *The Washington Post*, July 3, 1973.

"Senate Approves Iraq War Resolution." October 11, 2002. http://www.cnn.com.

Shadid, Anthony, and Rajiv Chandrasekaran. "US Forces Seize 2 Hussein Palaces As Armor Reaches Heart of Baghdad." *The Washington Post*, April 8, 2003.

Sheldon, Philip. "House Votes $100 Million to Aid Foes of Baghdad." *The New York Times*, October 7, 1988.

Shuster, Mike. "Saddam Hussein Museum—His Excellency's Personal Stuff." *Weekend Edition*, National Public Radio, September 21, 1996.

"Son of Iraqi Leader Is Target of an Assassination Attempt." *The New York Times*, December 13, 1996.

"Stay Iraq's Scimitar, Together." *The New York Times*, July 26, 1980.

Sulzberger, C.L. "His Kurds, and Why." *The New York Times*, March 29, 1975.

———. "Uncle Sam and Ivan in Iraq." *The New York Times*, April 2, 1975.

———. "A Voice Not Far Offstage." *The New York Times*, March 30, 1975.

Tatchell, Jo. "Heroes and Villains." *The Guardian*, July 6, 2004.

Theodoulou, Michael. "New Iraqi Literary King Is Not-Quite Anonymous." *The Christian Science Monitor*, December 11, 2001.

Trillin, Calvin. "Saddam: Can't Color Him Humble." *The Seattle Post-Intelligencer*, August 24, 1993.

"Tracking Saddam's Billions." *BusinessWeek Online*, April 3, 2003.

"23 Shot in Iraq for Plotting." *Washington Post*, July 8, 1973.

"Tycoon in Quiz over Ties to Labour." *The Observer*, April 6, 2003.

"UK Firm May Have a Hand in Saddam's Fall." *The Telegraph*, August 4, 2003.

"The Vicious War." *Los Angeles Times*, March 28, 1985.

"A Victim's Brother, Here, Laments for Iraqi Jews." *The New York Times*, January 28, 1969.

"Volcker Highlights Smuggling over Oil-for-Food in Iraq Inquiry." *The New York Times*, December 28, 2004.

Walt, Vivienne. "Saddam Won't Die." January 18, 2001, http://www.salon.com.

"The Words That Broke the Suspense: From Clinton and the Iraqis." *The New York Times*, November 16, 1998.

Young, Gavin. "Iraqi Leader Takriti Urges Good Relations with West." *The Washington Post*, July 15, 1973.

Younge, Gary, and Oliver Burkeman. "War in the Gulf: Blix Says He Wanted More Time for Inspections." *The Guardian*, March 20, 2003.

OFFICIAL DOCUMENTS, INTERVIEWS, AND SPEECHES

"Agreed Conclusions and Recommendations." Conference of Middle East Chiefs of Mission, U.S. Department of State, February 21, 1951. National Security Archives.

"Arabic Anti-Communist Pamphlet Program." U.S. Embassy in Baghdad to Department of State, Washington, September 9, 1952. National Security Archives.

"Bill Clinton on Sanctions Against Iraq: Amy Goodman Interviews Bill Clinton," *Democracy Now*. November 8, 2000, http://www.globalpolicy.org.

"Biographic Sketch of Saddam Hussein." British Embassy in Baghdad, November 15, 1969. Public Record Office, London, FCO 17/871, National Security Archives.

Blix, Hans. "Security Council, 27 January, 2003: An Update on Inspection." http://www.un.org/Depts/unmovic/Bx27.htm (retrieved December 15, 2005).

Bush, President George W. The President's State of the Union Address, January 29, 2002. http://www.whitehouse.gov (retrieved December 1, 2004).

———. Address to the United Nations General Assembly, September 12, 2002. http://www.whitehouse.gov (retrieved December 1, 2004).

———. Radio Address to the Nation, September 14, 2002. http://www.white house.gov (retrieved December 1, 2004).

———. Address to the Nation, March 17, 2003. http://www.whitehouse.gov (retrieved December 1, 2004).

———. Address to the Nation, March 19, 2003. http://www.whitehouse.gov (retrieved December 1, 2004).

Byrd, Senator Robert. "How Saddam Happened." Congressional Record: September 20, 2002 (Senate), Page S8987-S8998, Federation of American Scientists Web site, http://www.fas.org/irp/congress/2002_cr/s092002.html (retrieved December 15, 2005).

Churchill, Winston. "Middle East Government Policy." Speech to the House of Commons, June 14, 1921, in *Winston S. Churchill: His Complete Speeches*,

1897–1963. Vol. 3, ed. Robert Rhodes James. London: Chelsea House Publishers, 1974.

Clinton, President Bill. "The Iraq Liberation Act." The White House, Office of the Press Secretary, October 31, 1998. http://www.library.cornell.edu/coldev/mideast/libera.htm.

Cohen, Secretary of Defense William S. Department of Defense News Briefing, December 16, 1998. http://www.defenselink.mil.

Cornwallis to Foreign Office, June 9, 1941, *Records of the Hashemite Dynasties: A Twentieth Century Documentary History,* vol. 13.

Crocker, Edward S. of US Embassy in Baghdad to US Department of State, March 10, 1951, National Security Archives.

Export-Import Bank of the United States, Memorandum to the Board of Directors Africa and Middle East Division. "Iraq: Country Review and Recommendations for Eximbank's Programs," February 21, 1984, National Security Archives.

"Full Text: Azores Press Conference." *The Guardian,* March 17, 2003.

"Full Text of the Joint Declaration." *The Guardian,* March 6, 2003.

"Full Text: Saddam Hussein's Speech." *The Guardian,* January 6, 2003.

"Full Text: Saddam Hussein's Speech." *The Guardian,* January 17, 2003.

Hussein, Saddam. Excerpts of speech. *The Guardian,* March 24, 2003.

———. Excerpts of speech. *The Guardian,* April 4, 2003.

———. Interview with Dan Rather. CBS News, February 24, 2003. http://www.cbsnews.com (retrieved August 13, 2003).

———. *President Saddam Hussein Addresses National Assembly on the War with Iran,* trans. N. A. Mudhaffer (Baghdad: Dar al-Ma'mun, 1981).

———. Text of speech. *The Guardian,* April 1, 2003.

"An interview with James Akins: The Survival of Saddam." *Frontline,* Public Broadcasting Service. http://pbs.org/wgbh/pages/frontline/shows/saddam/interviews/akins.html (retrieved January 10, 2004,).

"An Interview with Saddam Hussein." In *Saddam Hussein: The Man, the Cause, and the Future,* ed. Fuad Matar. London: Third World Centre, 1981.

"I Was Saddam's Boyhood Friend." Interview with Ibrahim Zobedi, BBC News http://news.bbc.co.uk/2/hi/programmes/panorama/2399891.stm (retrieved July 29, 2003).

Memorandum of Conversation. Sadun Hammadi (Iraqi Foreign Minister), Falih Mahdi 'Ammash (Iraqi Ambassador to France), Henry A. Kissinger (Secretary of State), December 17, 1975, Iraqi Ambassador's Residence, Paris, France, U.S. National Archives, RG59, Department of State Records, Records of Henry Kissinger, 1973–1977, Box 13, December 1975, National Security Archives.

"Opportunities for Anti-Communist Activities, U.S. Embassy in Baghdad to Department of State, Washington, March 30, 1953, National Security Archives.

Powell, Secretary of State Colin. Transcript of UN Presentation, February 6, 2003. http://www.cnn.com (retrieved December 15, 2005).

Project for the New American Century. "An Open Letter to President Clinton: 'Remove Saddam from Power,'" January 26, 1998, reprinted in *The Iraq War Reader*, ed. Micah L. Sifry and Christopher Cerf. New York: Touchstone Books, 2003, pp. 199–201.

"Saddam Hussein's Iraq." A report prepared by the U.S. Department of State, September 1999.

"Saddam Hussein." Telegram from British Embassy Baghdad to Foreign and Commonwealth Office, December 20, 1969, Public Record Office, London, FCO 17/871. http://www.gwu.edu/~nsarchiv/special/iraq/index. htm (retrieved July 29, 2003).

"Secretary's Principals and Regionals Staff Meeting." Transcript, April 28, 1975 (Excerpt, National Archives, RG 59, Department of State Records, Transcripts of Secretary of State Henry A. Kissinger Staff Meetings, 1973–1977. http://www.gwu.edu/~nsarchiv/special/iraq/index.htm(retrieved July 29, 2003),

"Transcript: Saddam Hussein Interview." February 26, 2003, http://www.cbsnews. com.

20th Report on Progress of Program for International Cooperation in Peaceful Uses of Atomic Energy. Lewis L. Strauss to Dwight D. Eisenhower, July 29, 1957, Dwight D. Eisenhower Library, reproduced on Digital National Security Archive [DNSA].

UNESCO. http://portal.unesco.org/education/ (retrieved October 31, 2004).

UNICEF. "Nearly One Million Children Malnourished in Iraq." http://www. unicef.org/newsline (retrieved November 1, 2004).

Union of Concerned Scientists. Statement on the 50th Anniversary of Eisenhower's "Atoms for Peace" speech, December 8, 2003, http://www. ucsusa.org/global_security/nuclear_terrorism/page.cfm?pageID=1296 (retrieved March 23, 2005).

U.S. Central Intelligence Agency. "Iraq's National Security Goals," December 1988.

U.S. Department of State, Bureau of Near Eastern and South Asian Affairs Information Memorandum from Jonathan T. Howe to Lawrence S. Eagleburger, October 7, 1983, National Security Archives.

U.S. Department of State, Bureau of Near Eastern and South Asian Affairs Information Memorandum from Jonathan T. Howe to George P. Shultz, November 1, 1983, National Security Archives.

U.S. Department of State, Bureau of Near Eastern and South Asian Affairs Information Memorandum from Jonathan T. Howe to Lawrence Eagleburger, November 21, 1983, National Security Archives.

U.S. Department of State, Bureau of Politico-Military Affairs Briefing Paper, "Iraqi Illegal Use of Chemical Weapons," November 16, 1984, National Security Archives.

U.S. Department of State Cable, Alexander M. Haig to the Iraqi Interests Section, April 22, 1981, National Security Archives.

U.S. Department of State Cable, George P. Shultz to the Mission to the European Office of the United Nations and Other International Organizations, March 14, 1984, National Security Archives.

U.S. Department of State Report, "Saddam Hussein's Iraq," September 1999.

U.S. Defense Intelligence Agency Intelligence Report, "Defense Estimative Brief: Prospects for Iran," September 25, 1984, National Security Archives.

U.S. Embassy in United Kingdom Cable, Charles H. Price to the Department of State, December 21, 1983, National Security Archives.

U.S. Interests Section in Iraq Cable, William L. Eagleton to the Department of State, April 4, 1981, retrieved July 29, 2003, National Security Archives.

U.S. Interests Section in Iraq Cable, William L. Eagleton to the Department of State, May 28, 1981, retrieved July 29, 2003, National Security Archives.

U.S. Interests Section in Iraq Cable, William L. Eagleton to the Department of State, September 20, 1982, retrieved July 29, 2003, National Security Archives.

U.S. Interests Section in Iraq Cable, William Eagleton to U.S. Embassy in Jordan, December 14, 1983, National Security Archives.

U.S. Interests Section in Iraq Cable, William L. Eagleton to the Department of State, February 22, 1984, National Security Archives.

Wright, Frank Lloyd. Speech at San Rafael High School, July 1957, Frank Lloyd Wright's Architectural Drawings: The 1957 Baghdad Project. http://www.geocities.com/SoHo/1469/flw_iraq.htm (retrieved August 6, 2003).

VIDEOS, FILMS, AND DOCUMENTARIES

"Baghdad in No Particular Order" (USA, 2003) directed by Paul Chan.

"Gunning For Saddam" (USA, 2001), produced by Frontline, PBS.

"The Long Road to War" (USA, 2003), produced by Frontline, PBS.

"Saddam: A Warning From History," Panorama documentary, BBC, broadcast on November 3, 2002, transcript from the BBC News Web site. http://news.bbc.co.uk.2/hi/programmes/panorama/2371697.stm (retrieved July 29, 2003).

"Uncle Saddam" (USA, 2000) directed by Joel Soler.

NEWS OUTLETS

Al-Ahram
Al-Ahram Weekly
Al-Hayat
www.aljazeerah.info
American Forces Information Service
Atlantic Monthly
BBC News World Edition
BBC Monitoring Middle East
Boston Globe
Business Week Online
www.cbsnews.com
The Chicago Sun-Times
Chicago Tribune
The Christian Science Monitor
Columbian
www.cnn.com
The Decatur Daily
Forbes
Foreign Broadcast and Information Service (FBIS)
The Guardian
Harpers
Knight Ridder Tribune Business News
London Review of Books
The London Times
Middle East Online
Le Monde
Le Monde Diplomatique
The Nation
National Public Radio
New York Amsterdam News
The New Yorker
The New York Times
The Observer
PBS, Online Newshour
Salon.com
San Francisco Chronicle
The Seattle Post-Intelligencer

The Telegraph
Toronto Star
Wall Street Journal
The Washington Post
USA Today

INDEX

About the Author

SHIVA BALAGHI is Associate Director of Kevorkian Center for Near Eastern Studies at New York University.